"John Brandi opens this dazzling collection with a description of road trips he took through the landscapes of Southern California with his parents, who taught him how to see. In subsequent chapters, the boy becomes a bard, and we trek with him up mountain trails, drop into roiling cities, meet eccentric visionaries and return home to the wilds of New Mexico. Brandi leans into each experience of place with the open senses and curious mind of a sommelier, tasting deeply, distilling the essence. His peripatetic embrace of the world is passionate and contagious."

—Anne Valley-Fox
author of *The Household Muse* (with Tom Ireland)

"Eyes and mind wide open to unanticipated concurrencies of place and time, it's no coincidence that Brandi, a long-practicing artist and poet, is drawn to shamanic shapechangers; his favorite landscapes are transformative vistas where ongoing dramas of the natural world play out in moments and eons. *A Luminous Uplift*, the latest of his distinguished publications, charts numinous inner realms to illuminate a profoundly engaged spirit of place—both around the world and at home in New Mexico."

—Ken Rodgers
Kyoto Journal

A LUMINOUS UPLIFT
Landscape & Memory

A LUMINOUS UPLIFT
Landscape & Memory

selected & new writings
1979 - 2021

John Brandi

WHITE PINE PRESS / BUFFALO, NEW YORK

White Pine Press
P.O. Box 236
Buffalo, NY 14201
www.whitepine.org

Publication of this book was supported by public funds from the New
York State Council on the Arts, with the support of Governor Kathy
Hochul and the New York State Legislature, a State Agency.

Printed and bound in the United States of America

ISBN 978-1-945680-66-3

Library of Congress Control Number: 2022950768

for Renée
your constant love and friendship

and in memory of my parents
Lawrence & Regine, who set me on the path

CONTENTS:

III: INTO THE DREAM MAZE

IV: UNCOMMON COUNTRY: AN AFTERWORD

INTRODUCTION

It's a ten-degree morning in the mountains of New Mexico, the first rays of sun warming the adobe walls of our living room. I've brewed two cups of Tres Estrellas blend while Renée kindles a stove fire. Yesterday we split and stacked another load of firewood to carry us through the winter. Task done, a shot of cognac and a hot bath proved ample reward. My creaks and wobbles are escalating now that I'm nudging into my eighth decade on the planet. So many amigos are talking about back pains, knee surgery, hip replacements, and the cumbersome effort it takes to rise from a chair once seated (*Remain standing!* I tell them)—all of which cause me to question our evolution into cane-toting, walker-pushing two-legged mammals. Wouldn't it have been better to remain an amphibian? Forgetfulness enters into the picture, too. Does the desert tortoise forget? The Pacific salmon? But we do, and before it happens to me, I've thought to present a few instances of life on earth in the following chapters.

In *Rehearsal for a Sicilian Tragedy,* a film on the vanishing puppet shows of Palermo, which Renée and I attended in 2016, Sicilian author Andrea Camilleri talked of the necessity to preserve traditions. "In an age like ours, which is an age of epic transformations, the only way not to be afraid of all that's coming is to know who you are. If you know your lineage and your traditions, you will never lose your identity." His words initiated some contemplative moments on this end.

From boyhood on, books have been part of my tradition: the writing and making of them, the visual art accompanying them, journeys inspired by them. I grew up with the printed word, no television for the first decade of life; no bright little handheld device to dull the world. The books on my bedroom shelf were stirring companions, the radio a worthy server of voice and music. On my table, those marvelous instruments of wood and graphite—pencils —allowed my thoughts to become visible. Sometime later, I was gifted a second-hand typewriter from my father's office, which, though interesting, required clumsy gestures of the hand quite apart from that of pressing a pencil or crayon. When electric typewriters appeared, I opted instead for a Swiss-made Hermes Rocket, an ultra-light manual typer perfect for travel. Much later came the Apple computer, a boxy contraption that was supposed to make life easier. Its word processing program was useful, but I could already feel a bit of foreboding as to where technology was taking us.

In preschool years, my backyard rambles and indoor activities held me suspended, like a water strider buoyed on ripples radiating from a pond's center. As I got older, time in a circular sense ebbed, the center vanished, and my world was squeezed into linear, measured time. It began in the first grade and slowly escalated into the curse of our times: an ungainly increase in speed. The rev-up has now become insane, fueled by an out-of-control tailwind. The newly purchased computer will be obsolete next week, replaced by a speedier update neatly downloaded into the body's vital organs. The latest automobiles, self-driving pods on wheels, have the built-in option of hurling you over a cliff. Meanwhile the old monsters ply the road, their drivers doing ninety—seventy is too slow. You don't dare flip them off as they nudge your bumper, headlights blinking GET OUT OF MY WAY. You bet I will. Life is too precious. I'd rather enjoy the steady pace of my rusting '98 Toyota and sip my coffee.

In making selections for this book, a theme began to appear: that from an early age landscape was important to me. Those of *Treasure Island* and *Huckleberry Finn* in books, the slate-gray mountains seen from my treetop perch in the San Fernando Valley, the minarets of Old Delhi slowly coming into focus under the magic solutions in my father's darkroom. It was a privilege to have been given a double dose of the faraway and near-at-hand at once. My father's photos and stories, his souvenirs of silk, ivory, and brass made foreign lands real, while family drives through California's coastal chaparral, into foothill oaks, up though snow-dusted peaks, and down into the desert gave dimension to the nearby.

Encouraged by my parents, I walked with pencil and pad. The terrain came in through the feet, the ears, the nose, the taste buds, and rolled out from the hand. A journey was always an emotional experience, one of sensation rather than intellect. As a grown man, the act of travel, with its unpredictable encounters and mysteries, became a poetic venture born not out of need for entertainment or escape, but to engage with new geography, people, and culture. Curiosity played a part, so did naiveté. Certain people stood out, mavericks who didn't fit the norm. If you had ears to listen, they had something to say. The physical world, too, had something to say:

snow peaks—
a musical shimmer
on the raven's wing

And something to ask. Lawrence Durrell wrote: "All landscapes ask the same question in the same whisper. 'I am watching you—are you watching yourself in me?'" Perhaps I heard that whisper as a youth, for it began to come clear in my early California explorations that landscape was not static, but an ever-changing meld of heart, mind, and mirage that matched an interior geography. Emotionally, it was the spirit of the land—geologic alterations, shifting horizons, drama of wind, water, and cloud—that both kept me on edge and made me at home.

Beginning with my Peace Corps experience in the Andes, the landscapes that continued to draw me were semi-wild or rural places inhabited by people who preserved long-established traditions of secular and arcane rituals: the Bolivian altiplano, the American Southwest, Mexico, the Himalayas, India, Bali. As for India, my travels were not, as some believed, motivated by the quest for spiritual enlightenment that was fashionable in the Sixties. I simply wanted to see the places my father visited as an army private stationed in the subcontinent. But how could India's spiritual realm not seep into an itinerary that had me following sacred rivers into cities devoted to Ma Kali or Shiva, or to the grove where Buddha was born, or up zigzag trails to cloud-hidden monasteries?

I have divided *A Luminous Uplift* into travels afar and ones close to home. For many of us, home is a place we believe is permanent, a sanctuary written into the will to be passed on with those treasured possessions that often enslave us. The word "home" can be traced to the Sanskrit, *kayati,* "he is lying down"—any place we recline to sleep, dream, make love, give birth, etc. It may be a tipi in the high country conducive to contemplation; an off-grid cabin and garden where we discover the labor, joy, and neighborly exchange that accompany deep rooting; or a temporary residence in a foreign land, a tent in the field where we bear service to others.

On a wall in my study in our house hangs the following haiku by hermit-monk Ryōkan (1758-1831):

The thief left it behind
the moon
in my window

The image was ours to savor two nights ago when Renée looked up from the kitchen counter to a crescent moon in the window. Viewed from inside our home, the moon was another home, a skiff rocking in a starry sea—a headrest in the space outside, suddenly brought inside. It was also a smile, the eternal call of the far away. I've sometimes been teased by friends (and scrutinized by literary types) as "the guy who is never home." A misconception, for sure, since the majority of the year finds me right here, over the desk, in the garden, at the easel. The mesas, arroyos, and stony palisades offer plenty of trails to keep our feet happy. But if a voice calls from deep inside, especially when the snow flies, I'm ready to GO. Get lost. Revitalize the brain cells. Twiggle the nerve endings. Have an affair with the world at large. I've stoked the stove too long, it's time to fan a few flames inside the head. And how lucky I am to have an avid and curious poet at my side as a companion.

During the evolution of this book it was often tempting to compare the present era with the past. Sometimes I gave in, but for the most I tried to keep an even keel. Let the times and travels speak for themselves. The minute you write the present, it is past. Live long enough, and you watch all that you see, take for solid, perceive as unchanging, slowly disappear. You retain only raindrops of memory, hard knocks of hail on the head, tiny bits of crust and berry that hardly complete the whole taste of the pie. Get too far into "how things used to be" and you're ripe for disappointment, cynicism, even anger to the point of hostility. Allen Ginsberg reminds us: "Ordinary mind includes eternal perceptions."

I won't say that any of the writing in this book came easy. As a poet, what I like about poetry is that a storm brews a voice from the air. You fear no contradictions. In prose you risk the head getting in the way. Too much thought, tinkering, ball-juggling and you're dead, a gnat smashed to the page. In the journey—as Herodotus, Bashō, Kazantzakis, and the Taoist sojourners verified— two legs go forth, nudge the muscles, get the eyeballs rattling, the blood circulating, set the invisible free from the visible. You trust the feet, see where language goes—a magnetic pull, the third eye beamed into action.

In a painting, the paint never completely dries. You can go back, blend, move pigment around, update, flesh out, renew the view. Preparing a book, you realize the same: the first, second, third, ad infinitum drafts are never dry. A few chapters herein appear differently from their original versions. I've revised with the intent to fact check, clarify, and tune the engine for a better performance. I wouldn't say this gives a smoother ride. On the contrary, it may give a few necessary jolts—a bareback lift from the saddle that sets you back down with your eyes turned around.

jb / Río Arriba, New Mexico

I.
Young Blood: a Preamble

My childhood years are full of reeds. I spent a lot of wind growing up.
But only so did I learn to separate the slightest whispers, to speak
precisely among the mysteries.

Odysseus Elytis

So we too look into our past, treating it as far as we can with respect
for its own sake, because of the scattered fragments of truth it must con-
tain. With infinite consideration, with ceaseless care, we disentangle
them, and try to keep them intact in their integrity, as free, as far as
we can make them, from the twist of our own time and of ourselves—
never forgetting that somewhere in that knot is the beginning of a
thread that we must follow.

Freya Stark

YOUNG BLOOD

On my desk this morning I've spread out a few boyhood souvenirs: a topographical drawing done at age ten of an imaginary island with all its contours, elevation gains, hydrography, psychic isobars, and place names; four books written in the second and third grade, penciled on newsprint with drawings: *Good Health*; *The Big Book of Birds*; *Iron Guns*; and *The Little Engine that Won a Medal*; and two books authored and hand printed during my college years: *a nothing book*, and *Tehachapi Fantasy*, both with poems and hand-colored illustrations celebrating that Blakean state of innocence synonymous with Joy in the natural landscape.

My early childhood years were benevolent ones, as were those in college, the latter filled with inspiration from memorable teachers and a sundry pallet of students. It is my parents, though, who first awakened my curiosity for the world and provided the guidance that allowed that curiosity to achieve momentum. Neither were university educated, they had no aspirations toward the higher arts, and they had little money. My mother was a homemaker who dabbled in poetry. Judging from her few surviving writings, she was a keen and expressive observer. My father was a newspaper accountant; his hobby was photography. Everything he admired or found unusual was alchemized through his camera. But he never called himself an artist. That category he reserved for the van Goghs, the Garbos, the Satchmos. Or for outlaws like his uncle Joe Zito and Zito's cousin Danny Russo, the jazz violinist and big-band leader who co-authored the 1920s hit, "Toot Toot Tootsie."

During the last years of my father's life—he lived to

be ninety-one—I was fortunate to have a few journeys with him, traveling as companions and copilots like we did when I was a boy. Water was a prominent part of these adventures: the Big Sur, the Great Lakes, the St. Lawrence River, the myriad creeks, ponds, and estuaries in between. He highlighted his maps carefully, complained when I strayed from the route, and, with a slight grumble, enjoyed himself wherever we ended up. I would write and draw as I did as a boy. He would have his camera, pen and pad, meds and Life Savers. There would be discussions and confrontations. At appropriate intervals I would record his stories on a small battery-operated tape recorder.

My father outlived my mother by seventeen years. She died in her early seventies, bedridden, swollen, unable to speak after failed spinal surgeries and infection. "Regina Caeli," were my last words to her—"Queen of Heaven," her favorite prayer to the Blessed Lady, a mesmerizing litany when intoned in Latin. Regina was my mother's given name, though she clipped it to Regine. Her parents were born in Germany. There were glass makers and opera singers among the clan, though I'm the only one who recalls that tale; perhaps it was a myth invented to help propagate the roots of her ancestry. What is verifiable is that she had several sisters and two brothers, one of whom became a priest, the other a judge. I hardly knew her side of the family; I was brought up by my father's side.

My father was from a large Italian family, tailors and musicians. His mother's side was from a mountain town in Basilicata, his father's from Caserta, just outside Napoli. By the early 1890s the Brandis had settled in a Michigan factory town near the confluence of the Cass, Saginaw, and Tittabawassee Rivers. My father didn't remain there. While in his late teens, he had an intuitive calling to a geography more fitting to his Mediterranean roots: Southern California. My father once explained this calling as "inner governance," a term we mutually defined as "something inside that takes control." In 1928 he joined a caravan of men driving Buicks fresh off the Detroit assembly line to a Hollywood dealer. There he stayed with his uncle Joe Zito, who had followed in the tracks of his brother-in-law, Mario Di Trapani, who fled Michigan for California after being threatened by *La Mano Nera,* a pre-Mafia gang that arrived with fellow immigrants fleeing the poverty of southern Italy. Extortion was its trademark, a threatening letter and a black handprint on a victim's door its calling card. Pay up or die. Mario safely set up his grocery business in Long Beach, and my great uncle Zito established himself in Hollywood as a musician transitioning from Vaudeville to silent films. By 1926 he had already traveled with John Ford's crew to Wyoming for the making of *Three Bad Men,* one of Ford's great silent epics.

My father's deliberate shedding of the Midwest for California was karmic. It meant I would not be born among ice and snow, but in the balm of sea air and wild fennel. As a youngster I was fascinated by tales of his road trip from Detroit to Los Angeles, a tough, two-week journey, partly on Highway 66, unpaved in those days; partly through a storm-soaked stretch of mud in Texas; and finally, across Southern California's desert dunes on a wood-plank track. "On some days if we made fifteen miles, that was a lot." On a postcard of 12,000-foot Sierra Blanca, he wrote his parents: "Just passing through these mountains in New Mexico and you should see the snow. Stopping here for dinner then will leave for El Paso, Texas." The card was dated Nov. 25, 1928, Alamogordo, New Mexico.

In 1929, despite the Depression, my father found work with the *Los Angeles Examiner* newspaper. A photograph shows him at his desk in the Credit and Claims Department, backed by oak furniture, ornate grillwork, sculpted pillars, and lamps with stained-glass shades. As a nine-year-old, I would accompany him from Burbank to downtown L.A. where he worked overtime for the *Examiner* on Sundays, sorting mail and balancing books. Teletype machines clattered, linotypists punched out stories, typesetting rooms smelled of fire and lead, giant presses churned out huge rolls of printed news. My father explained each step of the process, from the reporters' field work to the final publishing of their stories in the daily paper. The *Examiner* building was a treat, a blend of Spanish, Moorish, and Italian flourishes. Blue and yellow tiled domes, grilled balconies, arched windows along Broadway, a Baroque lobby with brass chandeliers, marble stairways, and a gilded elevator to William Randolph Hearst's private tower. The building dated from 1914, the creation of Julia Morgan, who went on to design Hearst's San Simeon castle in the Big Sur.

After my father settled in California he began corresponding with his teenage sweetheart, Regine—"the babe I spotted on Genesee Avenue and offered a ride in the Model-T I had just bought for thirty dollars." In 1933 he boarded a train from L.A. for the Chicago World's Fair, then on to Saginaw, Michigan to surprise her with a ring. The following year they were wed at Our Mother of Good Counsel Church in Hollywood. They wore black, honeymooned in Mexico, rented a Hollywood apartment, and on weekends began exploring Southern California's diverse paradise: Palm Springs, Santa Barbara, the Malibu Hills, the dells of Griffith Park, the Franciscan missions—a favorite being San Juan Capistrano, for the annual return of the swallows on Saint Joseph's Day.

A photograph from that period shows the newlyweds in the Hollywood Hills, wild grasses at their feet. Regine leans against a softly contoured boulder, her arm around my father, who smiles bright-eyed, his black hair neatly groomed, his left arm around her petite waist, a 16-mm movie camera dangling from his right hand. Definitely a portrait of two happy Michigan transplants enjoying the warm Southern California air—a move perhaps as dramatic as Vincent van Gogh's relocation from the grays of Holland to the brilliance of Provence.

With a modest loan they purchased a newly built house in the San Fernando Valley. For my mother—charmed by Hollywood's palm-lined avenues, the clubs, and continuous action—it was a difficult move. The Valley was a barren, sandblasted place. It stunk of dairy farms, there were few neighbors, hardly anywhere to shop, only one unpaved road over Cahuenga Pass to Hollywood. But the house was affordable, with enough space to accommodate her relatives who had begun to visit—companionship that was vital, especially when, in March 1944, five months after I was born, my father was drafted into the army and shipped to India.

After World War II he returned to civilian life and reclaimed his job as a collections clerk at the *Examiner*, where he was upgraded to chief accountant. As my father settled into his marital obligations and the "good life" Americans felt they deserved after Hitler and Pearl Harbor, he continued his love for the camera. The state-of-the-art darkroom he built in the garage was testimony that he wished to resume his artistic creativity as a photographer, a hobby he had stepped up while in the army.

My father gave me an early sense of geography. As a youngster I accompanied him into the Hollywood Hills where he experimented with his 8 x 10 press photographer's camera. The road, edged with low wooden rails, was narrow and full of curves. Oak, eucalyptus, and peppery chaparral filled the canyons. Towards the crest he stopped to photograph the Valley, just beginning its irreversible postwar boom. To the east rose the Verdugo Mountains, behind them were the San Gabriels, a bit farther snowcapped Mount Baldy. I asked him what lay beyond the mountains. "Desert," he replied, "miles of sand." That was the first mention of the word desert in my life. I was five years old.

West, beyond the concrete sprawl of L.A., the view opened toward the ocean. Beyond the sweeping curve of Santa Monica Bay lay Santa Catalina Island, its wrinkled summits rising out of the salt haze. My father described it as an arid place with a big casino. "What's a casino?" I asked. "A place where you lose money," he answered. "What if you go past Catalina?" He filled his pipe and gazed over the sun-gilded waters that had carried him to the South Pacific, Australia, and Asia during World War II. "Keep going and you'll come to India."

On the first drives with my parents into the Mojave Desert, we stopped in gem shops to examine fossils and polished minerals, visited the ghost town of Calico, and explored a jumble of sandstone outcrops known as Vasquez Rocks—a former bandit's hideout that lent itself to a youngster's imagination. I hugged the window of our 1947 Hudson, a high-wheeled, turtle-humped model with a mysterious button below the dashboard which, when pushed, settled the wheels into Hydra-Matic.

The emptiness of the Mojave took hold of me: land and sky that just kept going: a lithic glint of scraped-clean hills—smoky pearl, faded lapis—and between them searing playas of white sand. My father's pipe smelled sweet. My mother had prepared sandwiches and potato salad. The beautiful big car was a pillow of air. Safety was not in seat belts or air bags but in a canvas water bag looped around the front bumper. The bag said "Mohawk" and on it was printed the profile of an Indian's head. It was a backup in case our radiator overheated, but that never happened—so I made up stories of us drinking from it, stranded in a dead-end canyon after running out of gas. At dusk the dashboard brightened with luminous dials. Desert ranges blushed, the land cooled noticeably. In the dark, the rain-like fragrance of creosote scrub intensified. My father stopped the car, flicked off the headlights, and we got out. Utter silence, and with it the awakening of a sixth sense, one enlivened by absence. For the first time, I saw the full span of the Milky Way, a white river rippling across the zenith.

My father's darkroom was an inner sanctum. You got to it through a garage filled with hand tools, a table saw, a jig saw, planks of pine, scraps of hardwood, cans of paint, bins of dowels, pegs, and metal fasteners. Sealed from the outer world, the darkroom was dimmed with amber glow, odorous with potions, set with enameled metal trays and a bellowed contraption known as the "enlarger." My father's large-format press camera yielded his most memorable work. He did all his own developing and printing and I was his eager assistant, holding white squares of paper beneath a chemical bath with a pair of tongs. Bathed in crystalline solution, blurred images magically came into focus. Alchemy! Under the weird glow of the safelights appeared a bee on a magnolia blossom, a crenulated line of Sierra Nevada peaks, neighborhood kids posed in Halloween costumes, the onion-shaped dome of the Taj Mahal.

Among my favorite photographs were those of my parents as sweethearts relaxing in their Hollywood apartment, or goofing with relatives at rowdy Italian picnics in Griffith Park. One shows the twenty-six-year-olds in a rose garden. My mother wears stylish white pumps, calf-length skirt, and a figure-hugging cashmere sweater. Her hands are folded against the slim tummy that would later bear her three children; she smiles upward at Lawrence, her handsome counterpart affirmatively posed in suit and tie, a shaft of sunlight across his heart, his luminous Italian eyes lovingly directed into hers—"like Valentino's" I hear myself say, though a note to his father on the rear of the photo puts it more mildly: "Just a couple of kids still in love. Looks like I was in a serious mood, but it's that darn sun again. Hope I get used to it."

A few of his photographs were framed, most were dutifully catalogued into albums by my mother, one of them devoted to my father's wartime stay in India. Unlike his brothers, he hadn't been sent to a battle zone, but was stationed in the India-Burma Theater, an Allied effort to prevent the Japanese from occupying the subcontinent. The year was 1945 and the war was almost over. With little to keep him busy, he finagled time off, rented a bicycle, and took to the countryside with camera and notebook. Instead of battles my father's photos revealed village shrines, mosques, a bullock and driver at a watering hole, a snake charmer, a yogi performing rigors. Each photo was arranged chronologically, with a neatly typed caption pasted below. These my mother would read to me, after having me study the photos. A typical one:

Street scene, Old Delhi: a woman with her bundle. Almost all shopping goes on the head. The naked man behind walks nonchalantly. He carries his only worldly possession: a bedroll. He is a kind of wandering priest or holy man.

Such people and places were impressed upon my psyche, as was my father's habit of complementing each image with a commentary. My parents were to emphasize this format as I was beginning to read and write, a couple of years before I began school. In a corner of our living room, I had my own table with pencils and a stack of 8 x 10 newsprint trimmed from the end rolls of the *Examiner's* printing presses. After each visit to ocean, desert, or mountains I was asked to draw something remembered from the trip, then write a line or two below. My mother, who taught me to read, was instrumental in the latter. If I drew a giant redwood, she would ask "How many steps did it take to walk around it? What did you feel when you put your cheek to the bark?" One or two lines, sum it up, kid! It was she who provided my first experience in haiku, though the term was never mentioned.

Once, after a bear rummaged through our camp, I tried drawing it, but failed miserably. Frustrated, I resolved the situation by drawing two yellow eyes at the center of the page and colored the rest black. After all, the bear came at night; all that was visible were two frightening eyes in the beam of my father's flashlight. What else had impressed me about the bear? It had struggled to claw open our metal ice chest and left two bright spots of blood on the lid. "Bear blood!" my sister cried. We bent low to examine it, after which my father explained that bears were mammals just like us. I've lost the sketch of the bear, but the writing that went with it I remember well:

> The thief that invaded
> our camp came and left
> on four legs.

When my drawings and writings accumulated, my parents gathered and stapled them together. "There, now you have a book." To which they added: "But you need a cover, and a title. Look through the pages. What is the book about, what do you want to call it?" It was impressed upon me that one traveled, observed, felt the world, transformed experience into words and drawings, bound them into pages, and shared them with others. Books were magic entities not to be taken lightly. They did not rely on the muse, but were inspired by simple yet deep travel observations. They captured feelings and preserved events.

They even kept people alive after they were dead.

One evening, after my mother read from *A Child's Garden of Verses,* she told me that the author, Robert Lewis Stevenson, was a traveler who lived and died long ago, but to hear his poems was to hear him still alive talking to us. As a child I loved his images of windy nights and quavering chimney flames "that could paint an empty room." He named the flowers and constellations: Hollyhock, Shepherd's Purse, the Hunter, the Plough. His rhymes of travel, "Where among the desert sands/Some deserted city stands," stayed with me when my mother closed the book and left me to sleep. At my young age I knew, as most children know, that one could invent kingdoms by shutting the eyes, or in a backyard garden find "fairy places among tiny tree tops, rose or thyme." Stevenson's poems spoke the truth.

When a neighbor gave me *Treasure Island,* illustrated by N.C. Wyeth, I turned to my mother upon opening it. "He's drawn a map for us!" It was an aerial view of the island printed in gold and red, adorned with a sailing ship, compass, and mermaid. Graduated lines on and around the island indicated woods, rivers, headlands, coves, dangerous riptides, and "areas of foul ground." The latter required some explanation. My mother filled in: "It's where rocks hidden underwater cause shipwrecks."

As for my reading skills, *Treasure Island* was in the stratosphere. But my mother read aloud selections that captured the story's essence. And Wyeth's illustrations! I couldn't wait for another page to be turned. He could paint young John Hawkins leaving home, walking into the shadows of the unknown, while his mother, painted in bright sun, wept into an apron held to her face. He could paint blind Pew tapping his cane on a moonlit road and you could hear the cane, feel shivers, smell the all-surrounding night, imagine the man's frenzy as he called out for his comrades.

Thinking back on Stevenson's "fairy places," I see myself reveling in my own poetic corners of our Southern California backyard: mossy shadows in a secret nook between the hibiscus and poinsettia; a sandy cove filled with eucalyptus leaves near the rear fence; the neighbor's exotic kumquat tree; a cluster of butterflies blending into the lantana flowers: all very Mediterranean. I was spoiled on this, had it all to myself, had inside our house the parental gift of a secluded space with table, paper, and pencils where I could sit, imagine, draw, invent.

One Monday morning I was cast from paradise. My mother dressed me in a gray uniform, combed my hair, and packed me into her '37 Ford sedan for a ride to the parish school. I was forced into an uncomfortable desk with attached chair, strangers on all sides. The room was stuffy, it smelled of other kids: cigarette smoke in their clothes, fried potatoes they had for breakfast, pomade in their hair, bodies unwashed, bodies overdosed in cheap soap. One girl, whose un-ironed uniform hung upon the thin rail of her body as if on a coat hanger, was sent home because of lice. The boy seated next to me (his last name, Tice, rhymed with lice) vomited his scrambled egg breakfast on my left shoe.

Over the blackboard was a metal crucifix. Drawn across the blackboard were lines of white chalk, three or four bars stacked vertically. Inside the bars were sample letters of the alphabet, each properly drawn. I had never learned to write this way. My marks were personal, not proper. They were not formed inside lines. When sample letters were passed out for the class to trace, I obeyed with annoyance. Repeated tracings were supposed to help me memorize the letter. But I had already learned the *A* by eyeballing my mother's *A* and copying it. It wasn't a perfect *A*, but once written it stayed in my head. So did the rest of the letters. I received admonitions because my letters were "messy" by scholastic standards. As for how quickly I learned and remembered their primary shapes, I garnered no accolades.

My desk was in the front row, too close to the black-robed nun with whom I was trapped for the rest of day. The contrast between her and my mother was a shock, as it was with another woman my mother had introduced me to: the Blessed Lady. She stood in a niche of our parish church, beside the altar with its crucified Christ, an image my mother disliked. The nun was stiff and menacing, draped in black, arms crossed over her chest. The Blessed Lady was calm, robed in blue, arms outspread and welcoming. She was my mother's envoy, a truly bliss-bestowing figure, her bare feet resting on a crescent moon flanked by two cherubs and trays of flickering candles. The image probably evoked a "bodhisattva consciousness" in my young mind, opening levels in the psyche that would be with me for the rest of my life.

In that stale school room, robbed of my freedom, left with a woman who resembled neither the Blessed Lady nor my own mother, I had but one recourse. Resist! Kick and wail until the lady in black was forced to call the principal, who called my mother, who drove her '37 Ford back to school to fetch her unruly son. I was persuaded into returning only after my mother explained that the school had art classes, taught by a woman who wasn't a nun. She was from Spain, wore colorful skirts, and her class would be fun. It worked—for awhile. The following year I balked at having to trace pictures, then fill them in with prescribed colors, none that fit my imagination. I longed for my kindergarten easel and water paints, the liberty to paint whatever came to me. As for tracing cartoon-like figures, better to draw from real life as my parents had encouraged: a bowl of fruit on the kitchen table, a portrait of my sister under the lemon tree, the Chinese characters printed on the paper inside a firecracker when it was peeled apart.

Third grade was the same as first and second—confrontation with authority, at odds with being asked questions, then silenced when giving answers that didn't fit the teacher's guidelines. There were uncivil punishments, too. A particularly nasty incident happened when I accidentally dropped a peanut-butter-and-jelly sandwich during our outdoor lunch hour. I fetched it from below the bench, saw the sand stuck to it, and tossed it over the fence. Caught in the act by a nun standing guard, I was forced to retrieve the sandwich—and eat it. Grinding the sand between my teeth, teary with anger, I held my rage. Further punishment would mean standing for an hour facing a wall. The poet in me, the fighting poet, should have risen right then and there. But at such a young age all I could do was feel the rage. A decade later, I would fully realize that my pencil or paintbrush could transform anger into art.

In the fourth grade, geography was my favorite class. One of the projects involved mapmaking, which allowed students to gain a topographic appreciation of the earth. Each of us chose a state, country, or continent and fashioned it out of a flour-and-salt concoction that dried hard on a piece of plywood, after which it could be painted. My choice was California. I loved the shape of the state, its long in-and-out coastline, the mountainous spine running north to south where it met the empty sands. I painted the Cascades deep green, the Sierra Nevada light green, the Sierra Madres smoky gray, the deserts camel. The volcanoes up north, the domes of granite mid-state, and the rounded baldies down south I topped with zinc white. At last, amid all my bad grades, an A enhanced my report card. Later that year, I was invited to show the class a map I made at home for my own pleasure. It was of Italy, and I gave a talk comparing it to California: its climate, the wrinkled coasts, the chain of mountains running north to south, the volcanoes. One kid gave a kind of sneer and asked how did I know all that if I'd never been there. I had to be quick. "My grandpa's from Italy, from right here," and pointed to a bay under a volcano called Vesuvius. Rather than from my grandfather, though, all my information came from making the map: kneading, pinching, and carving the landscape with my hands, asking questions along the way, realizing Italy was a peninsula, it had Alps, and islands that smoked.

Eventually that bane of a question arrived: "What do you want to be when you grow up?" It happened when relatives visited, elders who looked older than they were: some with big bellies and cigars; some shrunken, with cobwebbed faces; one in bow tie, suspenders, and wrinkled shirt, mostly silent for he refused to speak English. There was an aunt with a fuzzy, over-powdered face that I feared to kiss; another whose eyes were set in ashen rings as if they had been punched; and always a woman darker than the rest, blazing eyes, long legs—pretty enough to excite me. Uncle Zito, my hero, was in the mix, too—aloof and dapper, content to be out of synch with it all. He didn't ask what do you want to be, for he knew my replies wouldn't fit the family hopes: test pilot (danger, the unknown), ventriloquist (ability to speak in another tongue), makeup artist (alchemy, transformation). At the top of the list was ACTOR, which I considered to be very cool. Learn the lines, dress the part, become a temporary other: hero, villain, cowboy, detective, gladiator, mutineer, Casanova.

The movie industry dominated my home town: Disney Studio was three blocks south of the house, Warner Brothers a mile west, Universal Pictures a tad farther. Neighborhood kids were auditioning for roles, but my father warned that acting would not be a career option for his son. ("What's career option, Dad?") It did not represent steady income, and it could lead to the wrong crowd: rowdies, dopers, misfits of questionable morale. ("What's morale, Dad?") My father's attitude may have stemmed from Uncle Joe's success as a studio musician, a career that resulted in his losing his invested earnings in the stock market crash of 1929. "He fell in with the wrong crowd," my father would say. "They gave him dopey advice."

The extreme lives that Hollywood stars led didn't fit my father's idea that he had been born into a line of immigrants who came to America to buckle down, take life seriously. One was expected to rise above the tenuous livelihoods of the forebears: tailors, musicians, fruit vendors. My great-grandfather, when not tailoring, earned a few bucks as a musician playing at parties hosted by Saginaw lumber barons. Family stories recount his trudging through the snow with a harp on his back. Certainly the next generation could do better, spawn successful wealthy entrepreneurs.

When my elementary school All-Saints Day pageant rolled around, I thought my father might change his tune about me studying acting. The pageant required each student to choose a saint, dress like the saint, and recite a few lines about the saint's life. My mother suggested Saint Lawrence (my middle name), but backpedaled when she learned he was martyred on a spit. My father proposed Saint Francis. He crafted a small wooden crucifix to be tucked into the cord wrapping my waist to cincture the dyed brown sheet my mother had sewn into a monk's robe. During the play, I recited my lines perfectly. When the curtain closed, the director asked someone to go out and thank the audience. No one volunteered. "I will!" I leapt in, with no other motive than to part the curtain, savor the thrill of stepping out before an anonymous crowd, say a word of appreciation, and enjoy the applause. I pulled it off, but the event did not appease my father who remained adamant that the stage was not to be my calling.

About the closest I ever got to a Hollywood actor was when William Boyd, dressed in his signature all-black Hopalong Cassidy cowboy outfit, passed me on his white stallion, Topper, in the 1954 Pasadena Rose Parade. I was sitting cross-legged on the curb when he glanced down and tossed a silver dollar into my lap. The coin was actually aluminum, but it didn't matter. What mattered was that it was impressed with Boyd's smiling face under his big cowboy hat, and on the reverse was a four-leaf clover and a horseshoe with the words: "Good Luck From Hoppy."

At age twelve, I took a strange turn. I became an acolyte, an odd choice given my disposition regarding rules and authority, but not so odd given the theatrical aspect of such a role. If acting was out, here was a chance to learn some lines, don an outfit, and play a part in front of an audience. The performance involved carrying a big red book, indexed with colored ribbons, from one side of the altar to the other. This called for careful steps and a genuflection. The priest kissed the book and blessed it with incense. Each page—edged with gold, illuminated with fruit, flowers, and twining vines—opened into scripture, stories, poetry. When not in use, the book was covered like a baby. During ceremonies it was never far from the bread and wine. In the Mass, without the book, without the words, there could be no transformation. The book, in essence, was alive.

The priest opened the pages, intoned a song, and I replied in Latin. The meaning escaped me, but the rising of his chant amid smoke and candles—in praise, supplication, benediction—left an imprint. Perfectly intoned, one letter became many letters, one word many words. They levitated from the page, acoustic, unplugged, pure. When the priest finished his song, he bowed to the book and I jangled the hand bells. Their echo reverberated as he turned to face the congregation and raised the Eucharist. When he turned to the altar again, I studied the symbols embroidered on his chasuble: glyphs of Greek and Latin, a tree's forked arms outspread to receive the sun. The church was a theater. Aisles, ushers, seats, stage. The priest dressed for his part, I for mine. The spectators kneeled, shut their eyes, and stood to respond to the lead actor, the man in the sacristy who put robes over his shirt and pants while I went out to light the altar candles to announce the ceremony.

To celebrate my becoming an acolyte I received a gift that had nothing to do with religion, but everything to do with how words arrived on the page: a small rotary printing press and a set of rubber type. My first project was to print a neighborhood newspaper. I hand set the type into a 36-pt. logo, THE BULLETIN, and cranked out a dozen copies. On each copy I would print whatever neighbor-hood gossip I could dig up. This proved to be too much in-formation to hand set, so I decided to write it out. Much of the gossip my parents asked me to censor: the name of the kid who threw overripe persimmons at passing cars; the alcoholic who walked his dog onto neighbors' lawns for its nightly poop; the properly identified ruffians who ar-ranged after-school fights between rival schoolmates; the name of the girl who never came to school without her lice. "You will not publish news that will cause our neighbors to not like us," my mother warned. Exhausting my hand copying out the news, followed by the task of peddling THE BULLETIN door to door quickly became an ordeal. I wanted to be a writer, not a salesman. Make books for personal pleasure, I thought. One copy each, the best you can do. I had plenty of themes in mind: Climbing the World's Tallest Tree, Pounded by a Twenty-foot Wave, How to Write Chi-nese, The Meaning of Telepathy, How I Rescued Consuelo from the Tehachapi Earthquake. Man, I had to get going!

I wanted to realize them all.

In the seventh grade I experienced a crest of ire that would set the tone for further rebellion. During a U.S. history class, my teacher—a life-weary, self-possessed nun—assumed a righteous tone and announced that at age eighteen every boy in class would be ordered by the U.S. government to serve in the army. I ducked behind the girl sitting in front of me and shouted "Oh Yeah?" The nun clapped her hands. "Who said that!" The class went silent. "I did!" I answered, standing to assert not my culpability, but my defiance. That earned me a week's detention for "speaking against the law." I was to stay after school and scrape wads of hardened bubble gum off the playground—unless I apologized. I refused, carried out my sentence, and returned to class. But the idea of "obligatory draft," having to serve without question a country declaring war on another country, never left my mind. I had learned at least one lesson in school: to resist was to remain intact, to safeguard my drive. Were old people to determine my life, my politics? I'd rather speak out, even if it meant "bad behavior"—the authorities' term for subversion.

High school years—I'd rather erase them. Peer pressure to conform, dyslexia when it came to learning dance steps, lousy pay washing dishes at a local steakhouse, four years of questionable education at a school run by Brothers of the Holy Cross, each seemingly bearing his own cross as a recovering alcoholic or social misfit. I ran away from home during this period, hitching through the Mojave to the Sierra Nevada, where a hay truck dropped me on a farm road leading to Mt. Whitney. I walked until snowdrifts blocked me, then returned to the town of Lone Pine, spending my last two dollars on an all-day breakfast in an all-night cafe. Over endless refills of coffee, I wrote until my fingers ached: a story about a loner (me), the road (hwy 395), a ranching girl (Ginny), her overbearing father

(Judd), and the mountains (the steep flanks of Mt. Muir). The idea: a wanderer gets sidetracked by a pretty girl, ends up working on her father's hay farm, and one night (full moon, of course) runs off with his daughter.

I hid the story away, never mentioned it to my parents, or to my schoolmates where my stories about cars, hoodlums, and girls (think Tuesday Weld) were underground hits. As a Fifties' teenager—at odds with my parents, fraught with acceptance issues, done with the altar-boy stuff, lost in angst and boredom—I lived in the shadow of the anointed peers, hid the heart, became the class clown to gain acceptance. I tried out for sports but received the bench. R.O.T.C. wasn't my cup of tea, nor were straight-laced thinkers obedient to church, state, political bullshit, and consumer fads. Their lifestyles cloned TV shows like *Ozzie and Harriet*. The perfect American family. No quandaries, questions, pizazz. Effortlessly good people who enjoyed trouble-free lives, no loose ends, no fractured edges. It never seemed to get dark for these people, the kind of darkness that finally lets you see.

While I bumped along on a crooked path, unsure of myself, hoping for a bit of self-discovery through mistakes, I was beset by elders whose complacent mediocrity added weight to my shoes. It was a world of how you were supposed to act according to others' rules. The polished-shoe, wise-guy, better-than-you war mentality had seeped into civilian life with bigotry, racist jokes, pride. Patriots lived in the afterglow of their 1945 victory; I lived in the dark side of that victory. As a war baby I feared the Bomb's role in future conflicts. I was angered by Americans who cheered the bombing of Japan and supported the proliferation of nuclear weapons, believing they'd keep America safe and the economy upright. My teenage head burned with the idea of a youth culture that would stand up against the America I saw as self-centered, nationalistic, and little interested in the rest of the world except to tame and deprive countries that would be of use for military or economic gain.

Rock and Roll was a life saver during this stage. I was thirteen when Elvis Presley's "Heartbreak Hotel" was first aired, a real hair raiser. A bellhop whose tears kept flowing? A desk clerk dressed in black? Broken-hearted losers crowding into a derelict hotel to cry their gloom? The narrative thumped through my brain with imagery as powerful as Wyeth's cape-wrapped figures in *Treasure Island.* On the heels of Elvis came "Rip it Up" by the wildly flamboyant, totally unpredictable Little Richard—exactly the right fit for the times. So was Chuck Berry, true poet of the genre, with his soul-grabbing guitar intros and streetwise lyrics. I loved singer-songwriter Buddy Holly with his rockabilly West Texas twang, and Fats Domino's hard-driving New Orleans boogie-woogie. A memorable standout was Bo Diddley, son of a Mississippi sharecropper's daughter. His hypnotic guitar and funky riff-driven vocals hit me as an absolutely Black sound, a deep-rooted rap from another continent. His guitar was rectangular, with a reverb effect and a distorted amp that made it seem like he was playing in the back room. Bo's steady beat on "Pretty Thing," three or four notes for the entire melody, crackled through my body like electricity—a Willie Dixon song, my first real link with Mississippi Delta Blues.

While the household slept, I put my ear to a tiny Emerson transistor radio under my pillow and listened to "race music" on Huggy Boy's late night show: Hank Ballard and the Midnighters, the Clovers, Ruth Brown, Etta James, Little Julian Herrera. Rare lowrider hits from East L.A. Sexy R&B from distant brick-city ghettos. Whether I knew it or not, when Etta gave her raspy, elevated twist to "Something's Got a Hold on Me," I was getting a good dose of the Church. A perfect morph of gospel into rock.

Dick Hugg broadcast from Dolphin's of Hollywood, a 24-hour record store that featured Black music and drew a large Anglo-Latino audience. Rhythm and Blues was IN for white kids rebelling against their parents' listening tastes. Guy Lombardo and Mantovani were bad soundtracks for the times. A raunchy edge was a better fit for our clandestine parties and risqué escapades when parents left town. Huggy aired the first African-American all-girl groups, the Bobbettes, and the Chantels, while John Dolphin endorsed Sam Cooke and Charles Mingus. Stoking the fire were Aretha Franklin, Mavis Staples, and Gladys Knight.

It wasn't only music that saved my life. It was the holy ground of the West Coast. The dry heat, the sea out there like a promise. A thin balm of salt, sunlight, and golden chapparal working its chemistry on the senses. On those halcyon days when desert winds licked the ocean razor sharp and one towering swell after another rolled in, I'd hitch to the beach and ride the surf, often resulting in a good head-pounding beneath a wall of water—a psychological cleanout. You crashed around in the deep wondering if you'd see light again, and when you did, it was High Mass. You were delivered—baptized, fortified.

Farther north, beyond Point Conception, the water was too cold for a comfortable swim. This was pensive territory where one enjoyed the grand reward of walking: introspection. Otters backpaddled in aqua coves, tide pools revealed rainbow galaxies; the rare sighting of a condor was a mythic experience. You had plenty to see, and plenty to care about. In Southern Cal you looked past the volleyball players on the beach and the eyes stopped at Catalina Island. Up north you gazed across the Pacific through Monterey pine and imagined the tip of Hokkaido peeking through a fogbank. It was a mind-freeing horizon where thoughts unraveled toward the Orient. Luminous energy invaded the spirit. I wanted to wrestle something from it. Write, paint! Be van Gogh by age twenty. Later would be too late. I'd be too old.

At sixteen I passed my driver's test and bought my father's '53 Chevy Bel Air for $400. I would no longer have to bum rides from others or be held hostage by peers whose priority was to cruise the strip and party. I packed the car with camp stuff, drove across the Mojave to the Sierras, and hiked 14,500-foot Mt. Whitney, a relentless ten-mile climb with an elevation gain of 6,000 feet. Grasping huge sheaves of granite, I experienced solidarity, a bodily romance with the mountain—a desolate, mineral beauty. The "down below" was left behind. Scrambling over uneven talus, I felt stable. I was home! I now added Walter Starr's *Guide to the High Sierras* and John Muir's *The Yosemite* to my library.

A month later, I tucked Steinbeck's *Log from the Sea of Cortez* into my bag and drove the bare essence of a road down the Baja coast. The Mexican landscape put my head in a new place. A raw, quavering sheen bounced from the stony hills. The road was slow, it allowed everything in. When the route dipped from dry desert to an oasis-watered valley, the air filled with the yeasty bite of tropical refuse, drift of cook fires, tortillas baking on clay platters, corn roasting on grills. Mexican houses just seemed to happen. They were of clay, cliff rock, bamboo, palm thatch, tin, and cement. The human touch was everywhere. Ingenuity reigned. A saint carved into a stone lintel guarded a door-way; a stair rail became a hand-molded snake; a hubcap painted with a mustache and scissors announced a barber-shop; pebbles pressed into wet mortar dried into childlike designs of suns and stars. Household gardens had no par-ticular plan. Fruit trees, prickly pear, tomatoes, sun-flowers, corn, tomatillos, runner beans, bougainvillea, jalapeños, cabbage—all in one patch. Order in the disorder. It gave me comfort. So did the land, bone bare, its dun-colored hamlets breaking away toward the sea. A church dome crowned uneven rooftops, a noble silhouette against a burning sunset. Lamplit windows paraded along alleys of blue dust, each window like a tiny square in my childhood Advent calendar.

Twilight brought out food wagons with fiery offerings of salsa, cilantro, onions, and steak. Rancheras played from plaza speakers. Mothers way too young pushed baby carts. Old men conversed on benches. A stranger's invite might lead to a cold Dos Equis or fried squash blossoms and *queso asadero* heated in a tortilla. No matter that I didn't understand Spanish; it heightened my attention to its musicality, no syntax in the way. Lip smack, sandal clap, wing flap, wave slap, horn blow, sex moan: one big vibration. A burro wheezed, streetlamps fizzed, a puppy bawled, a tuba farted, bats beeped, a toddler cried, lovers necked in the dark, veiled ladies straightened their skirts and whispered secrets. A man with a bolo tie and fat sombrero stood at a mike singing salvation hymns. Another yelled political slogans, waving red sheets of paper. The whole world was out, one big talk. An amplified collectivity, all ports open, electrifying my pores. I began to scribble madly. In the commotion and communality, it hit me: forget the studied voice, listen up, capture real talk!

In my last year of high school I was browsing a favorite Hollywood hangout, the Pickwick Bookshop, when my eye caught a golden Buddha meditating on the cover of a Mentor paperback: *The Way of Zen,* by Alan Watts. I bought it for sixty cents and packed it into my bag for a trip to northern Cal with my best friend's sister and her fiancé. We drove his yellow '56 Caddy convertible through Steinbeck country—Monterey and the Salinas Valley—to San Francisco, then up the rugged Sonoma Coast. Among the redwoods, I waded into the Russian River, found a flat rock, sat down, and opened *The Way of Zen*.

Right away, I felt at home. Watts' explanation of Zen reaffirmed that life could be understood by direct intuition instead of in abstract, linear, representational thinking. Three terms in the book stood out. The first was *wabi-sabi*: the acceptance of imperfection, an appreciation of time-worn austere beauty. An axe handle darkened with use, moss greening the north side of a fence, a sudden whorl in the grain of a tabletop. The second was *suchness*: a no-thought state where a thing appeared "as is," unnamed, no interpretation to undo its true state of presence. The third was *wu-wei:* non-acting, simply allowing. Not bogged by purpose, a not going forward, a not backing up. Freedom to go with the flow. No safety belt, no constraint, no self-imposed barriers.

The river swirled about my toes. Was I moving or sitting still? I turned the page to a photo of Kyōto's Ryōan-ji garden. Raked sand symbolized water; rocks suggested islands. Landscape as a contemplative sanctuary. Yes! I heard myself say: the existence of nature, the nature of existence. When I took out my sketchpad and began drawing the river patterns, I realized my hands had eyes, my entire body was an antenna, everything was vibrating in, then out again through the bloodstream. It was not only a return to childhood exuberance, splashing color as I pleased, it was pure undifferentiated existence with everything in my immediate range, and within that range, all the black holes and distant galaxies, too.

In 1963, I was in my second year at the newly established San Fernando Valley State College (now Cal. State Northridge) when the poet Jack Hirschman walked into the art department. He was the first real poet I met, and he was on a mission. In hand was his latest manuscript, carefully typewritten. Bursting with energy, coat flapping, one shoe untied, flames from his wild head, he was a man totally new to my radar: enthusiastic, inventive, informed, vibrant. His head was in the language cloud, heart in the Kabala, feet firmly planted in the human swirl. He celebrated the poets of Europe, Russia, Greece. Politically outspoken, he railed against the American War in Vietnam, gave faces to underdogs, celebrated the marginalized, and filled my ears with lyrical, edgy, surrealist language: words turned inside out, phosphorescent, crackling with light, even when rising from the darkest fathoms.

The manuscript Jack wanted to see into print was *Interchange*, a poem dedicated to John Cage, one that Jack would later size up as "the 'mind' of a car in motion from the Pacific Ocean at, say, Venice to the Interchange or major freeway hub in downtown L.A." It was a crazy ride of speed, dotted lines, Mad Hatter billboards, babbling brake lights, standstill of exit ramps, dead-stop of backed-up boulevards. The poem was a fast-forward metaphor for our times, a juxtaposition of imagery that zipped into the eye as if through a windshield, and washed over the reader—the driver at the wheel—like a black-and-white rainbow.

As a wet-behind-the-ears undergraduate studying painting and graphic design, I was asked by my graphic arts professor, Harold Schwarm, to transform Jack's poem into a typographic journey. Baffled and intimidated at first, I had no choice but to settle in, put my foot to the pedal, and ride—follow Jack's concept of the poem, match the energy of his word flow, design a book unlike the sewn-and-bound books I grew up with. Instead, it would have no binding. I would operate the art department's flatbed proof press to produce an edition of 300 copies, which Jack would sign and read from at Zora Gallery, the official publisher, in Los Angeles.

The process required hand-setting metal type and vintage woodblock fonts, printing them on a small hand press, pasting them up, photo-developing metal plates from the paste up, locking the plates onto the proof press, and printing the poem on refrigerator-white sheets of semi-gloss card stock. The sheets would be cut into 7 x 7 inch squares and loosely collated into white 7¼ x 7¼ inch boxes which Jack had already purchased. They looked like reel-to-reel tape boxes, but Jack laughed and said no, they were leftovers from an importer who had them made to package women's stockings to be sold at high-end department stores. The boxes—each to be silk-screened with INTERCHANGE in bold italic caps—would hold the poem squares, each square like a page normally bound between covers in a traditional book.

When the project was completed in 1964, I was amazed to realize not only what had been accomplished, but what I had experienced as a young man during my meetings with Jack—sometimes at his Venice cottage, sometimes at Barney's Beanery in West Hollywood, an authentically "beat" place, teeming with the energy of artists, musicians, poets, and free thinkers. Over a beer at the Beanery, Jack told me *Interchange* was inspired by "the most far-out poem of the 19th century, *A Throw of the Dice Will Never Abolish Chance,* by Stéphane Mallarmé, a work that had a many different typographies and a spatial design that was unique for that time."

Jack's reading at the Zora Gallery to celebrate the release of *Interchange* knocked my socks off. Behind him was *Interchange,* removed from the box, each black individual card pinned to the wall. The poem made visual! A typographic black-on-white constellation that reverberated with Jack's deep, lyrical voice. Over his head was the central page, the only one having white typography against black. This was the intersection, a turnstile around which all other pages, arranged in any order, revolved. Random sensory flashes—white bars of highway lines, headlight streaks, billboard slogans—dashing back and forth against stark black—simultaneously hitting the mind in whatever order, even though, as Jack explained, "there was a beginning-middle-end of the poem as originally composed."

Jack's presence—his innovative mind, his politics, his poetics—had a tremendous effect on my life and art. To render visible the auditory charge of his language in *Interchange* might have seemed an impossible leap for a twenty-year-old art major, but there was a tangential aspect of my university studies that helped me understand where Jack was coming from. I was minoring in anthropology under the tutelage of Edmund Carpenter, Marshall McLuhan's distinguished collaborator who had just returned from field work with the Inuit people in the Arctic and was lecturing on his favorite subject: nonlinear reality—a direct echo of Jack's approach to the poem. Carpenter would sometimes baffle his students by citing Pascal's description of nature: "An infinite sphere whose center is everywhere and circumference nowhere." He was big on McLuhan's *Gutenberg Galaxy* and the first to introduce us to John Cage's indeterminacy in music.

My other teachers included jazz cellist Fred Katz, filmmaker Robert "Bobe" Cannon, German multi-media painter Fritz Faiss, and folklorist Bess Lomax Hawes. Together they encouraged students toward a wide spectrum of artists. Robert Flaherty to Fellini, Albert Ryder to Jackson Pollock, Man Ray to Dorothea Lange, Eric Satie to Thelonious Monk, Buddy Bolden to Fats Navarro, Ma Rainey to Billie Holiday, Walt Whitman to Allen Ginsberg, William Shakespeare to Ezra Pound, Thomas Hart Benton to Andy Warhol. A field trip to the Ferus Gallery in 1963 exposed us to the first showing of Warhol's painting of Elvis Presley dressed as a cowboy drawing a six-shooter on the viewer.

Fritz Faiss, who studied at the Bauhaus, and whose

paintings were destroyed by the Gestapo during the War, taught a class called "materials and techniques of the artist." He lectured on encaustic art, from Pompeii to Jasper Johns, and had the class read Paul Klee's *Diaries*. Bobe Cannon, an acclaimed animator, recommended *The Hokusai Sketchbooks* and Zen Master Sengai's *sumi-e* drawings. Fred Katz provided close listens to Oscar Pettiford and Jimmy Garrison. Bess Hawes tuned my ear to Leadbelly, Memphis Minnie, Blind Willie Johnson, the Georgia Sea Island Singers.

While the painting faculty celebrated Abstract Expressionism and Pop Art, I was drawn to artists who were often categorized as Regionalists. I finally got to see firsthand the works of Morris Graves, Mark Tobey, Emily Carr, Lawren Harris, Georgia O'Keeffe, Arthur Dove, Agnes Pelton, Marsden Hartley, and Albert Pinkham Ryder on a summer road trip with an artist buddy. With impromptu plein-air painting and museum stops, it was a ball—a chance to leave behind the everyday, especially important for my friend, who wanted out from the reins of his father, a stiff-jawed F.B.I. agent. We crammed his VW with art materials, sleeping bags, extra clothes, cook gear, and took turns behind the wheel on what turned out to be a 10,000-mile journey up the Pacific Coast to B.C, over the Cascades, across the northern prairies to Canada's lake country, around the Gaspé Peninsula, down New England's coast to New York, through Appalachia, the deep south, and back home across the Texas Panhandle.

In the art department, I worked late nights to nonstop FM jazz: Billie Holiday, Prez, Bird, Trane, Miles Davis; wild improvs by Ornette Coleman, Pharaoh Sanders, Roland Kirk. Billie's voice, heartbreakingly personal, bored through me with extreme sadness. A behind-the-beat Eternal Struggle. A far cry from the LPs my father primed me with before college: the Dave Brubeck and Stan

Getz an *Examiner* music editor passed on to him. But one album, *Focus,* hit me strong. Getz on tenor sax against Eddie Sauter's moody orchestral arrangements. His blowing was hot, cool, urgent, jagged-edged, abruptly going from dream-like curves to unexpected frenzy: a kind of tone poem that brought to surface what Ferlinghetti called "pictures of the gone world." It was both strange and reaffirming to find my innermost feelings being matched collectively. People revolution, jazz revolution, language revolution was in the air.

Kerouac, Ginsberg, Diane di Prima, Lenore Kandel, Leonard Cohen, the soaring oratory of Martin Luther King. And Bob Dylan: his raw-to-the-bone, biting attacks on the establishment, his stream-of-consciousness narratives and mercurial multiple-persona presence. His was "break-away" music, the real folk music of the era. Nothing held in reserve, plenty of room for personal affliction, a timely resurrection of deep-stream language, hallucinatory wordplay, surreal revolt, plain-spoken portrayals of everyday people. Dylan was the lonely genius, a hot-wired aerial receiving jangled receptions from everywhere, nowhere, and beyondwhere at once. As he channeled them into our world, we became lost in the imagery, carried by emotional heat waves and kaleidoscopic time warps. "A Hard Rain" was America's true anthem for the changing times. His angry striking out at the reckless war mongers in "Masters of War" cuts through me today with the same power and pertinency as it did in 1963.

Suddenly we had revolt, we had protest, we had stories in our songs: depth and dimension of LANGUAGE. It was quite a leap from "Mr. Lee," the snappy two-minute tune by the Bobbettes (1957)—over so quickly the feet hadn't a chance to reach the dance floor and the ears didn't quite know what they'd heard—to Dylan's Mr. Jones in his six-minute "Ballad of a Thin Man" (1965), or his dreamy eleven-minute surrealist love poem "Sad Eyed Lady of the Lowlands" (1966) which, instead of the snap, had the inescapable pull of a riptide. Or take "The Ballad of Hollis Brown," Dylan's portrayal of the squalor of an American farm family; or "The Lonesome Death of Hattie Carroll," a piercing tale of the deadly beating of a 51-year old African-American barmaid with a plastic cane by a drunken youth from a wealthy white tobacco-farm family. These were statements, not tunes. You didn't dance, you listened. And Dylan's voice, though affected, was a cracked and dusty worn-shoe hobo sound that had me glued to what he sang. The photograph on his album *The Freewheelin' Bob Dylan*—the young bard with his 19-year-old girlfriend hugging his arm as they walked a snowy West Village street— was for me, a crew-cut kid eager to flee the constraints of middle-class suburbia, a potent summary of youth, love, sexual yearning, and the potential freedom of all the unexplored roads to come.

In one of Dylan's early masterpieces, "Visions of Johanna," he unrolled a more personal story—a chronicle filled with hallucinogenic imagery as the protagonist moved through a nocturnal city in quest of his elusive muse. The subway, the empty lot, the museum, the watchman, the loft, the fish truck, the mule on the wall—all real, yet all of a ghostly netherworld. By the song's end, only the questor's vision of Johanna remains. Sometimes Dylan's lyrics were like whitewater rushing through the rocks, foaming, splattering, fracturing so quickly that the verbal pitch was overwhelming. "Subterranean Homesick Blues" was so odd and wonderfully dizzy that it popped you beyond words, through your cranium, into outer space. *Bang!* You appreciated language beyond comprehension. You *felt* your way through the song. You did not rely on the brain, the need to understand. It was Hello to non sense, Yes to the roll of thunder, the drift, the rockslide, the blow of lava:

a collective subjective non-linear word plunge.

Nobody knew what was next. That was part of the deal. Stormy weather. The eruptive Sixties. We had been flung forward, past ourselves, all sound, lyric, cadence. A meteoritic explosion. No beginning, middle, end. To drop out was to drop in—to be totally there with what had never come before. John Lennon and Paul McCartney's free-jam, invent-your-own-rules approach to composing was like Pollock standing inside his own canvas, dashing paint, lost in the action, stepping back to see what took place. A Gone-ness of not knowing. Head and soul dissolved into an energy stream of words FLARING with multiple associations. Song writing the writer. Existential recall, conversational debris, off-the-map fairylands, the Queen's speech, a car crash, a runaway child: grist for the mill. The Beatles' relentless experimentalism was a mind freer, a time-and-tense-shifting merge of dream and waking into found sounds, new structures of verse, overlapping tape loops. "A loosening up toward experience," wrote Michael McClure. "It is the surge that carries us through. It spurts and it radiates. It is the energy that defines poetry." A new system had been re-awakened from our deep interior, harkening back to William Blake's revolt. Word alchemy, language resurrected from the flesh. A rocking horse flung off its rails.

The mid-Sixties were fraught with serious questions over the capitalist economic system, the corporate-military-political engine that kept it going, the rise of consumerism at the cost of the planet, and the square generation's expectation that youth should abide by post-war values, fall in line for the betterment of America—no questions asked. But there was plenty to question. The Holocaust, for starters. The criminality of the use of the atomic bomb on Japan and napalm and agent orange on Vietnam. The lingering effects of McCarthyism. JFK's assassination.

Racism, hate crimes, apartheid. J. Edgar Hoover's illegal wire taps, burglaries, planted evidence, false rumors aimed at interrupting grass-roots political meetings, and the unabashed disruption of literature, publishing, and free speech through outlandish censorship.

If you wanted to march, protest, stand up for change, speak out against the war, you were subject to surveillance and harassment driven by Hoover's paranoia and ultra-conservative anti-Commie patriotism. This was not an era for sissies. You stood up or you died. Or you stood up *and* you died. Blacks were still in chains, Native Americans on the Long Walk. The Vietnam War was out of control. Gays were under persecution. Student revolts, civil rights marches, sit-ins, anti-war demonstrations were on the rise. Ginsberg's "Howl" had set the stage ten years previous; now it was Joan Baez, Buffy Sainte-Marie, Nina Simone's "Why," Coltrane's "Alabama," the polarized movements of Martin Luther King and Malcolm X, Mahalia Jackson's "We Shall Overcome," and Jimi Hendrix's screechingly distorted "Star Spangled Banner."

America was exploding. Amid the smoke and shrapnel, many of us were ennobled. We came together, we were cynical, we were not going to buy the Grand Lie. Others were shock-waved into their own trajectories, either to flame or fizzle. In 1965, about to graduate, I was torn between heading to San Francisco to join the growing literary scene and war protest, or going overseas to work as a Peace Corps volunteer. When I spoke of my hesitation to leave the scene for peace work abroad, Jack Hirschman lit up. "Go! What could be more important?" Jack helped me understand that I was not leaving anything, but going toward something: vital social work, ample solitude in which to examine one's thoughts, plenty of experience from which to write. "Get out of L.A. and do some good," he said. "Peace work will not only change your life, it will inform your poetry." I hadn't quite expected that advice from a senior poet teaching at UCLA, but, given Jack's increased anti-war activity, it shouldn't have come as a surprise. (Hirschman was eventually fired from UCLA for participating in public protests and giving A grades to draft-eligible students to assist them in avoiding the war. He would later move north, take to the streets of San Francisco, and become poet laureate of that city.)

Jack's advice was echoed by Pete Seeger, who one afternoon gave a mini-concert on the college campus: traditional ballads and anti-war songs. Seeger's life and work stood as a testament for social and political change. He recalled his folk- singer hero Woody Guthrie who performed with a slogan taped to his guitar: "This Machine Kills Fascists." These days Seeger was confronting President Johnson and the Vietnam War on his album *Dangerous Songs!?*. After the concert, I went up to shake his hand. He asked about my plans after graduation and when I told him of my thoughts about joining the Peace Corps, he gave a positive nod: "Any peace work that counters the violence of war is a worthy calling. Make yourself active!"

My peers in the art department warned me that leaving Los Angeles meant giving up the chance to get a gallery, boost my visibility as an artist, and establish a following. I appreciated the advice but tossed it aside as practical and limiting. My pressing need was to strike out toward the horizon. I didn't want to be deceived by the idea of keeping current, being up with what was fashionable, or ditching my desire for the afar to remain home to stay tuned with the latest art movement. An electrical charge was rippling through my nervous system—the "inner governance" once described by my father: a calling, a lightning bolt flashing GO!

Though I had applied for Peace Corps work in Bolivia or Nepal, my destiny became highland Ecuador, not a bad compromise. As part of a ragtag group of young volunteers brought up on everything from cherry picking in Michigan to civil disobedience in Berkeley, I was assigned to work in a "community development" program, a hazy definition, at best. It could mean building a one-room schoolhouse, harnessing water for electricity, suggesting new strains of seed for arid terrain. None of which held meaning for people who didn't own their land.

One volunteer, Jeffrey Ashe, who would become a lifelong friend, vented the shock most of us felt upon first arriving in Ecuador: "To arrive in the highland Andes in 1966 was as though I had been put in a time machine that was dialed back to 1570, a time before Cervantes. The relations between patrón and laborer and even the technology of farming had been unchanged for centuries." Instead of dispersing seed or building rabbit hutches, it seemed more important to examine Ecuador's feudal situation by listening to the people we were sent to work with. Let them tell us what they needed, not have it the other way around: Uncle Sam stepping in with a plan.

I soon found myself working with landless Quechua-speaking farmers with a small group of Peace Corps volunteers and Ecuadorians from the Agrarian Reform Institute in Quito. The landscape was visually stunning: verdant ribbons of barley, wheat, and quinoa climbed the hills into tawny grasslands that caressed the snows of 20,500-foot Mt. Chimborazo, one of the most beautiful mountains I had ever seen. For the indigenous who lived there, beauty took a back seat to the brutal social and economic exploitation that they and their forebears suffered under the governing privileged class. In backcountry hamlets Indian leaders were already at the early stages of organizing to discuss agrarian reform and how to get their stolen lands back. As Peace Corps volunteers, our aim was to help connect the dots, the hamlets, the community leaders, and expand the discussion. It was in the Andes in 1967 that I had a political rather than a literary experience with a book.

We were carrying copies of a 48-page paperback, *Reforma Agraria en Ecuador,* which spelled out a law passed in 1936 that abolished serfdom—mandatory labor by a peasant for an absentee landholder in exchange for the right to live on a tiny plot and grow a few beans. The plot, which could never be owned, was on the rockiest, steepest area of the hacienda, while the patrón held the level fields, and the water. The land, of course, once belonged to the people. It had been stolen over the centuries by the church, state, and privileged elite who had effectively kept the *Reforma Agraria en Ecuador* secret. Most of the peasants couldn't read anyway. There were no schools on the haciendas. Campesinos were kept illiterate and forced to toil the rich owners' fields to serve off hundreds of years of accumulated "debt." The plight of the Indian serf had been explicitly detailed by Ecuadorian author Jorge Icaza in his book *Huasipungo,* a tale of social protest akin to those of Zola and Dostoevsky, that garnered both censure and acclaim upon publication in 1934. It was required reading during our Peace Corps training in Puerto Rico.

In Ecuador we held clandestine meetings with landless farmers in which excerpts from the *Reforma Agraria en Ecuador* were read aloud. Laws were discussed and *hausipungeros* (tenant farmers) were informed that a branch of the Ecuadorian government—the Institute for Agrarian Reform—had been created to serve them. It was an intense period, my usual set of footholds dislodged. The serfs explored aspects of the agrarian reform law that provided legal justification for them to take action. They broke with four hundred years of oppression, joined with other indigenous movements, marched in the streets, roused public interest, accessed proper political channels, and—

after a prolonged struggle—obtained their land titles.

Like my father in India, I wrote detailed letters home from abroad. Some were lengthy political rants; others described the land, people, and Andean festivals with all the emotional punch I could muster. Some were accompanied with poems bordered with drawings of flaming volcanoes and mythical condors; others with photos taken with my Yashika-120 camera. Most were typed by candlelight in a cold adobe hut, my feet kept warm in a pan of water heated on a Coleman stove. My Hermes Rocket would accept only two sheets of carbon and three onionskin papers in its roller. To send one poem to a dozen people I would have to retype the poem four times. A "copier" was to be found in the Peace Corps office, fifty miles off, but I could only get my hands on it when the director was away, and even then it rarely worked.

One day a fellow volunteer, Don Briddell, told me of a hermit living in a remote valley in southern Ecuador where the climate had enabled a high concentration of centenarians. He described the recluse as an eccentric utopian steeped in Eastern mysticism and suggested we visit him. I agreed, deciding it would be a welcome break from my political work in the northern Andes. We hopped a night bus to Ecuador's far south, and woke to dry crumpled hills ringing a valley verdant with maize and sugarcane. A farmer indicated the path to the *casita del ermitaño* and shortly we found ourselves at a gate signed "Universidad Natural." The hermit was a longhaired forty-eight-year-old American ex-pat named Johnny Lovewisdom. He was dressed in a white cassock and walked rather stiffly. We sat outside his hand-built hut, where with a little coaxing he expounded on Eastern wisdom, yoga, Hindu saints, and Buddhist masters. On that occasion we were not invited into his hut, but some months later when I returned on my own, it was a different story.

In the manner of certain Asian ascetics, Johnny twice refused to open his door, but on my third try it creaked open and I was welcomed in. Lovewisdom was partially paralyzed, the result of working in the pesticide-contaminated orchards of California's Central Valley. Instead of enduring the long process of suing the grower, he took a freighter to Guayaquil and set out for the Andes. Living in a crater in the 1950s, he devoted himself to meditation, fasting, herbal remedies, and yoga—until his solitude was interrupted by reporters, who wrote him up as the "Saint of the Andes." A wave of curiosity seekers followed, but Lovewisdom slipped away to the bumpy terrain of the Andean basins near the Peruvian border. He settled in the Valle de Vilcabamba, which he proclaimed "The most radioactive-fallout free valley on earth."

Johnny lived on a diet of raw fruit, practiced his asanas every morning, and spent the afternoons cranking out his "Universal Life Newsletters" on an ancient mimeo press. These he mailed at the local correo, a tiny adobe, its porch post tied with a mule whose packsaddle held the daily mail. Lovewisdom died in 2000, by which time his books had become available on the internet, among them *The Buddhist Essene Gospel of Jesus* and several chapbooks on diet, including *Live Juice Therapy* and *A Master Course on Foodless Living*. I hadn't realized I'd befriended an iconoclast-dropout supreme, just when dropping out was becoming a viable alternative in the States. But Johnny wasn't always encouraging to people wanting to start a new life in Vilcabamba. I was with him in 1967 when he was composing a letter of response to a group of seekers from Seattle who thought The Valley of Longevity (as it was beginning to be called) would be an ideal place for a commune. His advice: "You don't have to travel 5,000 miles to start a commune. Begin where you are!"

It was Lovewisdom who suggested I abandon carbon sheets and type on wax stencils, which would allow me to make countless reproductions on his mimeograph. "Don't wait for the world to move," he advised, "move it yourself. Not in editions of three, but in three hundred. As many pages as it takes! Hand sew the pages into books!" I left Johnny's abode charged with glee. I had been taken back to boyhood when my parents bound my writings and drawings into my first books, and to the rotary printing press I was gifted at age twelve.

Weeks later I returned with my stencils. My usual letters had turned into prose poems, and I used a stylus to scratch drawings into the stencils to accompany the writing. Johnny and I printed up the poems, which I mailed to friends, family, the *Los Angeles Free Press,* and various underground mags. By serendipity, several thousand miles away from home, I found myself at the heart of the so-called mimeo revolution, a publish-it-yourself movement that preceded the alternative-press phenomenon. Johnny Lovewisdom had connected me to the precursor of the Worldwide Web. All he requested in exchange was that I haul printing ink up to his hermitage. Proper mimeo ink was unavailable in Ecuador. The "ink" Johnny was referring to was used crankcase oil that a bus driver saved whenever he did an oil change behind the Vilcabamba depot—a shack, really. Johnny laid a long pole over my shoulders, each end of the yoke dangling with an empty, recycled five-gallon lard can. I then trekked to the depot, had the driver fill the cans, and hiked the ink back up to Johnny's, my spine sore, my pants splashed with oil. In all, a worthy exchange.

These reflections bring a smile. In 1967 there was no googling Johnny Lovewisdom. You had to venture out to see him. Today one can stay in to go out. Sit at a computer, "bring it up" on the screen. In the Sixties, one embarked on a determined journey. You left home, and you were gone. You didn't know what to expect. Without email, cell phone, GPS, you were on your own. Bus ride to bus ride, footstep to footstep your mind stretched, probed, extended its feelers. Tangible, touchable, walkable horizons were mysterious and waiting. Who knew what was around the corner? Mystery was a preferable contrast to today's "see it before you get there" on a handheld screen. One entered the landscape as if submitting to the pages of a great storybook with its typographic projections of mountains, forests, deserts, and seas to be savored page by page. If you had a destination in mind, a slow entry was preferable. Sail, hike, ride a bus, bike. After the pleasures and frustrations of multiple sidetracks and myriad encounters with characters dubious or enlightened, one arrived at one's goal: the headwaters, so to speak. Here you basked in the presence of the source. A slow, quiet absorption of a new land. Lovewisdom called this presence *darshan*—"a beholding."

> *Trails go nowhere,*
> *they end exactly where*
> *you stop.*
> > —Lew Welch

My trail stopped at Johnny Lovewisdom's, but the journey continues to unwind. As I write, memory starts and stops, multiplies into branches, continues to redefine the past with events, images, personages that rise, fade, and are replaced by new ones. Where lies reality? In all of it! The hermit resides in the pursuer of the hermit. He is here, at his desk, typing up a past waiting to be told.

In 1997, after my father died, I found a cache of

letters he had written from India. Removing them from their box, a distinct sensation occurred: an olfactory hit of paper and ink accompanied by the tactile sensation of unfolding the onionskin letter from its envelope and enjoying the visual hit of the typewriter impression on the page. The letters were accompanied by my father's photographs and penciled notations recorded while visiting shrines, street fairs, and sacred riverbanks. They revealed my father's eagerness to "say what he saw," visually and verbally—an act of pleasure that remained with him the rest of his life. Three weeks before he died, my brother Jim and I drove him up the California coast, where he walked the Big Sur cliffs photographing poppies and surf. In a small inn, we drank cappuccinos while he penned postcards to loved ones, informing them where he was and what he was seeing. I know he missed our mother on that trip. Sleeping across from him in a Morro Bay motel, I heard him whisper her a good night, followed by a soft chain of words that sounded like he was making an appointment with her—as he had done when he first suggested they come to the California coast to live together.

At age thirty-six, the exact age of my father when he embarked for India, I made my first trip to the subcontinent. With no plan to duplicate his journey, I inadvertently found myself following his tracks—observing, conversing, taking photos and notes. Old Delhi, The Taj, Benares, the Deccan villages, the Himalayan hill stations; with each advance, with every revelatory fumble into an idol-crammed temple, dusty village, or chaotic marketplace, it became obvious that my father's written records and photos had set me forward on an artistic path—or, more simply, into the art of seeing. Without intention, he had tweaked my curiosity, instilled a delight for the exotic and an appreciation for the ordinary. He provided a sense of what true journeying can be: an awareness that the world is not only there to learn from, but to partake in.

Travel opened the door to surprising landscapes, common households, and to the many rooms of a beautiful if not brutal world. On sacred river steps where worshipers had prayed for thousands of years, he photographed the unbelievable in the everyday: minstrels in rags chanting holy songs, women in silks cupping flames in their palms, ascetics knotted in contortions, cows daubed with red handprints, babies with antimony eyes and brass amulets, a marigold vendor at the cremation ghats. Thirty-five years later, they were still there. The characters, the mishmash, the grief, the goodwill, the crunch of pilgrims venerating the sunrise. It was the first of a half-dozen journeys I would make to India, each journey just the tip of the iceberg.

My father was an accountant, not an editor. But when it came to the written word, he could set me straight. Once, after I handed him my latest book, he halted after the first couple of pages. "Why do you take so long to say something!" His "do more with less" comment I had heard many times during my college years. My father, though, wasn't a professor. He didn't read Emerson or Whitman; he liked *Popular Science* and *The Saturday Evening Post.* He placed great emphasis on loyalty and diligence, responsibility to family, obligation to community and work. He was meticulous with his dress and with his automobiles. He was socially gracious, often suspicious, frugal with money, yet paradoxically generous. An avid toy maker, his early gifts to me were a handcrafted wooden truck, a construction crane with pulleys, a tomato-can locomotive with bell and headlight. Toward the end of his life he dispersed his savings to his children in yearly segments. Two thousand here, three thousand there. I saved a few increments for a down payment on a modest house along the Río Grande. The next segment went towards an adobe studio. He proudly approved. He didn't want to die and leave his money in a will; he wanted to watch it satisfy the needs of his children while he was alive.

It is to my parents that I owe my early awakening to the natural world. I watched my father train flowering vines with tender concern, add eggshells to his heirloom roses, nurture fruit from the very first tree he planted in our backyard—a Meyer lemon, in the year 1934. The summer heat of Southern California was perfect for cooling ourselves with lemonade squeezed from this hybrid tree native to China, and my mother's lemon meringue pies were unparalleled. Behind the Meyer lemon and not far from my favorite climbing tree—a sprawling Dutch elm—my father built a small shrine from planks of redwood and in it he placed Saint Francis. In front of our house stood a magnolia tree, too delicate to climb. In the month of May its creamy petals filled the air with sensuous perfume. The effect—when combined with the neighbor's wisteria, sprays of golden poppies, and a bed of carnations—was exotic, if not erotic. Add the menthol scent of the eucalyptus along the rear of our property and the noble flare of a poinsettia under my bedroom window, and the sensation was overpowering.

In the kitchen I helped my mother with her Italian dinners, adding parsley and a pinch of nutmeg to the ricotta stuffing for ravioli. Her cooking was influenced by the Sicilian members of the family, her pasta sauce flavored with lots of garlic, a dash of cinnamon, and a medium-size onion pierced with cloves. Southern California was Eden, a breadbasket, the buzz of nature, the "Indianness" of the earth, red pigment in caves, phallic yucca exploding under a magnetic sky. And the hearth. Bawdy family gatherings. Clatter of silverware, sauce pans, serving spoons, clink of wine glasses. Food heaped on plates, The Italy of rolled-up sleeves, chianti, poker chips, cigars, loud political arguments, dark secrets, dark rings under the eyes of hushed aunts. And the cousins, a little too fat, always exuding sharp odors of adrenaline.

"The clarity of Cal," wrote Kerouac, "it'll break your heart." He meant rolling yellow hills against Pacific blue. Gold light at the end of day. Lazy clouds floating above white clapboard cottages, bougainvillea sprawling over tile roofs. Moonflowers and date palms in desert canyons. Oranges, almonds, peaches, and figs. Mimosa from South America, pepper trees from Peru, pomegranates from the Mediterranean. Hollywood with its Chaplins and Cleopatras. Rows of artichokes and grapes. San Francisco's fleeting sun, Orient-bound freighters through the Golden Gate.

> "Smoke and goldenness
> in the late afternoon of time."

When I climbed into the light between the leaves of our Dutch elm, I had the world to myself. I peered through my spyglass over neighborhood rooftops, followed a line of smoke from a Southern Pacific train moving across the suburbs, and followed, too, the slate-gray ridges of the Verdugos, the San Gabriels, the Santa Susanas. Thin highways wound through these weathered upthrusts and I was often with my parents on them, drawn into what John Muir called "the rose-purple zone," foothills "bathed in endless variety of fragrance and color, as if Nature had taken pains to gather her choicest treasures to draw her lovers into close and confiding communion with her."

My favorite road twisted over the Tehachapis into the San Joaquin Valley, where it straightened, narrowed through olive groves, and followed the Kaweah River into foothills dotted with see-through pines and fairytale crowns of oak. When the hills steepened into the Sierra Nevada, a new kind of air whickered through the wind-wings of our Hudson: a diamond-clear breeze fragranced with incense cedar, kit-kit-dizze, sugar pine, and *Sequoia Giganteum*. I explored acorn-grinding places on flat granite boulders, copied Indian glyphs into my notepad, plucked fool's gold from a brook where minnows darted under the shadows of flowering dogwood. My father gave me an Automobile Club map of "The Giant Forest," a miniature masterpiece of finely dashed topographic features, a throwback to the map in my coveted *Treasure Island*. Trails marked in tenths of miles and place names in 9-point font revved my imagination: *Pillars of Hercules, Bears Bathtub, Shattered Giant, Panther Gap*. I wanted to walk them all, and with a bit of begging I got my father on a couple of them.

A favorite path traversed a flower-studded meadow circled by towering redwoods, crossed a stream where a mother bear and her cubs dallied, and advanced into the most sky-reaching trees I had yet to see, their stately columns interspersed with slanted rays of sun. Eyes upward, I walked through a subdued and misting shadow world streaked with gold. And there, before a massive redwood, my father and I stopped. The tree was not standing. It had fallen long ago, was fire hollowed, and lay among the ferns and moss like the hulk of a beached sea vessel. One end was boarded up. "What?" I looked up at my father. "A hermit's home," he said, walking closer. "A man who lives away from things."

Hale Tharp, the hermit, was long gone. A herder who had drifted into the mountains in the mid 1800s, he had boarded up one end of the fallen sequoia to create a cabin-like extension and made it his seasonal home. When my father asked me to look inside, I timidly stuck my head through a crude doorway. After my eyes adjusted, a tiny earthen-floor room was revealed. Plankboard bed, stump for a chair, cast-iron pot hanging from a tripod in a fireplace that emptied its smoke through a stone chimney which ran up one side of the fallen tree. ("A noble den," John Muir called it when he visited in 1879.) I sniffed the musty darkness, took a photo with my Kodak Brownie, and felt a lift inside my flesh. That such a lifestyle existed was a revelation. In the tingling silence a seed was planted. Twenty-five years later it would germinate into the primitive cabin I built in the mountains of northern New Mexico.

Not far from Tharp's cabin, our family hiked a granite dome and I stood in limitless sky. An updraft of sun-warmed sequoias fragranced the air. A distant line of storm-beaten crags, snow in their aprons, danced without moving. A thousand feet below I caught the glint of the Kaweah River. I came down feeling up. It was the first time I had stood in eternity. I was ten years old and felt an exalted connection with all that I saw—Muir's "wild delight." The granite summit was not enough. I wanted to go farther: where a keyhole pass between 14,000-foot peaks held my gaze. Back home, I helped my father print a photo of those peaks taken from the top of the dome. I tacked "The Great Western Divide," as he called it, to my bedroom wall above a table decorated with a small felt-covered bear from the Giant Forest gift shop, and a few Sierra Nevada quartz crystals. Mountains were now a serious calling.

There is always the physical tangible aspect of a landscape in one's upbringing, an outer view which merges with the inner psychic landscape to shape a lifetime. The taste of lemon from our backyard tree was a nip of Paradise compared to the Forbidden Fruit in the Old Testament—an invigorating, palpable cleansing plucked from my private Eden. And the Dutch elm? To hoist myself up its trunk and climb into the branches was to rise transfigured into the Tree of Knowledge, free of bondage, all links to parent, teacher, and pastor clipped. I could peer between the branches and *see* beyond who I was and where I was, into the Great Circle of mountains and sky that held me. I *knew* the world was round, I did not have to believe the clumsy sketch on the blackboard chalked by my geography teacher.

One of my prized books, *Marvels of the New West*, was printed in the 1800s, a library discard, battered on the outside, but fine on the inside. I still have it on my shelf. The pages are profuse with engravings depicting the wonders of nature: *Snow Galleries of the Sierra Nevada, Cascade on the Firehole River, Cliff Palaces of Mesa Verde, Vishnu's Temple in the Grand Canyon, Danger above the Timber Line*. Two maps compared "The West As it Was" and "The West As it Is." I liked the West as it was: no towns, cities, political boundaries. Only topography: *Western Declivity, Plateau of Anahuac, Grand American Desert, Cinder Cone at Sunset*.

I couldn't keep my feet still. Maps were open invitations to ride the contours. The cartography on my California map dipped 280 feet below sea level in Death Valley, rose into the bristlecone pines, fell into jagged fault lines, and soared again to nearly 15,000 feet. A Himalayan map revealed peaks of almost 30,000 feet. They lodged in my imagination as unclimbable temples, their names mysterious and unsayable: Lhotse, Cho Oyu, Dhaulagiri, Nanga Parbat, Kanchenjunga.

One summer, digging through a box in a neighbor's garage destined for the Goodwill, I found Maurice Herzog's *Annapurna*. In the book were close-ups of the Himalayas. One showed a man with rope and ice pick dangling from an impossible cliff. The world around him was transparent, only ice and sky. Nothing between him and heaven but his own will, nothing to break his fall if he lost grip. It was death or the sublime. I added the book to my collection of mountain things: a *Sequoia Gigantea* cone, a glossy red manzanita branch, a flicker feather, a gnarl of driftwood from the Merced River. Impulsively, I took the stones I had placed near my felt-covered bear, and—without knowing why—buried them under the backyard lemon tree, as far as my eleven-year-old arm would reach.

Thirty years later, when my father put the house up for sale after my mother's death, I dug up the stones. They are in front of me now, under a photo of Annapurna from my twenty-day trek around the mountain. My journey to the Himalayas began with the burying of the stones. Surely it was an act of hiding a symbolic mountain; to place in safekeeping a desire to visit the peaks that entranced me in Herzog's book, and the wild feeling that overcame me on the granite dome where the keyhole pass held my gaze.

I look back now on many journeys that have merged into one journey. On trips to the Sierras, my parents spurred me toward the Himalayas. In the Mojave, they opened the doors to the deserts of Rajasthan. Through my father's travel descriptions and my mother's encouragement to "write a couple lines," they guided me onto a path to self-expression. Always pointing farther, they put me on the road to the Southwest —and to the far reaches of the world.

II.
Somewhere in the East

A journey, after all, neither begins in the instant we set out, nor ends when we have reached our doorstep once again. It starts much earlier and is really never over, because the film of memory continues running on inside of us long after we have come to a physical standstill.

Ryszard Kapuściński

the way through the world is more difficult to find than the way beyond it.

Wallace Stevens

THE TAJ MAHAL: ENIGMA & REALITY

"Sahib, look!"

The conductor on the Rajdhani Express, a chest-nut-skinned man with white eyebrows and a bright smile, taps me on the shoulder, pointing with his black glove out the window. Across the early morning landscape, a few kilometers off, the Taj Mahal glitters like a marble jewel box. Its sandstone plinth is hidden by waving fields of sugar cane, creating the effect that the Taj is floating just above a brushstroke of lavender mist rising from a broad ripple of green.

"A supreme sight, Sahib!"

The train chuffs on, spitting a blizzard of cinders through my open window. Crows fly into the calligraphed shadow of engine smoke falling across the canebrakes. Tattered children poke their heads from the reeds, rub their stomachs, and extend their hands toward the passengers. These skinny-as-a-rail kids are there to guard the ripening rice paddies. Armed with slingshots and pebble-filled cans, they are human scarecrows who earn the equivalent of a few American pennies a day to chase away the crows.

The train slows for a curve, then grudgingly regains momentum. As we near Agra city, the Taj grows in proportion, yet by some architectural mystery it gains neither weight nor solidity. The domes and minarets seem fashioned from a transparent material that both absorbs light and ricochets it into the beholder's eye. Around the gleam of opalescent marble, the air is mottled with mauves and violet-gray—as if Monet had added his brush. The paradox of this painterly effect is that it is created by pollution: thousands of charcoal hearth fires, the dust of goat and cow herds, coal haze and acidic fumes from Agra's industry.

There's another paradox, too. The more momentum the train gains, the more we seem to be standing still. It is the Taj that moves, a music box rotating slightly above a stripe of chartreuse fields, its measurements exact, the towers aligned perfectly. The sheer marble walls, inlaid with countless thousands of precious stones, reflect the rising sun like a master-cut diamond. If this could be my only glimpse of the Taj, it would suffice for a lifetime.

The locomotive slows into Agra Station. The Taj disappears. In its place comes a tangle of dusty trees, rotting shanties, clanging rickshaws, and fly-ridden sweets shops whose gloomy interiors hide behind bamboo scaffolding and tangles of electric wire. The whistle screams, wheels grind to a stop. In a vaporous frenzy of steam and grease, the passengers—so amiable and courteous during the journey—push and scramble for the doors. Farmers shove, upper caste swing parasols, children slither between fat bellies. A hundred red-turbaned porters rush toward the doors, waving down customers, grabbing jute-tied boxes, metal suitcases, bedrolls, bulging baskets.

I slip through them, only to face a horde of men waiting outside the station. Screaming like crows, they all want my business: to drive me to a hotel where they will reap a commission, or to "special factory" where they'll gain a cut on a marble chess set, or to "my friend's shop" for an Ali Baba snuff box or a plug of hashish mixed with dung. Firm, but polite, I tell them "just walking." A few alleys away, I find a cheap boarding house, freshen up, and hail a horse-drawn tonga away from bustle, past the 16th-century stone fort begun by Mogul ruler Akbar, then along a bend of the Jumna River where laundry wallahs and housewives gather with a great slapping of clothes and banging of metal cookware. Nesting birds circle the spigots to steal strands of hair where women plait their braids. Between the trees appears the famous dome of the Taj—a dome shaped like the bulbous haystacks across the river, a dome said to have its origins in the bell-shaped tents of Tartars, the mosques of Persia, the unopened bud of a lotus flower.

At the arched entrance through the south wall of the Taj, a sneezing skeleton of a man inside a kiosk collects money for the seventh wonder of the world. He hands me a ticket, walks out of his cage, takes it from me, tears it neatly in half, hands back the stub, and returns into the kiosk. Ticket in hand, I walk through the wall under a massive arch. All darkness, then a blast of daylight. A sanctuary of lawns, gardens, hedges, and trees bisected by a narrow, sky-reflecting channel of water that aligns one's vision arrow-straight with the Taj. The busy human world is left behind—the traffic craze of Agra, the traffic craze of the mind.

I stroll a few paces to get my bearings. The gardens, impeccably manicured, hardly resemble those pictured in the vintage photographs I saw on the wall of an antiquarian bookshop in Delhi. The original gardens were quite wild, profuse with cypress, almonds, figs, and fruit trees amid dirt trails overgrown with bamboo and tangled succulents. According to the book dealer, the unkept grounds were a haven for British and Indian picnickers who drank, partied, and chiseled out souvenir gems from the monument. I don't have any qualms with today's garden. Highly manicured, yes, but it leaves room to breathe. The trees are pruned and confined to clusters so visitors can view the monument unhampered. If you want a more intimate glimpse of the Taj, say a leafy camera-shot framed by branches, just step back into the foliage with the monkeys—which is what I do, while others make a bee-line for the Taj, racing ahead, cameras swinging, to grab a photograph without a single suit, sari, sunhat, or umbrella to interrupt their view.

Geometrical space, ornate flower arrangements, symmetrical walkways, scrolls of flora—they read like designs on an illuminated manuscript. The garden enhances the tomb, just as the tomb enhances the garden. Cypress trees for death, fruit trees for life, bands of golden poppies erupting like an Indian sunrise, a river of iris rippling with the color of dusk. Peacocks, egrets, a flock of parakeets skimming the trees. Marble canals, bubbling waters. The persistent praise of the rose. A narcotic attar of honeysuckle, jasmine, and narcissus. For the Mughals, dwellers of arid lands, the garden signified oasis; the oasis, paradise. A divinely inspired symmetry of pools, lawns, and meditative coves heady with hallucinogenic trumpet flowers. A prayer divided into stanzas, evenly spaced, and aligned.

I'm about to get out my notebook, when—like most times in India when one believes he is finally alone, but isn't—I detect a shape to my rear. A bristly-chinned groundskeeper eyes me from over his broom and is quickly by my side, speaking without hesitation. "You are impressed to be here, sir? It is not good to be coming from so far and not be impressed."

Sooner or later he'll want a baksheesh, but so what? I'll stay loose, see what he has to say. He is a jovial old timer who hails from Mathura, legendary birthplace of Krishna. On his forehead is a dab of sandalwood. "I see you noticing my *chandan* paste. Very important, sir. It cools my third eye and keeps my nerves composed."

For fifteen years, he says, the Government of India Tourist Office has employed him to sweep pigeon droppings from the 2000 square feet of walkway surrounding the palatial gardens and sky-blue pools of the Taj. This task he dutifully performs with the ingenious help of a dead crow tied to a branch of an acacia tree overhanging the main walkway.

"The crow is scaring away the pigeons. That way I

have not so many droppings to be sweeping. I have more time for talking to people like you. I am telling everybody the same thing: one time here is not enough. You must be coming many times. Early day. Sunset. Big moon. You must be forgetting what you have been told about the Taj. You must be looking for personal meaning."

The groundskeeper points to a verse from the Qur'an inscribed in jet on the southern facade of the arch through which I've strolled: *Enter Thou My Paradise*. He tells me that stonemasons and calligraphers labored jointly to make the size of the script seem uniform to the eye, even though it recedes further from the eye as it proceeds up the arch. True. From where I stand the size of the script, no matter where I look, equalizes itself within the eye. There is no diminishing perspective.

"We are having an illusion, sir. The size of the script appears the same. But it is not. It is getting bigger near the top of the arch. Everywhere here—in the gardens, in the chambers of the tomb, around the minarets—you will be finding attention to illusion. Excuse me sir, you are coming from which country?"

High noon. While the groundskeeper continues his task of chipping away the hardened pigeon droppings with a putty knife, I linger in the sensual formality of the Persian gardens. Eventually the walkways deliver me through a hedged labyrinth onto the main path leading to the mausoleum. I want to turn away from the Taj, forget its reputation, find something small to look at. But my eyes are drawn to the pearly architecture as if it were a magnet. My attempts to relax, ignore, or bring meaning to the Taj are continuously impeded by tricks of the mind.

First it goes about convincing me of the "importance" of being here. Then it tries telling me that I might not really be here at all. Next it floods me with details. How emperor Shah Jahan planned the Taj as a memorial for his

73

wife, Mumtaz Mahal, the Beloved of the Palace, who died bearing his fourteenth child while accompanying him to the battlefield. How within a month his hair turned white as he wept with remorse. How he called stonecutters, astronomers, and mosaicists from Persia, Arabia, Afghanistan, and the Mediterranean to build her tomb. How 20,000 laborers worked two decades to complete his vision. How he cut off the hands of his architects and blinded them to prevent them from making another Taj. How he was imprisoned by Aurangzeb, his third son, who didn't want the fortune his father promised him squandered on more public monuments—particularly the tomb Shah Jahan planned for himself. It was his wish to be buried across the Jumna in a mausoleum made of pure jet, a Black Taj linked to his wife's mausoleum by a bridge of silver spanning the river. Pompous, for sure, but what a symbol! The bridge as an artery joining husband and wife, suspending their love above the flow of time.

As the story goes, Aurangzeb murdered his brothers as he fought his way to the throne, jailed his father, and seized the Black Taj funds to build mausoleums for his own wives. Shah Jahan, locked inside the Red Fort, not far from the Taj Mahal, supposedly died of an overdose of aphrodisiacs followed by a minor stroke while attempting to seduce a housemaid. A good story, but more likely he overdosed on heartbreak. Half-paralyzed in the Jasmine Tower, the great Mogul king expired on a bed near a tiny window through which the marble dome over his wife's cenotaph was reflected by means of a mirror angled into his dying eyes.

Instead of burying his father across the river from the Taj, Aurangzeb had his tomb placed alongside Mumtaz's tomb inside the Taj. Not only did this disrupt the mathematical balance of the main chamber, it threw Aurangzeb's karma into a spin. Attempting to conquer the entire Deccan, a folly which lasted twenty-six years, he sacrificed hundreds of thousands of lives, depleted India of its grain, and unleashed famine and plague. On his death bed, Aurangzeb confessed to his son: "I came alone and I go as a stranger. I do not know who I am, nor what I have been doing."

The groundskeeper wags his head puppet-like as he ladles hardened excrement into his battered wheelbarrow. After he moves off, a postcard vendor appears, followed by a gaggle of masseurs with trays of oils and towels. The postcard man fans out "scenic scenes," but, seeing that I am uninterested, he quickly brings out "hot posse ladies"— Fifties-style Western women, naked save for cowboy hats, sequined holsters, and sheriff's stars over their nipples. Next, a masseur buzzes up like a fly, pummels my upper spine, and nods to the Taj: "Yes, splendid?" He proceeds to squeeze my ears. With disbelief, I hear them snap. Another masseur bends my arms backwards and kneads them like dough. A third greases my toes and cracks them one by one. Perhaps this is how Shah Jahan died, I tell myself, attempting a little comic relief as my body undergoes the assault. Perhaps the king was lured by a masseuse who removed her sari, lathered him with oil, and slapped him head to toe with a knotted towel. Noting my lack of interest, the masseurs abandon their play, and ask if I have something to sell. Watch? Levis? Coins? Stamps? Soon a cop is on the scene. He shoos them off with an enormous bamboo stick, but he too pesters me with the usual Indian repertoire: Where from? What do? Married? Children? Where staying? Change money? How long in India? What size feet? Smoke hashish?

Late afternoon. Heat waves evaporate into a blank sky. I remove shoes, pass through a short tunnel, then up the steps to the red sandstone plinth on which the Taj sits. A circle of tourists sip over-sweet sodas, sticking close to their Sikh guide. In orange turban and flowing kurta, he gestures emphatically, asking the group to look away from the Taj, across the Jumna River. His handlebar mustache flutters as he speaks. The tourists, drenched in unforgiving heat, fan themselves with pamphlets and plastic sun visors, struggling to pay attention.

"Now we stand above River Jum-naa. Best-known river in India except for Gan-gaa. Jumna is where Lord Krishna, eighth avatar of Hindu god Vishnu, played with his favorite cowgirls. Please put your eyes to opposite shore where Shah Jahan wished his own tomb, same as Taj Mahal but made of black stone, and connected to his wife's tomb by a silver span. Please take a silent moment. Try to imagine this bridge of pure silver over the Jumna connecting husband and wife."

The heat is stifling, the group becomes restless. A few saunter back to the main entrance. Others swat flies and search for relief, lifting one then the other foot from the sizzling stone. I take refuge in the shadow of a minaret, looking across the river to the hazy fields. The Jumna's flow is broken by a small raft being paddled from shore to shore where Shah Jahan's bridge would have been. A man and a woman sit facing one another in the raft, hyacinth leaves and melons piled around them. A slight breeze brings the scent of pampas grass and dung. In the fields, women walk single file, sickles tucked into saris, grass bundled on backs, babies slung around their fronts. In the lowering sun, chaff and dust raised by hooves and human feet add a golden hue to the air. "The light of evening when the cows come home," an Indian man once explained to me. "*Godhuli* we call it—kicking-up dust time. The kind of golden light in which a man should first see his bride."

When the tourists thin, I walk up to the Taj and put my hands, my face, my body against its smooth marble walls. My eyes are so close that each mother-of-pearl inlay, every carnelian rose, jade cypress, amethyst grape, and coral pomegranate becomes a galaxy floating in ice-white marble. Circumambulating the Taj, hugging the façade, I feel a reconciliation with nature, and with death. This is a tomb, after all—a luminous symbol of the afterworld, the eternal. The garden I entered this morning was the before-world, an ordered wilderness of temporal existence.

As the groundskeeper predicted, the Taj becomes personal. Its gleaming walls trigger the image of my father standing here in 1945 marveling at this same sight. His army tour finished, he returned home with gifts: a brass drinking cup engraved with hand-painted flowers, a bronze puja bell, a hand-carved alabaster box with a mother-of-pearl inlay of the Taj. I was still crawling at the time, but I remember my mother placing these souvenirs before me on a blanket on our backyard lawn. The metallic odor of the puja bell, the delight of its sharp ring; the delicate flowers on the drinking cup; the warmth of the alabaster box, its waxy smoothness: these souvenirs from a distant land were the seeds of my present journey.

I move around the Taj like a cat, studying the inlay: obsidian script accented with bloodstone, a row of crystal lilies, a cluster of garnet fuchsias with malachite stems, a swarm of tourmaline bees. Each mineral exudes warmth or coolness, vibrating with the energy of the site where it was quarried. The entire façade pulsates.

> *If there be a paradise on earth*
> *then this is it, yes this is it, this is it . . .*

The Persian couplet Shah Jahan had inscribed in his Hall of Private Audience in Old Delhi repeats itself in my ear. This is architecture at once real, at once ephemeral. Inside the Taj, daylight filters through screens of pure alabaster carved with fretwork. Softened, the light fills the huge curve of the central dome. Under it a musician plays a wooden flute. He's there for the tourists, but the effect is for everyone: guards, gatekeepers, ticket takers, sweepers. The melody spirals upward, amplified by the shape of the dome. It reverberates in circles, reaches the apex, then descends in ever-decreasing echoes. Shah Jahan's architects created this space for praise. Prayers would rise in swelling wavelengths, soaring to rest inside heaven's cupola, then slowly return with softening aftereffects. The worshiper was engulfed by prayer, a song that would not stop, but continue to begin. Perhaps this continuing echo of song is what gives the Taj its radiance: centuries of prayer dividing and subdividing into repeating breath rhythms that merge to transform the consciousness of the visitor.

As a guide leads a group of Japanese tourists into the chamber housing the tombs of Mumtaz Mahal and her husband, I overhear her refer to the Taj as "solidified music." The entrance, an arched marble portico, is framed with jet inlay of Arabic calligraphy extolling the splendors of Paradise. Inside, the octagonal chamber—with its perforated screens of fine-grained marble—is like a spider's orb. A weightless, liquid feeling. A muted translucence. The poet Ghalib:

> *Even God's Paradise as chanted by fanatics*
> *merely decorates the path*
> *for us connoisseurs of ecstasy.*

Each crevice, hallway, nook, and alcove is a chamber of the psyche. Lacework cornices. Spandrels covered with fire-agate poppies. Alcoves of parrots feathered with turquoise and opal. Galleries where pearlescent lotuses sprout from deep lapis. I walk through this architecture of lament, remembering the dead, calling forth the living—a purification, a unification. During a precious moment without sightseers, I stand before a marble lattice, soothed by a breeze that becomes a swarm of whispers as it divides through tiny apertures of stone. Through these orifices I spy upon the world outside as if through a pinhole camera, a precise and extraordinary focus. As clouds shift, the room goes from opal to olivine. In this phosphorescent honeycomb, I give a shudder. The walls of the Taj are the walls of my mind. I'm in my own head, a mineral storm.

Pomegranate seeds blaze like rubies. A purple fluorite tulip peeks from a snowbank. Crystal pink roses surround a bird made of pure citrine singing in a dusk of polished nephrite. These are see-through walls—mineraloid, organic, fossilized resin, decomposed plant, hardened sap. A flux of aural swells, a metamorphic trick of heat and pressure, limestone re-crystallizing into marble. The precious inlay is the result of tectonic pressure. A warp, a pop, a pull. Gemstones meant to praise the beauty of a paradise above also praise the earth below—the fire and ice from which they were born.

The enigma of the Taj is its reality. A reality that both lures and repels, gives rise to myth, marks historical and allegorical time, and simultaneously reveals Shah Jahan's passionate yet decadent fervor. The splendor of its whiteness paradoxically opens a door to our nocturnal selves. Within its chambers we go from sunlight to shadow, human to sacred. Exiting into the heat of day, the marble shimmers—the very effect of light on Himalayan snows. Like those floating peaks, the Taj is a mirage that one can touch. But as the fingers retreat, the Taj also retreats. With a sonar ripple it fades into the imagination, a bright echo conversing with itself.

This morning, from the window of the Rajdhani Express, the Taj was pure apparition. A resurrection of light, breath gathered in stone. Rising above the mist, spinning like a dervish, it danced imagination and reality into a blur. "Solidified music." Hymn turned to stone. Ethereal cantata whose lyrical brilliance implies life after death, a spiritual beginning. Now, in fading dusk, warmed by the still-radiating stone, I walk backwards from the Taj, whispering the closing line of Shah Jahan's couplet:

Yes this is it, this is it . . .

Agra, 1979

MULTITUDE & SOLITUDE

Mumbai's famous landmark, The Gateway of India, is an imposing eight-story arch of honey-colored basalt topped with minarets. The British constructed it in 1924 to commemorate the visit of King George V and Queen Mary in 1911. Through it arrived British colonists after their approach to the subcontinent over the Arabian Sea. Beneath it the last British troops departed onto their ships after India declared independence in 1947. An evocative spot, it is shared by tourists and locals, including dwellers from Asia's largest slum, and high class from the richest real estate in India.

The Gateway's broad concrete square is compressed pleasure, the stuff of theater, the jangle of the mob, the danger of liberty. A stage, a dreaming field, "an empire of beguilement," as Baudelaire would have it. It has you confused about your purpose; that you were born from a set of mirrors and into them you shall return. It lures you into a whirling spectrum of well-heeled, rag-weary, diamond-studded, footloose citizens whose lives have been stretched beyond limits: into wealth or debt, crime or lunacy, love or suicide. The swarm picks up with a certain ferocity by noon, climaxing at sunset—especially on Sundays. It buzzes like a cyclone, tickles your nerve endings with a fluttering crackle, a high-pitched whine. The pavement underneath tickles you, too. A beggar wisps his fingertips ever so lightly upon the legs, as if to keep you upright in the vertigo of overstuffed shapes, or very thin ones, or shapes in crisis —warped, elongated, puffed from the genie's lamp, pulled and stretched from their own reflections. A hidden dictum is in motion here: dare to achieve madness. A daily madness.

So many colors of sunlit skin. And brave revelations

through sheer cotton. Look up, and the sky is at once tense and beautiful, the sun amber against celestial blue, and from it a single chime of silver from which everybody is whirled: upright Bombay locals, soiled bumpkins, a spy (not so well hidden in his retro white linen suit and Ray-Bans), old couples from Rajasthan, young monks from Dharamsala, village women from Madhya Pradesh, Rajputs from Kutch—all parading in regional outfits. Backpackers, too—here for a week but pretending it to be forever—copying those outfits. Children dressed in frocks and pantaloons have faces candy pink and peacock blue from colored popcorn. Teenagers saunter coolly in contraband jeans, or walk tall in air-heeled Nikes. If for just one afternoon, one feels a bonding—sans worry. No suspicious eye, no out-to-get-you look, no condescending smile. Hindus, Sikhs, Jains, Muslims, Christians, Parsis, Buddhists—each with Sunday tolerance, as if they had put their hands into the fire in a past life, a life no longer applicable to today's afternoon of elevated pleasure.

A thousand million people in India! Impossible not to avoid the throng. Forty-five years ago I first came face to face with the multitude. It was in Benares, a holy day. In a tiny inn above an alley leading to the bathing ghats of the Ganges, I woke at dawn to a distant hum: a persistent, rapidly increasing rumble gaining volume in perfect synch with the increasing light of day. The room was shaking, my whole body vibrating. A steady slappity-slap of thunder filled my ears. I peered from the window to the alley below. Wall to wall bodies were flash-flooding through the alley: a roaring stream of pilgrims finding course to the river for morning puja—barefoot, swaddled in white, swinging water pots, carrying bundles of incense, oils, and flowers. It was not a river of individuals. It was one universal heartbeat, a murmuring madstream rhythm of flesh, a rub-ruffle of silk and cotton, a mantra of concentrated action.

Baudelaire claimed to be fortified by crowds. He saw rude alphabets in dissected faces, a prismed bouquet of feverish eyes—and felt equanimity, neither inferior nor superior, in the mix. He bathed in the multitude, saw it as an occasion to lose the self, disappear into others. A holy communion, mouth open, tongue rolled out to receive the body of—not some singular godhead—but that of the busy crowd. To become intoxicated by the Mass! To bend one's singular ray into the fluid dissolution of the horde's ever-separating, always-rearranging spectrum.

Kerouac felt it, too. When not alone on Desolation Peak or listening to the scrambled talk below the window of his San Francisco flophouse, he was drawn to the pack, the gang, the misfits: brouhaha of amigos, table-banging rowdies, chance-operational encounters with strangers. He knew what Baudelaire so well expressed:

Multitude and solitude: equal and interchangeable terms to the active and fertile poet. He who does not know how to people his solitude, does not know either how to be alone in a busy crowd.

Kerouac, that dedicated shambles of a man. Soulful, ill at ease, diligently observant, magnetized by women, men, ants, cats, the little Lamb, the holy sufferers—a guy who could swim the language wave and ride the undertow of slapping feet, barking drunks, madball orgy. He never made it to India, but in his imagination he saw "Benares, capital of the universe." He would have paddled into the masses, reporting the details of the "hum"—strangers "grooking in the streets." He had that same peculiar genius for abidement, enjoyment, makeusement of the closely packed urban realm—"the crowdy earthquake cataract"—as he did for the lightning crags of mountain solitude or a boxcar ride with the lamps of America rushing by in the wet cradle of night. Jack would have found some uncanny vision of eternity riding the Madhya Pradesh Express through the Deccan badlands, or looking out on old Bombay amid the fuzzily amped mullahs calling from their minarets. I can see him standing on a broken stairway sizing up the "Supreme Reality" pulsating beneath the sea-splashed boardwalk and torn sidewalks of the human parade:

> "The universe is a lady
> Holding within her the unborn light—"

Strange to be here, tasting the salt air of Arabian waters, hearing a clang in my head, remembering Kerouac and Baudelaire as I follow the myrrh of the veiled woman peering from her cloth eye-slits, or the wood-peg dance of a leg on broken cement, all the while whorling farther into the crossfire of the bald, the dreadlocked, the bandage-soled, the stiletto-heeled conglomerate. Hunkered gamblers, diamond-caned esquires. Ring-nosed, string-tied, sequin-veiled, dhoti-clad, jock-balled, bare-assed specimens of unconforming delight. Infants in baskets, boys on stilts, goats at the sweeper's bin. Everything bulging at the seams, sputtering like a wick. Obscene. Holy. Phony. All believable, absolutely genuine. Tattooed jailbirds and opaline movie queens side-by-side on the pavement, walking, hobbling, rollerblading.

> *The one wide street*
> *Lolls out like a giant tongue*
> —Jayanta Mahapatra

A fortuneteller wants to read my future. Do I want to see that far ahead? No searchlight scanning my personal sea, please. No lantern lighting the top of the stairs. "Okay, then I will turn the pages of your past. Just twenty rupees." No! And off he goes. And off I go, farther into the crowd. Such faces. A musical salad. Some are content to be who they are. Others imagine a life larger than their own, scripting clumsy lines, posing as Bollywood actors. Dust on their shoulders, gold on their toes, saffron veil, copper trident, ultraviolet wig. Tarot readers, scam artists, memory tuners, street gamblers, limo drivers. A lunatic whapping a branch to the ground, a sun-stroked willow of a woman rebundling her rags. The candy man babbling a birdsong twitter, a juggler rotating her arms into a child's scribble. An oiled-and-coiled human knot of a kid pulling snakes from his head for the camera-heavy Tokyo punk who quickly retracts his lens when the kid demands:

> *five dollar*
> *mister*
> *for my face*

A disoriented flight attendant walks up. "You speak English? Can you point me to the Taj Hotel? I'm from Miami, my first time in India. The rest of the crew told me: just go, walk out, see it. But I'm lost!" She is pale, perfect, petite, and *clean*. I try to help, but point her the wrong way. When I double check with a knit-capped man in a tunic, he waves me away. "Arabia, Arabia, no speak." The flight attendant dissolves into the crowd as if being yanked offstage. I am pulled oppositely, between the samovar-toting chai wallah and a gold-skinned girl with burning eyes, who—I say to myself, I will never see again—looks right at me as if this is again.

> Different histories
> the two of us
> like crossed knives.

Smile of hope, dread of knowing. A day of leveling where castes, creeds, singularities, hierarchies go opaque in the throng's single throb—all of it the first-time traveler's perfect prelude for India: to exchange identities, go aslant in order to stand straight, be pulled from oneself into the consciousness of many. At the waterfront a sign advertises HARBOUR CRUISE. Ten rupees for the top deck. I hand over my loose change, cross the gangplank, climb a rusty ladder, seat myself. A bell rings. We sputter into the sea, the ferry top-heavy with nuzzling honeymooners, tourists, a gaggle of extended Indian families, a couple of brats who keep stepping on each other's new shoes.

Mumbai skyline falls away behind foaming waves. City lights blink in prune-colored dusk. The harbor grows smaller, the crowd along with it. I offer a *salaam*, a *namaskar* to the loose-buttoned groom with his inert bride in a horse-drawn carriage; to the blind accordionist crooning a nasal lament; to the huge-head-of-a-man rolling backwards on his pallet; to the chic disciple of Allah in her sequined scarf and black *salwar kameez* giving a helping arm to her *burqa*-draped mother.

India, one juxtaposition after another. The strictly covered follower of the Prophet next to the unabashedly naked Vishnu worshipper. A tinseled whiff of patchouli above the stink of gutter-foam. Man on a laptop next to a scribe at his Olivetti. Someone starched, someone unwashed. Someone whip cracked, someone high on stilts. Someone running full speed, someone on remote control. The alchemic theater! It smells of hair gel and menses, roasted chickpeas and brass. It writhes with unshaven bards and the goddess in her sari. I hear the clockwork chant of the Puranas. See the betel-mouthed pimp unroll a carpet to the harlot's window. Every pore opens, my eyes dislodge. Memory steps ahead of reality, the future basks in the behind. On the promenade, a legless beggar sets out his bowl under a public notice: WALK PROPERLY.

Mumbai, electric tsunami—it catches everybody in its tow. Long-distance buses arrive with another load of villagers trundling a few utensils and blankets to make do until they establish themselves, win their fortune, return home. But how many will never return? How many will nail together slabs of packing crate and cardboard, reinvent themselves as trash pickers, scaffold climbers, twine twisters, pill peddlers, pickpockets? Or strip the garbage heaps, cast their magnetic sinkers between the sewer grates for precious metals, or crush rock, hoist cement, haul dirt, mow five-star hotel lawns with bare fingers?

The ferry wobbles in its own wake. On the prow, I stare into dusk, hear the faraway toll of the university clock, the grind of the cane juicer's mill. Kites tremble, griffins circle, vultures dine on open-air burials. A bar of fluorescent green bathes the sex worker in her doorway. I look over the glittering harbor and see the Towers of Silence, the double-deck buses, the men relieving themselves under the bridge, a newlywed setting out her dutifully polished husband's shoes, the monkey-faced philosopher sinking deep into theory, the ash-collector's bloodshot eyes, the bored pundit playing with his balls, a dribble of milk running down Parvati's hip, a rat slipping from its hole as the sea slaps the ferry's hull. It sounds like sex.

I open my mouth to the night. My tongue melts. Am I the crucible holding the fire that shapes the sword— or is it a key? The water becomes deeper as we pass the massive hulks of anchored battleships. Electric signs blink as we near The Gateway. Sanskrit, Hindi, English? They look like broken bones, glowing limbs of dismembered language. Above the quay, the sky is ablaze with electricity. Towers of glass dissolve into reflections. The hum, the human surge, is sounding its chaos beyond the breakwater. In this drift of human mix, I wonder: is it our fate to engage with mistaken identities? To seek love in mismatched eyes, each belonging to an aspect of ourselves, a person longing to be recognized? When the gangplank lowers, will someone be waiting after we disembark—or will we again find ourselves asking: Am I here, is anyone out there, or is the rudder off to stay?

Mumbai, 2008

ABODE OF THE PERFECT SUBLIME LOTUS

Om Guest House, Sikkim. I open the shutters to Kanchenjunga's floating massif, already showing a faint 4:30 a.m. glow. Quicker than a magician's wand, the color wavers into a musical score: mint, pewter, coral, gold. The mountain, forty kilometers as the crow flies, is the planet's third highest. The Sikkimese regard it as their Divine Protector. Out of respect, the first climbers, in 1955, halted their ascent just short of the peak. Ever since, mountaineers have done the same, stopping a few meters below the topmost of Kanchenjunga's five summits, four of which rise over 8,000 meters.

I lodge in Pelling, the village where outfitters embark for the flanks of the mountain. I have no intent to climb, just to gaze, fill my sketchbook, and hike a short ways to Pemayangtse Gompa, the Abode of the Perfect Sublime Lotus. Take any trail out of Pelling and you soon stand above the world, drawn to a vast, stretching impossibility of glaciated stairways, a blinding brilliance of cupolas, vaults, and thrones, each bearing a figure glinting in the early sun: Tara under an icy nimbus, Our Lady of Solitude wrapped in smoke, Athena with a frozen lance. Transparent and fleeting, they tantalize the eye in their state of undress. Then, too quickly, they realize their vulnerability and disappear under their veils.

"Everything from the Highest, everything from Above directs human imagination toward Light, toward sparkling urgency," wrote artist, philosopher, and Himalayan explorer Nicholas Roerich. One taste of the high country and the eyes are washed clean, the mind empties to receive. New vigor, new challenge. During long spells of mountain walking, what do you learn? That you cross a pass only to find the other side is this side? That snows are melting, tides are rising, little pockets of humanity need higher ground? That ours is a brittle existence, easily shaken by a single raindrop that turns all fixed notions into a boiling mudslide?

Ethereal mists of the mountain, yes. An elixir, a curative. Especially given the long bus ride up here suffering the heat of the Bengal plains after the clamor of Kolkata: its fanatical priests demanding coins from pilgrims, rushing them into Kali's temple, hastily sweeping their offerings—flowers, bananas, coconuts—into the mouth of the sacred cow. Give me the unbounded skies, the needle-thin summits. The frightful abyss, I'll take it! Let me brush off the dust, lighten the rucksack, climb into the Jeweled Realm where the mountain deities reside. Look to Kanchenjunga, you see them in fluorescent swirls. You trust in them after you leave the final teahouse and start up the eerie twists of darkness, break through the scrub, scramble the talus, hear the howl of your ancestors from a crevasse-pocked gorge of frozen ice fangs. You'll need the helping hand of the Goddess when your hairs stand on end as, just behind you, the foot-crunch of snow gets louder and from it appears a half-human shadow who's tramped out of the mist from some hell-twisted fissure stinking of sulfur.

I'm giddy this morning. I don't want to be mine, yours, or anybody's. I've written myself dry, sipping gunpowder tea served by Saraswati, a twenty-two-year-old charmer who rapped at my door with a tray of cookies and a thermos as I was opening the window to Kanchenjunga. A Buddhist family runs this lodge, their little puja room right next to mine, the altar set with bowls of spring water before Avalokitesvara's multiple arms extending rays of compassion to all beings. Downstairs, hot *tsampa* porridge awaits me in the morning. In the evening, it's *thukpa*, buckwheat noodles, and steamed *momos*. Upstairs, seven rooms each have mountain views. Bright and tidy compared to my last lodging—Hotel Retire, if I remember correctly. A grungy place on the Bengal plains whose paper-thin partitions didn't reach the ceiling, thus merging each individual's privacy into one collective blasphemy. Coughs, gargles, piddles of body fluids into chamber pots (each having a singular ringtone), rude emissions of flatulence unsuccessfully muffled, awful tries of travel-tired lovemaking, whispers of complaint too loud for secrecy, intermittent sighs of sleeplessness, and a continuous John Cage performance of zips, unzips, rezips of sleeping bags, duffels, night kits, and backpacks.

Kanchenjunga translates from the Tibetan as "Five Treasures of the Snows." A Sikkimese story says the tallest summit retains the gold of sunlight's first blessing, the summit in shadow holds hues of precious silver, the other three summits hide jewels, grains, and the open leaf of a prayer book. Nicholas Roerich painted Kanchenjunga several times, reducing its form to the essence of color and light: a stage of consciousness. He saw the mountain as the abode of the snows, yes; but also as the abode of understanding and social aid. When you climb, you rope up, become indispensable to one another. Watchful, patient, attentive. No life-or-death race to the top. Any meditative ledge will do, a temporary nook where you gather dry grass into a cushion, take a seat, gain a little insight above the human catastrophe of war, famine, and repetitive quest for power. When it's time to rappel back into the world, you return not with the treasures of conquest and bravado, nor with silver or gold, but with love and alliance—the real riches of the mountain.

After tea and oatmeal, I am not far onto the trail toward Pemayangtse, when, between a stand of Himalayan cedar, I see Kanchenjunga's mantel of snow riding a sash of cloud unraveling into a scroll of monastic prayer. Listen. The gompa must be near. A guttural vocal hum, muted timbre of the thighbone trumpet, a clash of thunder. Comes another sound, too, much nearer—the prattle of voices around a bend. Walking on, I find not the cluster of tourists I expected, but a group of Sikkimese schoolgirls. As surprised to see me as I am to see them, they don't shy away but digest my sudden appearance with smiles. Each wears a pressed navy-blue and white uniform, a necktie, a gold-buttoned jacket, knee-high socks, and black plastic shoes. Celestial youths, faces like open windows. Eager to practice English, they giggle, ask my name, and have trouble with it, as I do with theirs: Deorali, Tshering, Chori. I am too much of an entertainment, though. They've fallen behind the rest of the girls who are well ahead, standing with their teacher over a sign under the prayer banners:

> *These prayer flags are dedicated to sentient beings of six different realms for eternal liberation, chiefly for victims of world negative forces: twin tower 9/11, innocent war dead, Madrid train blast, Iran earthquake, world victims of mass murder, genocide, ethnic cleansing.*

This reminder of the world's condition, juxtaposed with the girls' beaming smiles, brings a flash of sorrow. I stop to sketch Kanchenjunga, but she is half-closed to the world, a veil pulled over her gaze. Is it in fear of our world, dangerous with perpetrators who believe they can start and stop time, harm and conquer others to get their way? Above the Buddhist flags, the sky is intense cobalt, the sun warm, almost hot. But there's a chill, a sort of explosion in me, something wanting out. What shall become of youth in this day and age? Tu Fu certainly had such thoughts in the eighth century, exiled to a remote shanty—sleepless, worried about war, his family far off, clouds darkening the four directions. I walk with the girls for a spell, doing my best to fall behind, to regain my composure. To no avail, until their teacher calls and forward they hasten, voices rising: *Good byyye!*

The trail ends at a yellow wooden gate, its swinging doors carved with the ornamental "lucky-knot," a Buddhist symbol for the Path of Longevity: May life be fruitful, unhampered by setbacks. The gate opens to a grassy square in front of Pemayangtse, a simple but colorful gompa crowned by a three-tiered golden roof. Its white façade is wrapped with a band of Mars red; the eaves and latticed portals are painted sunflower yellow; doors and windows bordered with pink and turquoise lotus blossoms. The gompa, perched on a rise of meadow, animates its surroundings with its colors, each hue a dash of modern jazz. And there's intimacy. The structure's compact size is less imposing than Ladakh's fortress-like monasteries built to house large groups of lifelong practitioners. Such palatial enterprises epitomized the wealth of a once-powerful religious hierarchy. The unique architecture and artistry I admire, but it wasn't achieved without a feudal system of labor and taxes, a hierarchy of privileged lamas, a subservient class of uneducated farmers.

Pemayangtse is of the humble gompas built near villages, allowing monks to live at home and gather in the abbey on important days of the religious calendar. It was founded in the early 1700s by the Nyingma sect initiated by Padmasambhava, also known as Guru Rinpoche, the 8th-century master who brought Buddhism from India to Tibet. On brightly painted *thangkas* framed with rich brocades, he is often depicted walking to Glorious Copper Mountain, a Buddhist paradise surrounded by the Cosmic Ocean. He wears robes the color of cinnabar and lapis lazuli and sports a triangular cap with an eagle feather, symbol of penetrating vision. Two consorts attend him: Mandarava, a Bengali princess and Tantric practitioner, and Yeshi Tsogyal, a Tibetan queen and spiritual teacher.

A stairway leads from the first floor prayer room, where the deities and sacred texts are safeguarded, to a large upstairs room lined with murals. All are veiled save for the one with two Bodhisattvas sitting naked in sublime Tantric copulation. (In most societies this would be the one that would be covered.) The Bodhisattvas are male-female archetypes seamlessly joined (it takes a keen eye to untangle who's who), a metaphor for the perfect union of wisdom and compassion, a core ideal in the Buddhist life path. Without such information, a casual visitor risks either getting a rise or taking offense. The ember-red male embraces the snow-white female who sits facing him on his lap, her head thrown back in a daze, her legs drawn up around his thighs. He clenches her tightly, her breasts pulled against him as she enjoys the ardor of climax, eyes rolled back in ecstasy.

A clatter of feet sounds from the stairway—the girls and their teacher. As they gather in front of the mural, I sense no embarrassment. All attention is drawn to the maestra's interpretation of the Bodhisattvas (the enlight-ened beings who've delayed entering nirvana in order to save others) who, she explains, are "wisdom and compas-sion sitting together." She talks about the prayer banners we saw on the way up, the unprecedented rise of human vi-olence in the world, and the need to bring healing through acts of love, consideration, and care. She explains prej-udice and fanaticism, followed by examples of the Bud-dhist principles of right thought, right word, right action. A tall order for youngsters to grasp, but I believe it gets through. It *has* to, to balance the chilling acts of terrorism that make the news daily.

I also wonder whether, beyond the wise words of their teacher, the girls aren't imbibing a hit of 120-proof tonic for future matrimonial reference, and something to talk about after school. These painted Bodhisattvas in the act of lovemaking! I don't recall any Catholic saints doing it on the walls of our parish church, though many of them had the look of having just done it. That aside, I often think of the gold-haloed saints and madonnas as Bodhisattvas, especially those whose enlightenment allowed for kindness toward all beings. Saint Francis was one, and he was duly pressed into my imagination at an early age. For my ninth birthday a neighbor gave me a book, *Famous Paintings.* I flipped past van Gogh's clumsy portraits and Chagall's donkey-headed angel to Bellini's *Saint Francis in Ecstasy.* The hermit saint was portrayed outside his cave, standing with outspread arms, at one with God and all earthly creations. A honeyed glow glazed his cassock, his bare feet, the leaves of a sapling, the glint of a bubbling spring. Pemayangtse's Bodhisattvas exhibit a similar glow, but it is not the glazed and honeyed effect that Bellini achieved. Here, male and female are painted in vibrant flat-toned hues. Surrounded by cloud-like nymphs, the two figures dissolve into a single flame, the pearlescent flame of Buddha nature.

The big surprise on the upper floor is a seven-tiered, ten-foot-high sculpture: "The Heavenly Palace of Padmasambhava," a surreal fantasy constructed by the late Dungzin Rinpoche. A former abbot of the monastery, he labored five years carving and painting each level of this wooden masterpiece with dozens of miniature dragons, nymphs, yogis, saints, buddhas, and dharma kings. Some scoot along on rainbows, some play hide-and-seek in fairy kingdoms, one waves goodbye to the world, crossing a bridge into a cave. Lower tiers are filled with humans at work and play. Upward, there is transformation of humans into angels, mythical birds, celestial beings. Dungzin Rinpoche really took it out there. No traditional monastic painter rules for this cat! His lacquered fantasy soars like an enchanted stalagmite, a Hobbit lingam. Myth given dimension: a peak, a spine, a central nervous system—a work of art that would fit perfectly alongside Ernst or Dalí.

A steady drumbeat from the hall below. Monastic prayers rise to a whomp on the drum. I circumambulate the sculpture, carried by the chanting until it fades . . . lower, softer . . . punctuated by a slap of prayer beads against the monks' palms. Outside, Kanchenjunga exits the day the same way she entered: wearing a gossamer cape. The Lepchas, who first inhabited Sikkim, called the mountain Konglo Chu: "High Veils of Ice." Behind those mists lay the Other World, the Far Shore.

From the upstairs balcony I contemplate the prayer-bannered trail up here, the Sikkimese schoolgirls— their immediacy, their lit-from-within spirit. I watch them disperse through the grassy courtyard, join hands, dance in a circle, and pause at the yellow gate through which we entered. They are opening it now, walking onto the Path of Longevity. Be thee safe, little Bodhisattvas, unimpeded by setbacks, guided by the many arms of Avalokitesvara.

As I step from the monastery, there is a new touch to the breeze. Rose and deodar. Fluorescence radiates from Kanchenjunga. The physical world? My own consciousness. The mountain's consciousness? My own breath. Mountain as monastery. Monastery as mountain. Crossing the grassy square to the yellow gate, I follow onto the path where the schoolgirls departed. From up ahead, through the waving prayer banners, comes a happy hop-skip song to carry me down.

It's a tough, bumpy road into higher altitudes. The trail zigzags up with precarious drops, slippery shale, rotten handholds, tenuous cul-de-sacs, scary overhangs— the works. But if you stay true, banish all woes, accept the false dawns, give reign to difficulty, there it is—a radiant enterprise of shining stone, well above the avalanche zone. But to get here you have to leave home, make time to stray from what you know.

Gangtok, 2006

HIMALAYAN SKETCHES

TAKING LEAVE

As a boy I fell asleep under a map of India my father had pinned to the wall. Nightly I traced the contours from the subcontinent's southern tip, across the plains, up the Ganges to its Himalayan source. And farther. To Nepal, where the sinuous topography became erratic ridgelines forming the world's tallest peaks. Sleep gripped me before I finished my journey, but to wake next morning was to dream of visiting that faraway land. Years later, filled with restlessness, I took leave. To be called by an inner force is to abandon everything familiar and follow a dream long buried in the psyche. "Follow" is perhaps too gentle. One is pulled. I think of Rilke's poem:

> Sometimes a man stands up during supper
> and walks outdoors, and keeps on walking,
> because of a church that stands somewhere in the East.

You open the door, say goodbye to the feast. Adventure is not the driving force, nor reason. Something in the genes alchemically combines with impulse and sets the feet forward. One is swept by a gale toward a compass point where stands a church, a country, a mountain, a sanctuary. Such displacement provokes a cellular reshuffle. A strange rush of air fills the head, eyes look everywhere at once, heels sprout wings. Rational intent doesn't compute. One is displaced from chronological order, shot arrow straight into the world's wideness. A flint-scented oxygenless realm, elusive heights that vanish into the jet stream.

> A world
> beyond this world
> we rake with plows.

STUMBLING OFF TRAIL

Unsure that the place where I began even exists, I give equal doubt to where I am bound. Destination is a tremor in the toes, a vibration up the spine, a cicada's metallic cry. Follow the breeze, paddle whitewater, go down, come up with a new set of shoes. Glide with a damselfly, wobble across a rope bridge, ramble the fields, every farmer gives a different direction. Finally, a bramble gatherer, arms full, lifts her chin to show the way. During it all, I momentarily escape myself. The heat thickens, the fields narrow, the hills lift into stark light where I feel the involuntary tug of my shadow pulling me off the map. When day turns lilac and a gentle wind begins to flow, I realize a good journey finds its own course. My feet are burning, so is my heart. A pleasant madness flames out of my head and lifts my hat as I tramp this uninhabited backcountry.

Full moon—
even the biting mosquitoes
have stopped for it.

THE DIAMOND OTHER

One into another mountains chime with glassy radiance. Among them, one stands out: the Diamond Other. A massive thrust of energy. Breath momentum. Visible echo of time. The mountain travels on ripples of heat, tides of ice and magma. My flesh shares its warp and weft, wrinkles and veins, shifting ravines. Dark subsoil, humus of thought, old lifetimes pulverized by the glacier's blade. Under a mountain so enormous, I am reduced to a weightless speck, no law but that of Mystery. Before me soars a granite wing bronzed by fire. Lone knife-edge of time, your empty eye a quietly potent thought-realm, your fault lines a visible echo of consciousness. My body your extension, an assembly of atoms who holds out a walking stick, and thinks he is going somewhere. Until boom! A snap of lightning, and somewhere becomes nowhere. Slap of wind, blur of rain, all is erased. And in a blink, put back together. I take a seat, run my eye over a wind-polished spur, feel my shoulders, the missing wings, the pulse of radiance under my skin. As I undo my bedroll and lay a sprig on the coals, a crimson glow brightens between the summits.

The highest peaks
no longer the highest
—parting mist.

STONE HUT YAK CAMP

A monk holds out a smoking juniper bough and tings a finger cymbal, his prayer echoing over ten thousand valleys banked against spires that cleave and tumble into a brocade of evening shadows, their glow caught far below in the glint of a winding river. At 13,200 feet, I've arrived at a cluster of huts wedged into a splintered cornice of rock. A peppery tang to the air. Flinty drift of hammered stone. Resin from beams adzed by carpenters still at work in the last light. There's a trace of yak-dung fire from the kitchen where Pema and Yangchen laugh and banter, knead dough, feed thistle to the fire. Even at work, they wear silver earrings, amber beads, rainbow-striped aprons over ankle-length robes. Potato soup dashed with garlic and wild spinach heats on a clay hearth. Shelves bright with platters and urns line the walls. Between bundled herbs the Dalai Lama smiles in a plastic frame. Next room over, through a door tacked with Sylvester Stallone, is a big plank table where guests take meals. The ladies warm me a cup of rakshi, the potent local brew. On the floor sits the old man of the house, his back against a wooden pillar, his legs stretched to the tin stove. He prays his beads, mind vigilant, a smile on his wind-worn face. When his eyes come round to mine, he holds them there. He's seen many like me come through the passes to yak camps like these, sharpening their song on the wheel of clear-medicine sky. Could be we've met before, in this life or another, in a stone hut like this perched under the stars above the clouds where the valleys take leave.

> Rise from extinction
> return to extinction—
> tipsy, I grab at snowflakes.

MESSENGER, REMINDER

Yesterday an earth-smeared sadhu with ochre designs on his bare-boned body appeared on the trail. He had that wood-smoke fern-and-mushroom scent of the timeless hobo. A nomad directed by an inner map, one who goes by foot, fasting on wild herbs, plenty of time for introspection and pushing the limits of the mind. High among glaciers or far below in the throngs of India, he is a standout, a spectacle, an anomaly in the human race. Yogi, impostor, nutcase, or true poet minstrel in the lineage of Kabir, the sadhu belongs to no nation. He exists in the state called *Bardo*. He does not marry, holds no job, carries no luggage, doesn't shop for apparel. Instead, he seeks frugal solitude: a cliff edge, a bend in the river where he can wash away worldly tendencies. While everyone does with more, he goes without. A walking enigma, renouncer, trickster, he plunks a trident in the sand, unrolls a mat, sings, bathes, eats a simple vegetarian meal, smokes a bowlful, and proceeds to the next cave. Rings of colored air vibrate around his sunbaked shoulders. Balls swinging, buttocks shaking, he is bare to the world, provocative to the max. All he needs do is stop, stand there without a word, his black pupils floating in crimson pools, and a thousand questions arise. From where, to where? Messenger, reminder, he is a metaphor for Time itself, the primeval flow of energy through the universe.

> Above the holy man
> thumping a drum, a monkey
> beats his chest.

CROSSING NANGA ICEFALL

The eyes, the body—this brittle trellis of bone, this wheel of sound we call self—spins with threads of sinew into a point beyond time, a point that refuses to be described, deified, defined as rising from cause or no cause. This thought (ice immediately forming on fragile perimeters) teases me with a shifting pose as I push through avalanche debris (otherwise known as karma), work my way around a yawning crevasse, and arrive in a berry-bright meadow silvered with briar. Here the trail loses itself to an uneven gain of ridge which can only be reached by crossing sharp, unstable scree. Rocks thump down, stars wobble from their thrones. A trumpeting aura blazes around the ragged brow of unmapped ice towers, a maze of cut-gem translucence honeycombed with tunnels. Yeti territory. Not to be fooled with. One could try and scramble the rubble like they do, quick and agile, powerfully traversing the snowfields. Or one could fix a thousand meters of rope (crafting a mind to go with it) and make way up the frosty aprons where zephyrs charge over the pass from the Motherland. But I'll stay, thaw my hands beneath my thighs, let the heights empty, and my brain provoke me with news of another world: one finally seen when the light dies, the lantern dims, and I slog through darkness, alone, without a beam.

> Dipper sinking—
> the depths of mystery
> begin to rise.

CHAMBER MUSIC

The monastery doors are usually locked, but this morning is an exception. Inside, the monks are cleaning. It's okay to enter, walk around, take a look, but rather than tripping over buckets and brooms in the half light and disrupting the work rhythm, I decide to return later when the lama's bell calls the monks back to sit before a long low bench arranged with loose-leaf prayer books. *Clinnngg!* A deep bass chant vibrates through my ribcage. *Uummph!* Voices rise. From the earth's vocal core a tectonic swell pulls terrestrial plates into acoustic plateaus. Honored lama, bumbling novice, snow leopard, lowly flea: all float into the universe. The mantra is not meant to be understood, but to take you in. Turn you inside out. The chant lowers. A soft *phlumph,* followed by a *crash-tink* of brass cymbals, a drone through the conch, steady thunder from the yak-skin drum. *BOOM! UMPH! BHARR-UMPH AHH HUMPH!* Dropkick of skipped beats. Elephant roar from ten-foot horns. *Dhrroom. Ghraawrl!* The chant ascends to the *katta-ka-takk* of the hand drum. Whirl of *dorje,* click of beads, finger snap. CLAP! The axing of consciousness. A drum-*clump* obliteration of self. No I, no other. Only no-thing-ness. A dissonant detonation of the everyday into the extranormal. A sound out of time before time. Call it "Chamber Music for the Liberation of All Beings." And to score it? The Himalayas themselves seem best. Run a bow over the strings of Nanda Devi. Strum the stone fishtail of Machapuchare. Let the airwaves seize you. Blue cloud boiling, bedrock swelling. The everyday cracked open, a geode exploding to reveal the Unseen.

> Heart sutra
> mountain weeds
> in full bloom.

WAKING FROM A NAP, LATE AUTUMN

Plum branches fill the window, spidery light glazes each limb. Fields out beyond are brown and done, at rest from the trials of their cattle. Maps, letters, trail guide on the table. A dog-eared page with a pencil-traced line over Cho la. Is this my ragged script that says "last point reached," or am I still in the dream that set my head with sails in sleep? All real, those icy streams erupting through wind-varnished rock? Young bamboo bending with black-masked monkeys? The Sherpa girl on the swinging bridge, mulberry cheeks, bright smile. Where is she when I return her look? And the woman in sheepskin cape, warming her back against the monastery wall? The farmer with missing teeth that perfectly matched his rake? The lone monk raising his song through the clouds? Too long I've stopped in deep wooded sleep. Everything spins in a reel of footage bleached by time.

A lightning flash
through precious stone
this life.

WRITING POSTCARDS, KALIMPONG

I've promised myself to unroll some paper and brush a few sketches before evening sets in. But first I've a few postcards to write while the sun is still warm on the overgrown garden below the steeply angled gables of the Raptor Inn. With the postcards rise a few feelings—those concerning correspondence in general. I wonder why letter writing didn't put on the gloves and have it out with e-mail? Why is the act of finding a nook to sit in when the light is just right and taking pen in hand to write a letter, a card, or even a note all but disappeared? What an honorable act it is to place a thought, a woe, an ingot-hot revelation on paper, give significance to daily life, provide a real and psychic portrait within the curve-ball journey we fumble along on. Only a handful of correspondents remain in my life. They often approach the page as did Michelangelo his block of marble, bringing out hidden forms—joyous, poignant—from everyday experience, letting the chisel slowly reveal a transient presence within the stone. It matters not the mood—cynical, exuberant, desperate, roaring in hellfire, juiced with new love; it's the on-fire intimacy, gut-grabbing doubt, deep-spiraling questions, exact details of things seen that provide a sanctuary where I can kick off my boots, live for awhile, take a plunge, bathe my brain. It's simple. Empty tea leaves from the cup, put a new pot on the fire. Draw ink from the bottle, draw light from the pen. That's it. A nice little cloudburst. And then, a lilac silence.

Evening cool
the sound of ink
brushed across paper.

CHANGING THE STREAM'S SONG

"He goes too far," my father once said of me to my wife. Her reply was a repeat of the refrain I often spoke to her: "Not far enough!" And they both laughed. When in doubt, I always thought: Forsake the reasonable option. Go for broke! When feet are moving, mind is absent. You hear the chime of bells on insomniac nights or the Siren's trade-wind call, and far is as close as you want it to be. Maybe it's swimming a 120-meter drop-off in the Java Sea just to know how frightening the Abyss is (and that it's possible to navigate it). Perhaps it's the dutiful pleasure of hiking a 16,000-foot peak to release a friend's ashes in the Himalayan wind. Or getting down on your knees in your own backwoods like my compadre Steve Sanfield, who found himself

> changing the stream's song
> simply by moving
> a stone or two.

You don't have to go to the world's other side to change your song. But if it helps, why not? Kick away the barriers and fly like the gods. Size things up in a buzzard crag. See what you weigh in a hanging valley. Test for an echo in the rues, calles, cloisters, cirques. Try a new language, get another head. Sound your name in the Empty Quarter. Seek the center of Incandescence. Travail? Sure. Wobble the entire belief system. Paddle outside the ropes and take a look around.

> A crooked walking stick
> keeps the path
> straight.

THE SHATABDI EXPRESS: RUMINATIONS

The 6:15 Shatabdi Express leaves Delhi Station on time. Our bogie fills with sunlight and the smell of ink as porters pass out *The India Express*, followed by tea and boxed omelets. The Shatabdi are the best of the Indian trains, cheaper than hiring a car or flying; more comfortable and safer than buses. The fare includes a/c, reclining seats, a meal, newspaper, and drinks. The trains are fast, punctual, and make very few stops—inconvenient if you're village bound. For that, you need the hard-bottom third-class trains, agonizingly slow locals that are only doable for the fun of an occasional short run, plenty of color and brouhaha. In the old days I rode them 'til my ass was raw. Now I settle into a comfortable seat, but not without the usual undoing of plans that a true venture requires: a state of readiness where expectations are abandoned and the spirit is allowed its own course, the mind sabotaged by unexpected turns. All that's required is a willingness to follow the meanders. "Big schemes only bring grief," said Chinese painter-poet Yuan Mei:

> *Carry only what you need*
> *a light skiff takes the wind,*
> *rides the water lightly.*

Travel light, the best mantra. With little on your back and lots of enthusiasm, you're free to sleep where you feel, wake in undefined territory, sit at the feast, break bread with strangers, amble the garden. Amid joys and discomforts, travel realigns perspective, engenders poems; but mostly it breathes as an end in itself, rich with camaraderie, new views of old cities, shared experience with new companions in the tangles of the ghetto or on the uncut trails of the backcountry. When Bashō wrote:

> *come see*
> *the real flowers*
> *of this aching world*

was he not asking poets of all ages (especially the clever ones who seek high profile) to get down off their horses and seek what is low: beauty in common experience, ache in the plight of the underdog, the war ravaged? Nothing hallowed or brainy, just unpretentious images that reveal what convention cannot reach.

Out the window, bronze light, fuzzy clouds. Deluged fields where royal-blue rollers skim the reeds and white herons stand motionless. In the swales, cattle give off steam. A temple spire appears, its pennant limp in the haze. *No mind No mind No mind* the iron wheels rattle. But mind is here, and the repeating clickity-clack of the rails sets thoughts in motion.

After landing at the Indira Gandhi Airport, Renée grabbed our bags while I found an ATM machine to withdraw a hundred dollars of rupees to begin our trip. Bleary from the all-night flight, I put on my specs, took out my Visa, inserted it, and nothing happened. Turned the card around, re-inserted, still nada. Removed my specs, wiped them with my shirttail, prepared for another try. Out of nowhere, appeared Mr. Courteous to help me. "Please sir, I shall try for you?" He takes my card, polishes it on his pantleg, swipes it, and it works—out comes the rupees, and, as I am counting them, into his pocket goes the card. But I'm a seasoned old timer, quick on my heels, and sharp enough—despite my sleep-deprived state—to grab his wrist, though gently, because he is a man dressed in coat and tie (well prepared for his role of the gentlemanly savior), and I'd rather be a gentleman, too, but firm. "Er, I believe that's my card?" The man feigns surprise. "Oh, sorry sir. My mistake, good sir. Only trying to help." Uncanny, the way the world works. Lots to be learned as the days fall into place.

Bags in hand, money tucked into our secret breast pockets, we taxi to a perfectly spotless Old Delhi hotel at the end of a dark alley lined with rickshaw repair shops and a monkey on every balcony. Very few tourists from abroad would overnight in the heart of Old Delhi, the Chowk as it is called; nor would Indian vacationers. Too crude and frenzied, too old and in the way. The Red Fort, the Jama Masjid, the hectic bazaars are not priority for the casual tourist or the eager-to-get-ahead VIP, busy with conference calls and spreadsheets. Forts, mosques, collapsed *havelis* are ghosts of the bygone—remnants of failed dynasties. Such highlights are reserved for tour groups, though to see them they must wade through dire poverty, and the sour fact that absolutely no progress has been made to resolve such poverty.

The India Renée and I pursue is the one most Indians wish to avoid—parts of the cultural anatomy that bring embarrassment or apology. Much of what we are interested in—street markets, folk art, handicrafts, village ceremonies, ritual music, small-press publishing, co-operative farming—is shunned by the eager-for-profit clan. Anything non-profitable, or not profitable enough, is irksome to the technocrat who sees a double ikat weaving made by a tribal artist not as technology, but as a time-consuming "craft." In the face of the slick, quick, and upgraded, Henry David Thoreau takes his stand: "Most of the luxuries, and many of the so-called comforts of life are not only dispensable, but hindrances to the elevation of mankind."

Giving audience
the Swami halts his blessing
to answer his mobile.

A few years ago, when Renée and I told a student from Shanghai that we were planning a visit to the hill tribe areas of Southwest China, she looked at us as if we were going to the wrong China. "Oh, those places. Not Han people. Not China." On our trip, visiting a Dong village—now touted as "top-class scenic spot where fishermen fish with cormorants"—we witnessed a group of eager (and thoroughly drunk) Chinese businessmen who had come to organize a test-run of a dance performance that would be sold to European sightseers by a Beijing eco-tour company. During the recital we were embarrassingly singled out and ushered into a front row by the promoters—one of whom swaggered into the village performers, patted a dancer on the head, and drunkenly stammered (with a spittle-dripping smile): "How do you like *our* China?"

Who knows what has become of that Dong village? If there's another to be found, I'll leave it be. Photograph it, talk about it, post it, and it'll be off the hidden path for good. Thinking back, those villagers had little interest in leaving their fields to accommodate tourists. The village was so unpretentiously "there," with a kind of nothing-happening, nothing-to-do-ness, that it didn't fit most travelers' itineraries. Too rustic for more than an overnight stay. No English, no wi-fi, no café au lait, not one flush toilet, no reliable transport. Which is why I felt we had actually arrived somewhere. Within the nothing-to-do-ness, a lot was happening: tilling, sowing, harvesting, threshing, shearing, carding, dyeing, weaving, brewing, feasting. Everyone active. Stonemason, midwife, blacksmith, tailor, butcher, coffin maker, tanner—anyone fit and able—joined in house-raising, bridge repair, ditch cleaning, and hay stacking, with time left over to dance at a wedding or get drunk at a wake. Would the village hold to its traditions? Or fall to investors laying out plans for luxury hotels, mini-bus tours, and a visitor center with exhibits showing "the old ways"?

Romantics about to visit India, be warned. If you don't like having the cushion pulled out from under you, the mind unraveled, every rational plan sabotaged, best to stay home. People wonder why there are so many heads on Indian gods. Well, they are a good back-up system for tens of thousands of situations in which one head is not enough. All too soon everything comes undone. The many-armed Shiva dances you off the wheel. Whirled about, you either go mad or slowly regain stability. Peel away the modern veneer, get to the core, and you'll find what you seek is alive and well. All you have to do is slow down, find a crack in the wreckage, slip through.

> Under a gate
> marked No Trespassing
> tiny wet frog tracks.

Within India's diverse peoples and geographies, millennia-old shrines bake in the sun, pictographs speak their painted messages, ritual labyrinths (imitating those in the psyche) are walked upon by millions every day. On the shore where Buddha bathed, monkeys open newspapers and scan the "available for marriage" page. A boatman on the Ganges talks with his hands and steers with his feet. A boy learning English asks: "How many years are you old?" The show goes on with unceasing contrasts. The flower vendor wears plastic roses in her hair. A naked sadhu smears himself with ash and replaces his Rolex. The old monk pruning plums has the thin arms of my father. A narrow ramp onto The Grand Trunk Road reads: "Tight

Entry Go Slow." Mother Kali's tongue is rolled out in defiance. Goddess Lakshmi's privates are darkened by a thousand years of prayer. India. I wait to arrive but I am already here.

> In the crooked mirror
> my face
> finally straight.

I think of the young couple in Delhi we took under our wing, their first time in India. They were from Los Angeles: he, light, ruddy, dressed in jeans and T-shirt; she, a dazzling Latina, ablaze in a royal blue jumpsuit, eyes faultlessly made up. Both wore fanny packs and held to them tightly. Their passports, tucked into their outfits, were attached to conspicuous black cords wrapping their necks. They were eager for experience, to have something happen. But walking the streets with them for a couple hours I could sense danger ahead. He had patience, adaptability. She, a short fuse, quick boundaries. He would work his way tolerantly through the touts; she would swat them away. He would put up with a cold water shower at the Shanti Lodge; she would demand a Marriott. He would dig train travel; she would plug Cafe Tacuba into her ears and escape the ride. He would walk into the unexpected; she would hire an air-conditioned car. Already he was trying to calm her over the flies attacking her legs. Already she was opting out of the Pearl Mosque to shop for jewelry and new clothes. The flies and the touts wouldn't stop in Old Delhi, either; they'd be waiting in Agra, Jaipur, Benares, and Kovalam. It would be a test for him, a bane for her. (If India didn't meet their expectations, she confided to Renée, they had funds to go elsewhere.)

"What's the quickest way to know India?" he asked. "Take a third-class train," I advised. "Get off to the side."

She overheard, grimaced, turned to Renée and asked about the beaches of Goa. I thought to help them off the trail a little, but why rob their experience and replace it with mine? Perhaps they would weather the rough edges—the shock of squalor, the foul gutters, the ribald devotion—and find themselves submitting, the walls cracking, new discoveries pouring through. Who am I anyway to be offering advice? A cornball who prefers a paper map, no GPS, plenty of sidetracks where I can leave myself behind, enter a reality beyond my imagination? What this young couple will experience, if they don't hide in an ashram, hang with a tour group, or sun bake on a beach with towels over their heads, is an India that will pull the cataracts from the eyes, shatter the mirror, shake all sense of time, change one's life forever.

I always liked Thomas Merton's response in his *Asian Journal* to the question: "Did you find the real Asia?" You can see him scratching his head before looking up with a twinkle: "I am at a loss to know what one means by 'the real Asia.' It's all real as far as I can see." Maybe thirty years ago you could find an India that was a world apart from the rest of the world—things done exactly the opposite of the way the West was doing them. These days, questing to find the real Asia, a first-time visitor's big surprise is that the smallest corners have been gotten to. Nearly every hill, temple town, heritage site, has its cellular tower. The erotic temple, the bazaar with strangely dressed natives grilling wild boar, the astrologer with his hand-drawn charts? The erotic temple is now famous for its up-market sound-and-light show. The natives, dressed just like us, are enjoying fast food in the new McDonald's. At a plastic table, the astrologer opens his laptop and burns your horoscope onto a disk. It's easy for somewhere to be nowhere at all, a place just like every other place. Money driven. Spiffed up to satisfy the tourist's yen for the photogenic.

There's nothing like traveling on your own. If you need to find another, go with a rogue, a lock picker, a clairvoyant, a jaywalker, an advanced lingerer, a ragtag soul yet to be born. If a poet, find another poet to look up when you arrive at your destination—someone who walks on the edge and isn't afraid of heights. You won't meet the rebel on a *Condé Nast Traveler* cruise promising "something different in a distant paradise," a place no longer remote that has suffered over-invasion since the advent of tourism in the Seventies. "Hill trek to lost tribes using Stone Age tools. Raft into untamed jungle. See ring-necked beauties of yesteryear." Are you really interested in buying a souvenir penis sheath from a native paid to dress naked-and-painted, who's doffed his everyday jeans and T-shirt for a grass kilt and boar's-tooth necklace moments before your arrival?

Funny, and a bit sad, to see a tourist walk Old Delhi's streets, camera held high, oblivious to what the market lady is hawking, what the lathe-turner is milling, why the housewife is chalking strange interlocking designs on her door step, or how many coins the beggar has just removed from his begging bowl to make it look empty. Once we traveled simply to let things happen, to let questions rise, to chance a new identity. Now, it's the know-before-you-go syndrome. Circle Mt. Kailash on the internet, snorkel the Red Sea on YouTube, peek through cyberspace into the forbidden sanctuary of the Sri Jagannath Temple. And *Lonely Planet?* It's just the facts, M'am. It's not there to remind you: let dust fill your boots, instinct point the way. A haiku by Santōka Taneda:

> *Wet with evening dew*
> *I slept—*

A friend once told me she felt Santōka's contentment on a journey in the 1960s from London to Istanbul, by train, bus, and thumb—staying with families in Iran and Afghanistan, dining on the floor, sleeping on rooftops. Aloof at the world's heart, she was happy for a simple blanket and a thin mat under the stars—all possible a half-century ago, unlikely today. If there's a comparison between the act of traveling and the act of poetry, I'll take my stance with Renée:

> *The poem has no plan,*
> *it's a plunge!*

Give me a sleeping-by-the-road, eating-from-the-berries kind of journey. A loose plan blissfully astray from rational schemes. One that follows deep currents: the Nerudas sobbing in front of barbershops, the Lorcas drinking at the Dos Hermanos bar, the Herodotus purposeful in his journey, a real listener. Where are the fugitive meanderers—the Xuanzangs, the Cabeza de Vacas—raw from footloose years through terra incognita? I once met a man on a bus on the rain-sodden curves of equatorial Sumatra, reading aloud passages marked by dried flower petals pressed between the pages of *Finnegan's Wake*. Along the road to Mandalay, a traveling musician told me of secret metals used to cast kyeezee, a gong with a supernatural tone. On the Perfume River an entomologist studying iridescent beetles was equally taken with Ho Xuan Huong's poetry:

> *Where is nirvana?*
> *Nirvana is here, nine times out of ten*

Most of us who sought travel in the early days were called into distant lands by heightened curiosity and a questing spirit. We took to the road with minimal equipment, seeking source and renewal in the act of travel with its inevitable encounters and mysteries. Bare to the world we had little contact with those back home save for letters miraculously received at a general delivery counter in a disorganized post office. The journey had mythic roots: a trial (more often than a trail) of confrontations, challenges, and a good dose of unpredictability to shake the belief system. Occasionally there would be a head knock, a revelation. To leave home was to discover another way back, and along the way become someone new.

"Life is the long lasting intimacy of strangers," wrote biologist Lynn Margulis. I'll raise a toast to that. And another to Antonin Artaud among the Tarahumara ("optical miracles confronted me at least once every day"), Isabelle Eberhardt in the Sahara ("absolutely dependent upon chance"), Tom Laird in Lo Manthang ("exploding horizons, as if we were no longer in a restricted or linear world"), Marilyn Stablein in Nepal ("I compiled a list of positions for lovemaking, positions the deities preferred"), Richard Schultes in the Amazon ("adventures happen only to those incapable of planning an expedition"), Freya Stark on the Lycian shore ("No happiness if the things we believe in are different from the things we do"), Alexandra David-Neel in Lhasa, Colin Thubron on the Silk Road, Dervla Murphy in Karnataka, Renée on a sagging bridge above the Dudh Kosi ("no layer of comfort to make us at ease"), or Milarepa hiking to his Himalayan cave ("the unfrequented path is the shortest way").

People often think I "go" because I've money to spare. Tiresome to clarify that I'm only able to board a plane to Delhi because I've saved every dime from those poetry-in-the-schools stints I've been doing since before I was born. Besides, the answer to "Why go?" is a real head-scratcher. I'm tempted to wax poetic: "To leave the familiar, surrender to what I don't know." For most people, that won't do. So I ponder other possibilities: Do we go to climb a distant peak? To feel the truth of history while standing in the rice fields of My Lai, or over a bend in Sand Creek? Are we out to meet the waifs, prophets, tillers of the soil (and the soul) in countries banned by immigration authorities? Bashō wandered threadbare, sleeping in fields, huts, and barebone inns. So did Santōka. "The mountains, the water, and my friends—these are what console and help me survive." He could be drunk, serious, meditative, often Chaplinesque:

> *How must I look*
> *from behind, going off*
> *in the drizzling rain?*

With so much of our environment wrecked, sabotaged, altered for profit or over-preserved like a gorgeous cadaver on ice, it is no wonder that disillusioned travelers recoil to cyber-cafés (where once were rice paddies) to chill at the keyboards, tick off places visited, or post their latest bellyache. Hardly anyone writes in a journal at day's end. Instead, rows of travelers are hunkered over screens clicking away at lightning speed, anxious to find out what's happening at home—chained to the humdrum they could have left behind. Writing in situ seems to be a lost art, too. On the streets, from the taxi window, riding a zip line, from the flaps of the trekker's tent, out comes the camcorder. Later, over an open laptop you're held hostage to the electronic slideshow—no talk required. It's as if the digital age has blown the fuse to details and feelings. Everyone's walking around with a mental bypass, an information gap. Why talk when you can text?

As a sojourner I'm happy to be unreachable. Wake on a straw mat in a new land, start from scratch, learn a new way of speaking, let the raw bumps of the road shake my beliefs. If I don't survive the challenges, so what? Does one always need to come clear, reach an end, regain footing on the same old path? Nothing wrong with returning home in absolute befuddlement—worth a Pulitzer Prize!

> Sign at the bottom
> of a stairway:
> Head Free

A fellow traveler talks about visiting places "because of the JUICE." In Sanskrit, juice is *rasa*—sap, taste, essence: the "life force" you feel in a place that bounces you from the ordinary and drops you into the slipstream. An emotional rise that happens when feet and psyche go astray, and the rhythm of the land carries you farther than you can walk, paddle, or fly. As when you spread the bedroll under Orion in the Thar Desert, brave the whirlpools of the Komodo Sea, or summit Gokyo-ri and see Chomolungma a fingertip away. *Rasa!* The JUICE. If it calls you, drink!

Aloof aloof aloof rattle the tracks. In motion, I step outside myself. Engulfed by newness, interior difficulties, exterior quandaries, mad scribbles erupt. Every mark on the page is a mileage post. Strange aspects of the new land beg the pen: in the heat, a little girl bends over a pond to fan the goldfish; in the cold, a butcher warms himself between slaughtered carcasses; in a pavilion once reserved for storytellers, villagers watch a sitcom; through a blossoming frangipani comes a drift of pyre smoke. I think of Joseph Campbell fleeing the madness of Old Delhi's streets for the a/c of the Imperial Hotel: "India is a land where one is forever surprised by things previously unseen."

In Campbell's time there was more room to see the unseen. Less people, slower modes of travel. A few centuries back it took six months for Europeans to reach

India. In 1786, Goethe and an artist friend traveled five days by ship from Naples to Sicily (a fifty-minute flight today). Reaching Palermo, they were reluctant to land. "Instead of hurrying impatiently ashore, we remained on deck until we were driven off. It might be long before we could again enjoy such a treat for the eyes from such a vantage point." Goethe scanned the new landscape, adding details to his journal: "The delicate contours of Monte Pellegrino to the right were in full sunshine, and a shore with bays, headlands, and promontories stretched far away to the left. Graceful trees of a tender green, their tops illuminated from behind, swayed like vegetal glowworms."

These days, a tourist scans the Internet and considers the options. Perhaps one doesn't need to go at all. Easier to open the laptop, tap a few keys, and travel virtually. Ascend Annapurna, snorkel the shipwrecks off Mykonos, ride a zip line through the rainforest of Costa Rica, zoom in on the turquoise sea of Bora Bora. If one does opt to brave the world (with its increasing human mistrust, random shootings, disappearing forests, war, global inflation, and new strains of viral disease), it's easy to tap a few more keys, buy a flight to Reykjavík, Timbuktu, or Thessaloniki. And, while you're at it, Google room #22 in the Golden Silence Hotel, suggested by *Rick Steve's Pocket Aegean*, and see if it really does overlook the temple of Apollo. Afraid to travel alone? There's MateMyAge.com. Need a guide? Bring one up on the World Wide Web, arrive in Kathmandu, and there he is, the guy you booked in cyberspace, waving a sign in the airport: Welcome Jhon & Rinne.

A trip planner roaming the Internet is subject to unforgiving misconceptions. He points the cursor, gleans an idea of a faraway land, and arrives with a preconceived picture show: tribal women dressed in mirrors, a camel dozing in the souk, a charmer calling a snake from a basket, an evening raga drifting from a fretted window. Prepared for what he thinks India will be like, he hits the streets and discovers the India that isn't—the one rapidly being left behind, the one hell-bent on replicating the country he just came from. The tribal girl wears a Madonna tank top. Rap songs blast from motorbikes racing through the street market. Flower ladies hawk plastic roses in traffic exhaust. The snake charmer's cobra is battery-powered. "Child-safe," he assures his bystanders.

Instead of griping about how India has changed, one could toss the latest guidebook with its planned walks and must-sees, and choose an outdated (re: food and lodging) but perfectly valid (re: natural history) guide to regional cuisine, textiles, gardens, music, religious traditions—and explore alternative paths: those of chefs, scientists, nudists, mushroom hunters, throat singers, fly fishers. Come to think of it, why not travel with a book of poems by Nanao Sakaki:

> If you want to know the land
> Learn the weeds.
> If you want to know the culture
> Check the craft.
> If you want to know the future of the land
> Listen to the folk music.
> If you want to know the people
> Know yourself.

Karnataka, 2009

KERALA'S THEATER OF THE DOUBLE

On the bus north into Kerala from Kanyakumari, the southernmost point of the Indian subcontinent, there is an easy-to-miss outcrop crowned by a small banner. The knobby peak, overgrown with medicinal herbs that have been collected for millennia, figures prominently in the Ramayana. As the story goes, when Rama's wife, Sita, is abducted by the Demon King, Rama's brother arrives to help rescue her, but the evil king wounds him with a poison arrow. To save him, Hanuman, the monkey god, is asked to fly to a Himalayan mountain to gather curative herbs. But Hanuman, in a hurry and unsure of which herbs to gather, decides to grab the entire mountain. Flying home, he accidentally drops a piece of it just north of Kanyakumari. From the bus window, Renée and I catch a glimpse of the outcrop through waving palms and rubber trees. Marunthuvazh Malai, it is called: Abode of Medicinal Herbs.

The mountain is a destination for Hindu pilgrims—the kind that have tread South India for thousands of years. Some arrive on luxury sleeper buses, but the ultra-devoted and the poor prefer to walk. At a brief stop in our bus journey we see a band of wayfarers sharing snacks at the roadside. The women are dressed in bright green, canary, and scarlet saris. Some are tied with babies. The men, blue skinned, daubed with turmeric, carry tridents and gourds. They wear lungis, a loose wrap similar to a sarong, tucked and tied at the waist. They may be on a *yatra*, a group pilgrimage, perhaps to visit holy sites that figure prominently in the Ramayana; or to circumambulate Mt. Arunachala where Shiva changed into a pillar of fire; or, if childless, headed to the Sri Nagaraja Temple, hoping to be made fertile by the auspicious serpent lingams.

Kerala is a long sliver of luxuriant green wedged between the Arabian Sea and the lush flanks of the Western Ghats, which rise steeply to the east. It is tropical India, a rainy, laid back land known for unique food, architecture, ritual drama, and bone-jarring percussion bands. It's the farthest south of India's west coast states, abundant with coconut palms, bird-filled lagoons, webbed waterways, rubber plantations, and an influx of trophy homes built by Keralites who've returned from work in Dubai or Kuwait. On my first visit in 1979, the rice paddies were remarkably intact. Now many are missing, drained by those who have money to spend on glitzy dream palaces.

After a couple nights in Kerala's capital city, Thiruvananthapuram—to visit the Sri Chitra Museum, home of a modest but striking collection of Nicholas Roerich paintings—we board a train for the ten-hour journey north to Kannur, a market town on the Malabar Coast. We have no fixed plan when we step off the train, although our primary objective is to attend a Theyyam ritual—the arcane ceremony of spirit-possession held in village shrines throughout northern Kerala. Usually it is an all-night affair, and secretive unless you are alerted to the whereabouts by a local, and given the go-ahead by the family hosting the event.

We could chance a stay at a suggested private house on a nearby beach, but we know nothing of the owners or what kind of tourists we'll encounter there. We could also plunk ourselves in a hotel near the train station. Tired from the train journey, we opt for the latter. We'll stay a couple nights, then give the beach house a try (when in doubt, do both). Meanwhile, Renée spots a tourist kiosk outside the train station. The affable man behind the counter is enthusiastic about our visit. "Kannur doesn't see many foreigners." He flips through an events schedule and jots down a couple villages where Theyyams are happening.

"But," he holds up a finger, "if Theyyam is your focus, you must begin at dawn tomorrow at the Sri Muthappan temple in Parassinikadavu on the River Valapattanam." A mouthful, but he writes it in Malayalam so we can give it to a taxi driver. Good, because Malayalam—*mala,* mountain, *alam,* place (or *azham,* ocean)—Kerala's prevailing language, is very complex. Over the centuries its script has been reduced from 900 characters to fifty, a few at least we should learn to avoid complete befuddlement in the bus stations.

We settle into a bright, new, inexpensive hotel, shower the dust from our bodies, and hail an auto rickshaw to a no-frills South Indian eatery filled with locals. The interior is spacious and cool, ceiling fans whirling, tin-topped communal tables wiped clean between customers. We head for the spigot where hand-washing is mandatory, then seat ourselves and order a prawn *masala* and vegetable *biryani* from the menu. The meal arrives with complimentary tumblers of *karikku,* purified coconut water, and is served on a banana leaf, from which the food is taken with the right hand. After eating, we follow others through a rear patio and do as they do: empty our banana leaves down a wooden trough into a pen where a fat sow gobbles it.

It is dark and thundering when we return to our hotel room. I give Adesh a call, the man who owns the beach house with his wife Ravina. Quiet-spoken and very polite, he quotes us a reasonable tariff that includes three daily meals of home-cooked Keralan food. The place is just south of Kannur, isolated on an estuary leading to the sea. Adesh says there's plentiful bird life, a canoe to explore the estuaries, and his neighbor just up the hill is a Theyyam aficionado. It's a deal! We'll see them after our visit to the Sri Muthappan Temple.

It rains through the night, often violently. At 3 a.m. we wake the sleeping hotel porter who opens the door to

Kannur's empty-wet streets. Near the market we rouse a cab driver from his front-seat slumber. "Parassinikadavu?" He sleepily mumbles. Noting the hour, and seeing that we are *firangi,* he already knows our destination. The forty-five-minute ride, with oncoming candle-dim headlights bouncing into our eyes and bony phantomesque dogs sleeping in the road, recalls night rides through pot-holed Cambodia, or the midnight heat of misty villages in Java. Cockeyed streets, blurred profiles, lone lamplit windows. I keep hearing Coltrane's plaintive "Tunji"—a good match for the musical wobble of rain beads on the windscreen, the rippled imagery of witch-like trees overhanging the glossy tarmac.

Dawn is breaking when we arrive at the Sri Muthappan temple, a modern whitewashed three-story edifice with tiled roofs capping each tier, and black-painted elephant heads sculpted under the eaves—definitely more snazzy than we expected. A few kiosks selling devotional goods are raising their shutters. Flower sellers are wetting down loops of jasmine. Children, already trained in the art of business, are setting out framed lithographs of saints and gurus. We join a few pilgrims seated in the temple cafe for dosas and coffee, and learn that in an hour the drums will call Lord Muthappan and his attendants to the inner court. After coffee we descend the temple steps to the river. In the semi-dark, devotees are taking quick, prayerful dips—a peaceful scene remindful that rivers are sacred in India—liquid shakti.

When the drumming begins everybody hurries into the temple—most, but not all, of the women stand on one side, men on the other—facing a miniature vermillion shrine edged with gold. The wooden structure, with its pointed roof, might be a clone of ones found in Keralan villages, or perhaps it is an original and has been relocated here. Either way, it's a rather incongruous sight inside the oversize, purely functional main hall. There is a brass pillar in front of the shrine, each of its five tiers filled with flaming wicks. A ceremonial pole juts through the temple's roof, and next to it four drummers join a lead drummer, all of them rocking back and forth, beating upright drums hung from purple sashes looped around their necks. The musicians are bare-chested, dressed in gold-bordered white lungis. They soon begin to move in a slow spiral toward the shrine, accompanied by a *shehnai* player.

This is our first experience with the energetic percussion that dominates Keralan music: a crashing shake-rattle-and-roll that wakes every nerve-ending in the body. It is ritual music, like Pueblo drumming back home, but not the soft calling-the-rain-from-the-sky kind. No, it's thunderous, all surrounding. A climb-up-high message urging worshippers to ascend on rungs of sound, leaving body and mind behind. Pure Keralan world-class music, totally unlike the West's classical music based on European folk melodies, or the stuff of Mozart composed to inspire contentment. This is primeval sound, meant to uproot you. It finds origin in rain forests, frog croaks, bamboo clonks, woodpecker knocks, monsoon thrash, falling trees—the energy of a "world becoming." The mind-loss experienced during furious lovemaking. A chaotic *oomph* that births order. A ten-thousand-decibel ricochet. The onslaught of epilepsy, as if you were about to go under, into a Bosch-like subterranean self.

When the drumming reaches a pitch point, in walks the elaborately dressed Lord Muthappan, a Theyyam representing Vishnu and Shiva combined—so we've been told. But who knows? Some say Muthappan is simply an old ancestor who roves the woods drinking toddy. To query in this situation is like asking a question at a Hopi ceremony, only to be assertively answered with seemingly valid information—which often turns out to be a spin on reality, something the tourist can chew on. The informant knows he has given "deflective information" to protect the secrecy of the rite. In a Jungian sense, it is what the rite means to the observer that counts, what it brings into consciousness for examination.

One of the drummers steps out to accompany Muthappan as he moves about the room with jerky gestures, his speech muffled, his concentration elsewhere. He wears a gilded red headdress, a white cloth beard, and a swath of blond wig falling down his naked back. His torso is earth-smeared, dotted and spiraled with abstract designs. His belly is big, ringed with a bulging red waistband under which a brilliant vermillion wrap is tucked. He is adorned with bracelets, gold-fringed armbands, and brass bells around the ankles. His most noticeable attire is a pair of silver goggles over the eyes and a small mirror-disk held in an upraised hand. When the performer—dressed and made up as the god he is to impersonate—holds up the mirror-disk and peers into it, he sees the god that has come to dwell in his body. In turn, when the performer, now the god, goes public and holds the disk toward the assembled pilgrims, they each see the god in themselves.

At one point, I feel completely dislodged from measurable space. What moves before me is not a giant costumed figure, but a language of creaks and flutters, a hieroglyph of reassembled perspectives. Muthappan flips the mirror towards us, then sprinkles us with water—like spring rain drops; like the priest of my youth whisking the congregation with holy water. (With a smile, I recall one of my duties as an acolyte was to fill the priest's ritual vessel with chlorinated tap water.)

While Muthappan continues his walk-around, we take note of the large sculpted dogs at the main altar. A dog was wandering around inside the temple when the ritual began, and he seemed to be allowed there, just as dogs are allowed to wander the plazas during New Mexico's Pueblo rituals. Later we learn that the dogs are Muthappan's body-guards, and that so many village dogs were once allowed into this temple that they became pests. The priests decided to ban them, but keeping them out also kept the spirit of Sri Muthappan from entering the performer's body. It was not until the dogs were allowed back in, that the performance went on as usual.

As Theyyam rituals go, this is an abbreviated one—no more than a couple of hours. But it is an authentic introduction to northern Keralan ritual drama, and it is perfectly timed so that just as Lord Muthappan is giving his final blessing, pointing the disk toward the queue of persons waiting to direct their concerns to him, the sky comes alive with light. As we exit the temple doors, the Valapattanam River—a muted gray at dawn—is now fully illuminated, the sun a molten wafer rising in soft hues of pear and honeysuckle. We bathe our feet along with other pilgrims, enjoying a solemn quiet infused with a refreshing undercurrent of joy, an "everything okay" vibe. Back in Kannur, we ride an auto-rickshaw ten kilometers out of town, then turn down a steep, winding dirt track to a village scattered in lush palm groves, separated from the sea by a few dunes. We are pleasantly surprised to find Adesh waiting on the footbridge over the narrows of a freshwater estuary lined with coconut trees. He is immediately likeable—wild haired, big smile, dressed in saffron lungi, red shirt, leather chappals. He greets us with soft-spoken warmth, bright eyes twinkling under unruly curls—a mischievous air of youth coupled with a trim, agile body. Right away Renée senses something. Could he be a practitioner of the *kalarippayattu* martial arts indigenous to Kerala? "Yes," he answers, which makes her happy. As a longtime aikido practitioner, she could already sense—from his body tone and centeredness—that he was trained in some form of martial arts.

Shortly, Adesh's wife Ravina appears, wearing a simple cinnamon-brown sari. With a smile, she greets us in perfect English. She reminds me of young Joan Baez. We cross the estuary footbridge and are shown to their 100-year-old house, a white two-story Mangalore-style place: tile roof, swept-earth courtyard lined with potted herbs, attached guesthouse looking out through the palms toward the sea. We unload our bags, wash up, and return to the main house for mango juice and muffins. Adesh draws a map with trails of the area and offers his canoe for bird watching. In a couple hours we'll return to the dining room for the first of many memorable Keralan meals designed by Ravina and prepared by her talented cook.

While Renée goes through *kalarippayattu* moves with Adesh, I stroll the estuary on a path fringed with massive palms. At ten-degrees north of the equator, the day's end bathes the sky with Turneresque hues: moist tints of mauve, brushed chrome, and peppermint—great thunderheads boiling into it, casting a fuchsia glow on the deep green of the coconut palms. The atmosphere is semi-transparent, aquarium-like. Several children are fishing on a grassy bank. In humble homes half hidden in the palm groves, villagers are lighting oil lamps hanging beneath the eaves. Pinpoints of lemon yellow glimmer in the gauzy, tropical dusk. Soft mantras fill the violet-blue hour. As if I were not alive. As if I were under my own skin, my feet not touching the ground—a specter slipped into the Beyond.

With the call of a cuckoo, chatter of kingfishers, dwiddle of tree frogs, the lagoons turn rose, then pearl. Misting rain wets my shoulders. I don't see anyone, simply hear hushed voices through the woods, children playing, crack of kindling, bang of hollow urns. Fireflies mingle with the first flicker of candles in windows. I exit to the *thump-and-swoosh* of breakers behind the dunes. The thunderheads, now moved by the winds over the Arabian Sea, have turned dark plum. On the estuary footbridge, a man is leaning against the rail under an oversize umbrella, his silhouette a perfect Chinese brush stroke.

Ravina has prepared a sumptuous dinner: fish in *masala* sauce, *jeera* rice, *dal,* curried potato, parboiled forest herbs. We share the table with a twenty-three-year-old French woman studying computer science near Kannur, a Swedish woman in her seventies, a five-time India veteran who visits yearly, and a woman from the U.K. who has just come from the tea plantations of Munnar. Over dessert of sweet beans, melon, and strong Keralan coffee, Adesh asks us to recite our poetry. Renée does a mix of tanka and a poem from *The Storm That Tames Us*. I do a few haiku. Ravina's favorite:

> Not knowing
> what to say, he mails
> only the envelope.

Adesh bounces off an image from Renée's reading with a line from a Keralan poem: "A veil of gold covers your eyes from truth." We ask him to recite something in Malayalam. Ravina translates the poem into English, from which it goes to French and Swedish. English sounds so unmusical compared to Malayalam. Adesh annunciates every sound increment with razor-sharp quietness. He's a master performer in his own modest way. Renée and I are knocked out. Not that this kind of spontaneity over poetry doesn't happen back home, but that it has happened so quickly here.

Back in our room, Renée reflects: "Amazing to come to a place so far from home and sit with strangers an hour later, laughing together, reciting poems. Sometimes you have to go to where there is nothing to find everything." Suddenly, a rap on our door. Ravina has brought an unexpected potion for Renée's cough: fresh ginger tea spiced with local peppercorns, fenugreek seed, and jaggery. "An Ayurvedic remedy." We wrap up in our sarongs and dim the lights. At dinner, Adesh explained that the oil lamps I saw on my walk are a Saturday ritual in Hindu households. "They light them at dusk for the recital of prayer. You were fortunate to have taken your walk at that time of day." His words bring to mind a haiku by 18th-century Japanese poet Buson:

> *Spring evening—*
> *lighting one candle*
> *with another.*

"The softest poem I've ever heard," Rénee dreamily replies, then falls into deep sleep. Tomorrow Adesh will to talk to his parents about just where to see a Theyyam that is supposed to be in progress. I hope we'll receive an invite.

In the morning we borrow a canoe and paddle into the backwaters. Tiny pockets of sunlight fill the vitreous sheen, one circle overlapping another, a coinage of gold. As we row, songbirds chatter up from the trees in front of us, moving off, landing again, moving off: flecks of graffiti wheeling into periwinkle blue. From dark brackets of reed we hear *chuk-chuks, kwaaaonks, uh-wooo-hoos* of what creatures? At length we make a list of the birds we can identify: brahminy kite, cormorant, pond heron, bittern, sea eagle, blue-bearded bee eater, a Eurasian golden oriole. The Malabar Trogan is supposed to live in these parts, but its territory is up higher in the deciduous forests. That would be a bird to see, but the stork-billed kingfisher—rusty head, blood-red bill, pale yellow breast—isn't a bad stand in.

In the last light of evening, a gentle star, alone and blinking bright, glows low on the horizon. It seems to have gathered the florescent green of the backwaters, the whispering music of the reeds, and the joy of the birds into one liquid radiance. And with it our own joy, that of being inseparable from all that surrounds. I think of the Navajo *hózhó,* that perfect state of balance and harmony expressed in the poetry of the Blessingway ritual: "With Beauty before me may I walk, with Beauty behind me may I walk, with Beauty all around me may I walk."

We've been given the go-ahead by the family hosting the Theyyam ceremony. This morning we wake at 1:30, dress quickly, cross the footbridge, and meet our driver, who's wrapped in a blanket inside his Ambassador taxi. We squeak and bounce up the cliffs in the darkness, take a number of wrong turns, and finally discover the proper track into a web of backcountry villages. The driver asks for directions, turns up a potholed lane, and halts. We find our way through randomly parked cars, tramp through a spooky copse of dripping trees, and exit into a cluster of houses whose tiled, steeply-angled roofs overhang stuccoed walls made airy with latticed windows. The houses front a large earthen courtyard where, in one corner, a bonfire is shrinking into coals. In the opposite corner a small wooden shrine is strung with colored lights. At the peak of its roof is a mask of Yama, god of death, guardian of the south. As one of Shiva's envoys, Yama is also known as Kala: "time," whereas Shiva himself is honored with the title Maha Kala: "Great Time." Eternity.

A noble tree spreads its crown over the courtyard's far corner, oil lamps blazing under its fairy-like branches. This enormous beauty may well have been the original shrine, an arboreal pillar uniting heaven and earth, its roots reaching into the Underworld, its crown filled with stars. Beneath the tree is a plaited palm-leaf shelter, a makeshift dressing room where the Theyyam performers apply their makeup and don their attire. The adjoining courtyard is empty right now; the ritual is in the in-between time. Villagers mill about, some have already taken their folding chairs to a raised platform fronting the courtyard.

Entering the family compound was like approaching the heart of a spider's orb. Blinking lights, dripping trees, shadow-puppet silhouettes. Humans or monkeys? In the darkness, who could tell? Giant insects and bats, too—clicking wings in a spun-candy kaleidoscope. For a second we were transported to Bali, a village séance, a place "out of time," a realm connected to one's own heartbeat—to mist, darkness, a blur of melding worlds. The spell was broken when we realized that people were beginning to check us out—not with that north-Indian nonplussed stare, but with concerned politeness. Suddenly, an official dressed in a white lungi and plastic sandals walked up and showed us to a pavilion where a couple dozen people had gathered under a thatched roof—everyone relaxed and congenial. We sat down on a rock embankment, but almost immediately two plastic chairs appeared and we were made comfortable. "You have camera?" a man asked. "Oh, too bad. Good Theyyam." Being accustomed to the camera ban at Pueblo ceremonies back home, it didn't occur to us to bring one. Looking around, we realized that most of the extended family gathered had either cell-phone cameras or compact digitals. Not only were we the only *faringis* present, we were perhaps the only guests without cameras.

The man who first welcomed us appears again, almost apologetically reminding us that tonight's Theyyam began "long time past"—just before midnight. We've obviously missed a good part of the ritual, but he assures us it won't matter. "Theyyams tell stories hard for me to explain, but you will enjoy what follows—like you enjoy opera without understanding their foreign language." He hesitates, then adds: "Of course, our opera is different. It is medicine opera." One of the Theyyam troupe now calls him to their dressing room. Another performance is about to begin.

BAM! BAM! BAM! Deafening cherry bombs light up the darkness, louder than the loudest crackers in a Mexican fiesta! A quick silence follows. A nervous unrest. Two drummers, barefoot and bare-chested, walk into the square and begin to beat out a clattering rhythm on their *chendas,* upright drums slung vertically over their shoulders on bright red sashes. The drums are about three feet high, made from jackfruit wood, and stretched with hide. Beaten with hardwood sticks, the sound is tight and powerful. The drummers are accompanied by a man keeping time with finger cymbals. All of them wear cream-colored lungis wrapped over longer saffron ones. Draped against their cinnamon skin, the effect is regal.

Soon an elderly priest wrapped in a waistcloth appears. Seen through the heatwaves of the bonfire, he is distorted into a wavering genie. He hunkers over a brass vessel on the dirt courtyard, placing offerings of coconuts, rice, and bananas on freshly wetted banana leaves. He brings his palms together above his forehead, prays, and vanishes into a sudden pall of red and green pyrotechnic smoke. When we look again, six drummers are drumming and two Theyyam performers are approaching the open square from the dressing area. They wear skirts of young palm fronds sliced into thin ribbons. Their faces and bodies are whitened with rice paste, eyes ringed with soot. Wielding long wooden poles, they jump, twirl and mime; variations of *kalarippayattu* moves. Lifting and lowering their heads, they meet and separate in reptilian-like encounter, stamping their feet, shaking anklet shells. Impulsive and unpredictable, they are one moment graceful, the next angular and ajar. Then, a sudden halt. The Theyyams stand as if tethered by a supernatural force, giving only a slight quiver as they banter irreverently, then speak commandingly. A few drops of rain begin. I look up into phosphorescent sparkles as if looking down into a tide of glittering plankton.

The Theyyams are now sitting on a bench, hidden by a red cloth held up by two attendants. All that can be seen are the impersonators' bare legs and feet, which remain very still at first, but then begin to jiggle as the drumming ascends. The toes twitch, energy ripples from earth to ankles and up the legs. Their bodies begin to shake with pure shakti vibration. The performers have entered that realm between death and rebirth where normal reality vanishes and the gods take possession. Incarnation, surge, resurrection. The triumph of Mystery.

Behind the red cloth, the Theyyams are being tied with tall bamboo standards, six or more meters high, laced with plaited palm leaves. When the drapery is dropped, their faces are covered by large, flat, red-white-and-black masks with huge eyes and scrolled fangs. When they rise to dance, they are giants, standing straight, then leaning forward on hardwood poles, akin to the jo used in aikido. Angled toward as such, they balance themselves precariously, headdresses and all, and slowly lower their board-like bodies to the ground. It is an extended bow, an exaggerated gassho expressing gratitude and reverence for Mother Earth. The drumming continues, heightening into crescendos, quieting again, then strengthening into a thundering blast of hail, a deafening roar of insects.

We've done little reading on the Theyyam, preferring to absorb the ritual in a personal sense. It seems, as in Hopi ceremonies where the gods descend into the bodies of the impersonators, that the Keralan gods do the same.

They step from a mythic realm to inhabit the flesh of the impersonators. Theyyam ritual is meant to call an other-worldly ancestor—a hero or protector—into the body of the dancer, who in turn transmits that presence to those gathered. The rite is a collective séance where people can leave the everyday and enter the sacred world of their cosmic divinities.

Adesh explained that Theyyam deities are pre-Hindu tutelary spirits overlaid with Hindu concepts. Mostly they survive untainted, a throwback to the "Time Before" when Theyyams walked out of the Keralan forests to mingle with humans and give counsel. In contrast to Hindu gods that sit with blank stares in clammy temples, Theyyam gods are active. They have voices, give advice, are capable of bringing good cheer to villagers, and a bit of mockery, too. "Often their stories question the idea of caste, hierarchy, the Untouchable, the all-superior Brahmin. The irony is that the upper caste are always in the audience. They love being entertained and advised by the Theyyams. Yet, behind the masks are men of the lowest level of the caste system, the *Dalits*, most of them excelled artists."

The young man next to us speaks good English and says tonight's Theyyam is sponsored by one family, but the event is open to anyone who wants counsel, or simply wants to enjoy a good story from the time of the gods. "These are serious dramas," he explains. "The performers come from a long line of artists who are highly trained and paid for their performances. They must learn the stories that go with each deity, know the martial arts, and have athletic skill. Each Theyyam demands mental and spiritual preparation. A performer must give up the human body for the god's body—fast, keep from liquor, and no sex. If he is not pure, a mistake will be made.

"The make-up men are also capably trained. They

are face writers who apply colored patterns that identify the deity about to be invoked. Along with the priests and performers, they must forego the worldly and prepare for the unearthly. The drummers, too, must be pure. Their job is to help call the god into the flesh of the impersonator by drumming him into a state where his speech and gestures give the drama the intensity expected not only by the spectators, but by the very god he has invited into his being."

❧

The priest who earlier vanished into the smoky haze of the pyrotechnics now reappears, although he is "gone," in trance. He is being urged into the compound by another Theyyam who has joined the ritual—dressed in tasseled red skirts flaring out from an elaborately pleated waistband. His arms are lined with metal bands and wraps of red cloth, eyes darkened, face smeared with ochre, a short white beard around the mouth. With long silver fingernails accenting his gestures, he implores the dazed priest forward, grabs his shoulders, props him in the center of the compound, and recites magic words to break the spell. The priest snaps awake. He walks normal again, and leaves the courtyard. The Theyyam, however, dashes about with frenetic advances, clattering his bells and ornaments while the drums ascend. He approaches a bed of red-hot embers, raked into a square by an attendant. Around us, people quickly back into the rear of the seating area. We take note, rise, and follow. The barefoot Theyyam walks onto the coals, kicks them into the air, and spins wildly away, only to charge back again. Hot embers fly, a few sizzle and die at our feet.

Theyyam performances are remote from the West's notion of theater on a raised stage, the audience neatly seated in an auditorium. Here, the earth is the platform. Characters roam helter-skelter in a courtyard, disappear into the trees, return through the crowd, vanish into mist. As in the Javanese shadow puppet play, the audience is free to roam. There is no fixed place where one must be. A chair is fine, or sitting on the top of a wall, or walking around to view things from various angles, even from behind the stage to watch the musicians and puppet master at work.

As in the shadow play, the Theyyam audience is often addressed in the trance lingo of the gods. The "Before Speech" of growls, mutters, raspy utterances, and high shrills that bring spectators out of their static realm into that of psychically-active participants. Powerful and capricious, the Theyyams are often contradictory, full of double entendre, yet capable of wise advice. They can insure a good rice harvest, make fertile a childless couple, heal village discord, keep the world turning in harmony. Antonin Artaud, who wrote about a Balinese dance he saw in Paris in 1931, but could have been writing about a Theyyam, said: "in the midst of a whole ferment of visual or sonorous images (we are plunged) into that state of uncertainty and ineffable anguish which is characteristic of poetry."

Dawn breaks into a morning of sultry heat. Seven hours have passed. We return to our homestay, take bucket baths, drink a mango juice, and relax with our Keralan hosts. When we describe the fire-walking Theyyam, Adesh says it was probably Bali, the monkey god from the Ramayana. When I tell him the costume hardly resembled a monkey, he laughs. "It is not about appearance. It is about energy. How the monkey acts. He is full of whim, changeability. And that is what lies beneath all Theyyam rituals: unpredictability."

RHYTHM IN STONE

The Khajuraho Night Train rattles through Madhya Pradesh, India's tawny heartland. I wake to a cherry-red sunrise, sit up, pick sleep from eyes, make way down the aisle to brush my teeth at the tiny metal sink in the rear loo. When I return to our berth, Renée is awake in the fold-out bed above me. Out the window, biscuit-brown hills swell and heave between tangled greenery. The land is heat washed, tumbled in sculptured masses of stone and sandy drift. To the Westerner, a biblical landscape; but to the Indian, a cosmogram of myth, history, ancient drama. Even a farmer cursed by drought will look upon a certain sun-parched hill with folded palms, knowing it to be where Shiva married Parvati. The suggestive cleave that a sage has marked with a stripe of pigment is a sanctified place where matter joined spirit to beget a sunrise. And the monolith half-buried in a stony ravine where herders gather dry grass? It is the carapace of the Cosmic Tortoise, an avatar of Lord Vishnu.

A purity of sun bathes this land. Rough, yet compelling, it wakes the eye and gives a surprise. Every so often a gleam flashes through a screen of trees: a metal pennant topping a Hindu shrine. Fields of flowering cotton follow, then a long stretch of blinding sand. Under an errant shade tree, pilgrims have paused to plant their staffs around an unusual ripple in the hardpan. A yoni? A birthing place? A reference point on an astronomical compass? Similar sojourners wander the high desert back home, Native Americans headed to the Emergence Place, the Salt Place, the Fluted Rock where the Holy Beings dwell.

Potentially, any place within the landscape can be sacred. As a child I was told of a Holy Land located in a desert across the sea, a lush valley set between the Tigris and

Euphrates rivers. When I looked up this so-called Garden of Eden in my atlas, it seemed too far away. Why there and not here? I felt robbed of my own Eden, the perfect oasis of my backyard with its central axis: my favorite climbing tree. Eventually I learned that the Eden handed to me in books was only one of many places on the planet identified and mythologized by people as their Ancestral Home, the Original Land.

Dust sucks through the carriage window. It carries the mineral taste of earth trodden by conquerors who plundered quickly and moved on. Thinly hidden beneath their tracks are foot-worn trails of prehistoric people who moved more slowly, gathered more sparingly, hunting only what they needed. The land passes, and with it the geologic ages: explosions, submersions, extrusions; the human histories: rise and collapse of empires; the diaspora of families on the run from heatwaves, failed wells, earthquakes, war, genocide. Sunbeams dapple muscular rock forms, a morse code of heaves and bulges through which the train marks a straight line, speeding not through emptiness but through a multi-ringed sphere of time. Historic, metamorphic, catastrophic. Personal, allegorical, rhetorical. Fundamental, mythic, divine.

I'm always at home on a train. Roll, bump, and sway. Swing, waltz, and tap dance. New motion in the mind. A wheeze, a pressure drop, an up-tempo recharge, a flash, a revealment. As a touring bandleader, Duke Ellington composed in the mental isolation of his train compartment, savoring the ever-changing sounds of steam and steel. George Gershwin said "Rhapsody in Blue" came to him on a train to Boston. In Madhya Pradesh my eye follows rhapsody of light on stone, a breathing of song lines, topography shadowed by clouds writing a score in the dust. Held by it, thoughts crystallize, boundaries dissolve. Motion! The *maww* and moan and *rapp-rapp* of the rails; a horn blow, whistle slice, a laser beam through all barricades. "I don't want to be stopped by anything," Renée says, "especially by myself."

Along the tracks, villagers wait for the slower, cheaper local trains. Men hunker in circles, tuck in their lungis, play cards. Women stand, strapped with babies, plastic jugs of cooking oil, portable stoves. Their daughters play by the rails. Dressed in ruffled frocks, they'll soon be girls, the baby-pink skirts replaced by silk saris. A milkman wobbles on his bicycle. Two cowherds casually hold conversation while letting loose their bowels in a ravine. Morning light brightens the cactus fences, warms a damp cluster of mango trees. The sesame crops turn gold. I open the carriage window to minty updrafts of fields and woods, a thread of cooking smoke. Renée spots a low-flying pheasant, its bright-fire colors painting the dull underbrush as it glides.

Inside the coach comes a steamy drift of sweet milk tea. A chai wallah makes way down the aisle. No longer does he tote the fragile from-the-earth/back-to-the-earth clay cups once common on India's trains. Instead, he pours the chai into non-recyclable plastic cups, through which the hot tea burns the fingers. If you don't drink quickly—which means burning your lips—the cup melts into a grotesque curl and the tea spills onto your lap. The profanity of change! Why should an improper tea cup bother me? Then again, why shouldn't it? Those old baked-earth cups were essential to the taste buds. Nothing like the rich combo of cardamom-spiced, sugar-sweet milk tea and the earthy flavor of the cup. Add, too, the pleasant pop and smash when the cups were tossed from the train to melt back into the earth. Besides, the cups gave local potters a chance to market their wares for extra income.

After tea, hotel touts ply the train, popping up from nowhere, slapping down their cards to remind us they will be awaiting our business in Khajuraho. "Take card, please, sir. Reduced-price massage, madam? Pamphlet for temple? Private, no-problem tour, sahib? Please, you will come see?" Jolly Inn. Xanadu. Hotel Bright. Royal Bargain Guest House (advertising "Free lawn"). I politely indicate I don't wish to begin my day like this, and the touts evaporate. (It saves a lot of hassle, being a crank.) Meanwhile, the woman in the opposite berth turns out to be a man. He rattled his beads—I thought they were anklets—all night, shifting under his blanket. Now he's up, ready for business. "Yoga master," he says. "You must take my exercise. Big benefit for thinking. Find me at Home Sweet Home." When his mobile rings he darts to a doorway for better reception, but not after quickly passing on his card:

> Worshipful Master
> Please Donate

The air quickly warms. Renée and I share a plate of potato-pea *samosas* flavored with curry and chile sauce. I reach into my daypack for *Mountain Tasting,* the haiku of Santōka Taneda, the failed Japanese sake brewer who became a wandering monk, lived without modern needs, and suffered for it too. His journals describe his being mistreated for begging, scorned for wearing grass sandals, mocked for being old-fashioned, and deliberately splashed by arrogant drivers as he walked the rain-wet roads. Disregarding the restrictions of his era and the confinements set by peers, he walked, held out his begging bowl, grabbed a radish from a roadside field, raised a cup with itinerant fellows in a tumble-down bar, slept among blooming grasses, and wrote the uncensored truth of the moment.

> *Frying fish,*
> *Sometimes frying the hand—*
> *Life alone.*

Putting one foot in front of the other, a dragonfly riding his *kasa*, seldom brought to a halt by unnecessary pondering, Santōka was content to enjoy "this moment, this immediate impression I want to express." A tired farmer on a rickety carriage, a child lugging charcoal through the day-labor of Tokyo, ants marching through a bamboo grove, the winter trees stretching out their branches: they were temporary companions—his to contemplate, rather than merely observe. Poetry, he surmised, is a "useless thing, something that cannot be bartered or sold, but does it not have value as an idea of what lingers on?"

> *The cold sound*
> *Of a one-sen coin*
> *Thrown my way.*

Suddenly I recall the image of a homeless wreck of a rag curled up on a sidewalk in Agra. A well-dressed man stepped around this shadow of death, fiddled with his mobile, and walked on. Was he calling for aid? Texting a client? No ambulance showed. No police, no Mother Teresa. Another man stopped, but only to hold out his phone for a photo. In the country where Buddhism began, where was Buddha? Only Shiva, in the form of a kid in shorts, danced by, rolling a bicycle rim with a stick, kicking up a little dust in the Karma Wheel. On the same block, a woman stepped from the frayed curtain of her shanty. Poised for a moment, a brass pot under her arm, she walked from the shadows into her routine. Crouched at a public well, she steadied her urn under the pump, worked the handle with her free hand, all the while giving a glazed stare into space. In her busy day, was this her only moment of pause? Lifting the urn to her head, she regained balance, a practiced labor, her movements precise. With the urn above her, she carefully turned and walked back into the shadows.

I would never know this woman's situation, her caste, her unending labor, the toll of her expected role. I was the voyeur, retreating to the cool patio of my inn to order tea and pen a few thoughts. In a journal entry from the year 1930, Santōka wrote: "Accept all that arises. Sometimes tears fall, sweat flows; at all times we must savor each experience and move on without being obstructed by circumstances." But what I had seen in Agra had obstructed my journey. My thoughts turned jagged. The ink in my pen thickened. I was at a standstill, unable to gain traction. Too many days in India two experiences are one too many.

The train squeals and brakes into Khajuraho Station. Time to lace the shoes, grab our bags, find some lodging.

❧

Ten centuries ago, Khajuraho's temples overlooked a densely packed city. Residents might have glimpsed the temple towers through the crowds of a bazaar, much like the modern traveler catches sight of Madurai's many-storied temples through a tangle of shoppers in the street market. Today Khajuraho is a UNESCO World Heritage Site. The old city has crumbled back into the earth, its temples now surrounded by mowed lawns bordered with evenly-clipped hedges.

In the bright afternoon, the golden stone soars upward, carrying the eye toward rounded summits meant to replicate Mt. Meru, the sacred pillar joining heaven and earth, the axis mundi central to the cosmologies of Buddhists, Jains, and Hindus. The latter know it as Mt. Kailash, Lord Shiva's abode. Located in western Tibet, rising from the arid plateau behind the main Himalayan range, its

22,000-foot dome of shining snow is a remote but much sought destination for pilgrims.

Of Khajuraho's eighty temples dating to the seventh century, twenty-five survive. I first learned of them when Gary Snyder wrote about Khajuraho during his India journey in 1963. One of the temples he described was the 100-foot-tall Kandariya Mahadeva Temple, a prototype for Mt. Kailash:

> ...a kind of geological-paleontological system of strata, moving up through animal friezes to the "human" level—fossils of dancers, lovers, fighters—temple wall like a human paleontology laid bare—rising; to the Divine Couples seated in shrines on sub-pinnacles—vegetable, mineral, and animal universes—complete—to the mountain summit, spire of pure geometry, a rock crown like the sun...

The Mahadev Temple is one of the most celebrated of India's medieval temples. Staggeringly ornate, it rises from a granite plinth, its burnt-ochre sandstone undulating skyward in distinct vertical progressions, light and dark exchanging places as day proceeds—like cloud shadows patterning a mountain's face. The effect is realized by ornate rivulets and foliate abstractions incised into the stone, little trappings for sunbeams that transform the temple into an airy, floating presence. This dreamlike effect was further enhanced by a shallow lake which partially surrounded the temples in ancient times. Defined allegorically, this was the Cosmic Ocean—the primordial waters that gave birth to the world.

We take a seat on the steps of the Mahadev Temple. Behind us, an austere inner sanctum holds a lingam, symbol for Lord Shiva who meditated in a cave, danced his way into light, and squelched ignorance. The entrance to the sanctum faces east, as do all the temple entrances in Khajuraho. A thousand years ago, a yogini might have performed her asanas where we sit. Perhaps she was one of those high-altitude hermits garbed in thin cloth who came to Khajuraho to escape the Himalayan winter. A Tantric master might have sat here, too, chanting mantras as the sun rose above the Cosmic Ocean. The sacred intonations attributed to Shiva and Vishnu (to whom Khajuraho's temples are dedicated) would have originated in the bellow of mountain winds, the whisper of a river coursing through reeds, the sizzle of a raven's wing, the throbbing voice of a Himalayan cascade.

Trekking the high summits, one experiences the *craack* of frozen water deepening a cut through granite. The mountain talks as it soars. It howls, gives a hissing spit of hail, clears its throat with a rasp. Boulders crash and explode as melting ice releases a landslide. The thrones are never quiet. There is the sonar activity of light. God is close. Audible clings to the inaudible, a wise lama once spoke. The mantra is a play of force, eruption of substrata. It's aural colors are present in the drone of the monastic clergy, in the meld of sound increments in the Hopi Niman ceremony, in the metallophones of the Balinese gamelan.

Khajuraho's setting, on the dry plateau of northern Madhya Pradesh, is attractive, but without any apparent geographical feature that would have led settlers to establish themselves here. No provocative outcrop or meeting of rivers. No grotto from which an oracle voiced her instructions. Perhaps the Chandelas, the rulers who migrated east from Rajasthan and founded Khajuraho, saw the site as isolated enough to prove safe haven. Where no mountains were to be found, they had them created from blueprints handed down by the gods.

The Chandelas must have enjoyed a stable moment in history in which they could comfortably actualize the mythological mountains into stone and embroider them with potent symbols of procreation. They would have needed royal patronage and wealth collected from vassal states to employ the masterminds of their great temples: skilled geomancers, expert architects, schooled builders, experienced quarriers, stone cutters, and teams of common laborers, scaffold builders, cooks, cart drivers, porters. All of this reached a zenith between 950 and 1050, until Muslim invaders began their approach in the thirteenth century. Luckily, the aggressors overlooked Khajuraho. The temples remained overgrown until T.S. Burt, a British army officer, discovered them in 1838. In typically Victorian terms he reported the façades of erotic carvings to be "a little warmer than there was any absolute necessity for." Perhaps he was a man who kept his pants on all the time.

Exploring Khajuraho, we look to the friezes above us, and smile. We are not overseen by saints or some godly judge refereeing our whims, as in a cathedral. We are looked upon by amorous couples dancing and lovemaking their way into heaven among parrots, elephants, flowering gourds, and a host of full-bosomed *apsaras* flitting from the clouds, each rendered with such lightness—as if the sculptor whittled a breeze from the heavens, gave it a whisper of mist, and brought to life a timeless angel. The mere sight of these temples and my eyes begin to well. They are fashioned in the same tan-buff stone of my homeland. Right out of the earth they rise! Same glow, same color of the soil. Same prism of mineral, same heatwave of breath from the hollows where life started. Stand close, and you feel the sun from a thousand millennia ago warm your face.

Khajuraho is a hologram. We walk through oscillating stone, experiencing all angles in one. The temples are a sound field of vibrating atoms. Their façades—quarried from the ground, lifted into the sky—are wrapped with organic motifs carved in high relief: buds, blossoms, leaves, birds, snakes, mythological beasts, and everyday mortals softened by centuries of monsoon rains. In the lowermost friezes, humans are at work and play. Higher up, they abandon their tasks to undress, bathe, caress, loosen their boundaries, and playfully unite into abstractions of bliss. Male becomes female, female male. In a fury of undulations, love is wedded to light, flesh illuminates space.

Khajuraho's famed erotica comprises less than ten percent of its sculptured panels. Yet, it is the big draw, especially for sex-obsessed Western tourists tethered to Puritan restraint, suspicious of ribald sex—the joys of doing it in the open, on the beach, lapped by the forbidden tides of freedom—praising God, legs in the air, screaming litanies of climactic joy. At Khajuraho, the spiritual does not exist apart from the sexual. The wonders of sex are realized without shame under the cobalt lens of sky. Alan Watts cites a passage from the *Brihadaranyaka Upanishad*, "When a man is in the embrace of his beloved, he knows nothing as within and nothing as without," adding: "nothing, indeed, of any other dichotomy." The climactic surge of pleasure during sexual intercourse—that thrust of primordial vowels—is a mantra. A sonic vibration of male and female joined, self and other dissolved.

Some guidebooks propose that Khajuraho's explicit friezes were meant as a manual for newlyweds, a Kama Sutra rendered in stone. Even the blind can read these storyboards, running fingers over soft Braille of lifted breasts, swollen vulvas, bold phalluses. Others suggest the erotic sculptures relate to Tantric practices. Do the lovers represent a spiritual fusing of male and female as they meld in ecstasy to meet the Divine? Or, are they simply keyhole glimpses into the bed chambers of the courtly? Playful, unhampered sex. Men twanging their phalluses, wives jingling their bangles, opening their charms—as did the milk-maids for Krishna.

Questions are best left as arousals. Explanations are as endless as the panels themselves. Big-breasted, wide-hipped Mother goddesses. A leaping stag under Kama's bow. A lotus-eyed girl, her sideways glance teasing a farmer from his plow. A cowgirl behind a blossoming tree, covering her mouth to feign embarrassment as she spies two lovers in orgasm—just look at their rolled-back eyes and clenched toes. And the shepherd girl with one hand fondling a man's lingam while her other hand undoes her sash? No inhibition, she's ready for it.

Mr. Kurian, our wise and easygoing guide, points out a princely figure enjoying sex with three favorites. Two of the girls help the third onto him, her rear toward his face, his member thrust deep. His free hands stroke the yonis of the two maidens who smile as they look on, obviously enjoying the transmission of sexual passion through the woman they support. According to a book Mr. Kurian loaned us, *Guide to The Sacred Places of Northern India*, most of Khajuraho's sculptures have double meanings. The author, Alistair Shearer, theorizes that Khajuraho was indeed a Tantric hub, which is why so much erotica appears on the temples. Other scholars dismiss this, claiming Tantra is a highly esoteric cult whose arcane teachings are transmitted orally in secret settings and would never be revealed on a temple façade. A "whispered transmission" would be more appropriate.

A triptych of carvings shows a woman bending over, her yoni seen from the rear, expanding to receive the lingam of her lover who gradually enters her, until, in the final panel—the one highest up—she throws back her head with a scream. Mr. Kurian cheerfully allows us on our own for this, distancing himself from what he calls "a 12th-century porn show." The panel, though, carved in pink stone sparkling with feldspar, is too stylish and graceful to be lewd. Its radiant vitality reveals an act of mutual devotion between god and goddess: Shakti, the female creative force animating the universe, joined with the fiery heat of Shiva, the male force. The image is probably loaded with esoteric meaning for the initiated; but Renée and I are not of the initiated, we are poets—and we approach Khajuraho as we do Indian love poetry:

> *The night was deep*
> *the lamp burning with heat*
> *my sash unloosened on its own*
> *He touched my body*
> *I slipped out my breasts*
> *my skirt left my hips*
> *What happened next is all a blur*
> *I can't remember who he was, or me*
> *or what we did or how.*

Khajuraho's artisans could animate this moment in stone, give charge to the arousal with chisel and hammer, shape and smooth the fermenting desire of two lovers about to consummate their longing. Filled with anticipation, they step closer in each finely chiseled panel, stroking the flesh, snuffing the camphor lamp, undoing the hair, baring the goose-bumped flesh, casting off jewelry in a fit of zeal. Casting off names, too, in a fury of pleasure. The swollen kiss, the liquid eyes, the opulent breasts lifted high, the impossible backbends into pleasurable acts of cunnilingus—they are rendered with precision. Beneath them, sculpted with equal care are musicians, dancers, and open-mouthed singers. Everybody is invited into the blissful elation of the lovers. A lotus unfolds its petals, blooming tendrils wrap each other in steamy ringlets, a cloud swells with heat, a purple banana pod, engorged with seed, bursts into flower.

   In one panel a monkey hides in a tree. Like the mind, he cannot remain still. Swinging through the foliage, he pairs with another, is about to copulate, but is too agitated, too distracted. A branch of mangos hangs nearby. The two monkeys go after the fruit instead of themselves, even though their flesh bristles with desire. Below the monkeys is another set of panels. The first depicts a hearth-bound wife contemplating a caged songbird. The second shows the bird free of its cage, and the wife free from the hearth. In the final panel, she meets a lover in the reeds. Her anklets are off, her back is marked with scratches, her hips grow ample, you can hear her sighs. What the artist carves in stone, the poet renders into words:

> *Oh don't*
> *or all my treasures*
> *hidden deep shall open*

   Someone should publish a collection of remarks made by Western explorers at Khajuraho. A bestseller for sure. One 18th-century traveler, Captain Edward Moor, wrote of "monstrous delineations . . . human nudities in the most indecent, uncleanly situations exposed in the most shameful combinations that a brutal imagination could suggest, in all the filthy attitudes of unnatural depravity." Had he looked closer, the "human nudities" weren't naked, but cloaked in gossamer silk sewn with jingling pendants. Not only did the carver intend the illusion of bare skin to compel the eye closer, he aspired to portray with exactness the courtly attire of the era: sheer draperies styled to emphasize the body's curves. Renée recalls the holy city of Kashi, where she watched women at the Ganges perform their morning ablutions, praying to the sunrise while dunking into the water. Their saris pressed to their bodies, they splashed out of the river in stained-glass hues of silk, all features of the flesh sumptuously revealed by the very cloth meant to hide them.

In Western classical art, god puts restrictions on the artist. In the East, god, or better said—the goddess—gives permission. Writings by the first foreigners to visit Khajuraho, those who claimed its erotica was an "error of the senses, an ocean of carnality lashing against the shore of our spiritual natures," make you wonder: did these guys take their own lovers to bed with such brainy condemnation? With a little chutzpah they could have inhaled some bhang, loosened their belts, and stepped into the minds of Khajuraho's artists who submitted to bliss and went to work with their chisels. There is no word for "obscene" in Sanskrit. Nor in the language of monkeys, dolphins, elephants, eagles or pandas.

It is difficult to re-create the life of the Chandelas without a hefty amount of reading or an expert historian who can paint a picture of then as now. Mr. Kurian has been crafting his knowledge as a guide for forty years. He's gifted with investigative thinking, has a sense of humor, and provides ample room to ponder. He understands when enough information is enough, and doesn't answer every question. He knows if we work a little, we'll find the answer inside us. A native of South India, he was raised as a Christian, is well read, and doesn't shun the erotic iconography with its myriad implications: worldly, spiritual, esoteric. Every evening he rides the bus from Khajuraho back to his village, where he is received by a loving wife. "One who is smart," he adds. "She helps me see what is false in what is true." At dawn Mr. Kurian returns to Khajuraho, settles in, enjoys a cup of chai, and goes to work in his open-air office. "Some Khajuraho guides taint the visitor's experience with their own religious backgrounds," Kurian warns. "They slant you this way or that—Hindu, Muslim, or Christian.

Some will tell you Aliens built the temples. Others say the erotic sculptures are relics of a bygone culture. But yesterday is today. Flirtation and procreation are present affairs."

Many highlights we wouldn't have noticed without Mr. Kurian's help: the superb craftsmanship of dry-walled stone interlocked and held in place with resin; a pair of coupled dragonflies hovering above two dancers inhaling to broaden their bosoms; a wasp at the nipple of a naked courtesan brushing make-up around her eyes; a woman lifting one leg, applying henna to the bottom of her foot, her private beauty purposely revealed; a young bride letting a see-through veil fall from her thigh, onto which a scorpion with a raised stinger has crawled.

A baffling moment occurs when Mr. Kurian shows us a carving of a man inserting an acupuncture needle into his lover's spine as she lifts her behind. "You must account for the position of the needle. It corresponds to the position of the moon. Arousal has many forms." But we detect no moon on the carved relief. Was the moon in the sky? Did we miss it? Was the arc of the woman's back meant to represent a crescent moon? We'll consider it our koan for the day. "Maybe while you nap, the answer will be revealed."

At sunset, we return to the temples by ourselves, long after the departure of the last tour bus. Sightseeing crowds arrive at predictable hours. Indians zip through in noisy gaggles, assemble for family videos, and vanish. Foreigners gather in compact groups around their guides. A few tourists are history buffs. Most are simply curious. Some come for a peek, perhaps awed by those slippery acts they are reluctant to perform at home. Maybe they'll depart with a little inspiration to spice up their lives. Others arrive totally unprepared, Khajuraho is just another stop on the itinerary.

"What is it about this place?" I keep asking.

"Rhythm captured in stone," Renée suggests. "The grace of it."

She's right. There is an obvious warp-and-weft energy in these temples. Each wrap-around frieze can be read both horizontally and vertically. The eye goes two ways at once. Side to side, bottom to top—from indoor scenes: cooking, bathing, coiffing the hair; to outdoor scenes: hoeing, herding elephants, drumming, honoring the king, praising the gods, preparing for battle. Higher up, humans abandon the everyday for the exotic: tender fondling, explicit coupling. Male and female are impossible to untangle. Their interlocked figures are beyond intercourse—they are mutations of energy, the awakening of Kundalini, the rousing of dormant psychic forces. One of the earliest Upanishads reminds us:

> From Joy springs all Creation
> by Joy it is sustained
> towards Joy it proceeds
> into Joy it returns.

Evening is the best time at Khajuraho. The stone gives a tangerine glow, slowly turning rose, then a dusty cinnamon as the fading sun aligns the human spirit with the divine. At this hour we find ourselves not visiting the temples as spectators, but swept away as participants. Mountains of light. Luminous mantras. Rhythm captured in stone.

Khajuraho!

Blake's "eternal delight."

Khajuraho, 2010

TIME, TRANCE, AND DANCE IN BALI

The great volcano, Gunung Agung, is Bali's cosmic mountain. For the Balinese it is the Navel of the World, the central axis associated with Mt. Meru in Hindu mythology. From its 10,000-foot summit flow the rain waters, tier to tier, irrigating the rice paddies terraced around its slopes. Every village, each home, has a shrine to the mountain gods, tended daily with flowers and incense. And in each village—except those of the indigenous islanders known as the Bali Aga—people sleep with their heads facing the cosmic mountain.

As the home of the gods, Gunung Agung is an important orientation point on a geographical compass for every villager who dwells in its presence. From birth through daily labor to the end of life, the Balinese share an intrinsic and permanent relationship with the mountain. While working the fields, sitting to weave or carve, planning a religious ceremony, constructing a new house or temple, they are intimately aligned with the mountain, drinking its waters, receiving its power, observing its moods, fearing its eruption. A cab driver once told me how important a person's home is to this compass point. "As a teenager I went with a relative from my village to another village to buy seed. We drove into an unfamiliar valley and I lost my direction. The mountain was missing, I got sick. I tried to stand up and steady myself. Everything had changed. We bought the seed, and when we returned home the sickness left. My head was fine, I knew where I was." At the story's end, he laughed. "Now I drive tourists to and from Bali's International Airport."

One morning, I take a walk with Ketut, a shadow-puppet master who has invited me to have a look at his village temple. We zigzag uphill through terraced rice fields, walking a mud-banked irrigation canal—a real balancing act since the levee is so narrow. Occasionally we step aside to let gaggles of bebek pass, the young duck herders following behind, waving thin sticks tied with white ribbons. The route sparkles with dew, the morning sun already strong through waving stands of bamboo. At the temple we wrap our waists with the customary cotton-polyester sashes, his gold, mine blue, and approach the *candi bentar*, a ceremonial "split" in the wall that surrounds the complex. Both sides of this doorless stone gate are elaborately carved with writhing organic designs—a complex DNA of uncoiling tendrils rising into twin peaks—the open space between them perfectly framing Mt. Agung in the background. Stepping through, we leave the material world and enter the sacred. The presence of the mountain is paramount, a deified link between heaven and earth. Inside the open-air compound are several courtyards, each with a *meru*—a multi-tiered, thatched roof pagoda symbolizing both Mahameru, the Buddhist mountain of heaven, and Gunung Agung, Shiva's abode. According to Ketut, the merus are homes for the gods when they visit, but even in their absence, I notice the gods have been honored with offerings of plaited palm leaves, jasmine, and bougainvillea flowers. Each has been sprinkled with water and set with sticks of smoking incense.

To either side of the gate we entered, two boiling-eyed creatures chiseled from volcanic stone stood guard, their fat bellies draped with black-and-white-checkered cloth. "No fear," Ketut says. "They are reminders to maintain your balance through life's doorways. They also ask you to enter the temple pure. Forget money, forget worry, forget yesterday, forget tomorrow, leave the self behind. Enter without mix-up." The checkered cloth, he explains, is called *kain poleng*, a cloth that wards off evil. "Black and white represent the opposing realms in the mortal world.

Good thoughts, bad thoughts. High deeds, low deeds. Peace, war. We constantly move between them. Good and evil are always fighting. You have to be on guard. You can't let them knock you off course. This is the theme of the *wayang kulit*, our shadow puppet plays: how to keep balance amid confusion."

Ketut is an accomplished *dalang,* a shadow-puppet master. He performs not only for villagers who know the ancient tales by heart, but for the deities who visit Bali during the year. As a *dalang* he works his flat, hand-held puppets with diamond-flash speed while his voice careens from the heights of a whining siren to the depths of underworld growls accented with a cascade of shrill laughs. As a trainee, he apprenticed for years, cutting shadow puppets from buffalo hide and painting them, learning the stories, and the voices of each character pertinent to the telling of the stories. Watching Ketut backstage is to witness a multi-talented virtuoso. He sits cross-legged on a wooden soundbox, working the puppets in front of a lantern to cast their shadows on the screen, punctuating their actions with rhythmic *thonks* on the soundbox by means of a mallet held between his toes. Simultaneously, he is speaking a mix of high, low, and middle Balinese, plus a smattering of Kawi—the ancient literary language of early Javanese poetry. All the while he is directing the gamelan members as to where a change of tempo or a sudden stop and start is needed.

Accomplished in the high art of ventriloquism, Ketut goes from one voice to another, like Coltrane riding unexpected notes through the register: clown voice, princess voice, ogre, magistrate, benevolent ruler, impoverished servant. "All these voices must be kept separate inside the head, but when the story has many characters talking at once, that's hard." Even after twenty-five years as a *dalang,* Ketut admits that sometimes during an all-night *wayan kulit* he screws up, gives a princess an ogre's snarl or a ruffian a nymph's voice. "If this happens, I have to be quick to invent a story that gives the character an excuse to have that voice. Usually it works and I can hear a big laughter from the audience on the other side of the screen."

Ketut relates how his guru taught him to meditate a solid week before a performance. "He had me go off and blow air from the mind, then sit naked in a cold stream and go through all the stories and voices. The water's sound carries all other sounds away, so you hear only the talking of your characters. You hear it over and over and it stays. You don't visit or receive people that week. You save yourself for the night of the *wayan kulit*—six or eight nonstop hours. My teacher was a master *dalang,* also quite a prankster. One time he wanted to show me how to expand the voice into the elasticity needed to impersonate the sneers of evil villains and the sweet phrases of court ladies. He brewed—how do you call it?—a milkshake. And said go sit in the river and drink it. So I did. It went down into my stomach and came up. Three times it came up! For one month I lost my voice. I thought my career was done. But slowly my voice returned. When it did, it was large enough to hold the voices of all the characters in the hundred-thousand verses of the Mahabharata! What was in that milkshake? I asked my guru. Ground chile pepper, he laughed."

After our temple visit, Ketut suggested I visit Tenganan, a Bali Aga village in the southeast of the island. "To best understand Balinese ritual, you need to see their solstice ceremony. It's happening right now." Tenganan is one of the oldest and most traditional villages on the island, a ceremonial enclave inhabited by three hundred families whose pre-Hindu ancestors were driven into the mountains when the Javanese invaded Bali in the twelfth century. Known as Bali Aga, "Original People," they maintain their own kinship system, religion, dance, and music. As a communal society, they practice a continuous cycle of rituals in honor of their gods and ancestors. By keeping alive music, the craft of weaving, and the art of telling the stories bestowed upon them by their divinities, the Tengananese insure that the sacred time founded by the gods will remain alive.

In good trust, I followed Ketut's recommendation, grabbed a *bemo* to the tiny port of Padangbai for lodging, then arranged for a motorbike taxi to drop me at a trailhead where I could walk to Tenganan. I wanted the entry to be unhurried. A new environment needs to give you a look, send out its pheromones, elicit a pull.

❧

The trailhead is located on the outskirts of a ramshackle hill town, muddy and smelling of cattle. Today, Wednesday, is market day. Before setting off, it's worth having a look. Farm families have been filling the village since sun-up, milling about the lanes where women serve roast pig from outdoor pits. Men have lined up their wares, eager for a sale. They hunker next to yokes, plowshares, mattocks, and hoes. Calves bawl in the inspection corral. Herb sellers call out remedies: aromatic leaves, pulverized roots, nameless concoctions in recycled bottles. A basket maker displays strands of *ata*, the vine from which his baskets are woven. Some of the prized ones are shaped like Greek amphoras, patterned with zigzags and diamonds.

One fellow is getting a haircut from an itinerant barber. He teeters on a bright yellow chair, constantly bumped by a Chaucerian crowd of shoppers eager for a first-come selection of the best fruit, meat, and vegetables in the stalls. Under the barber's sheet he clutches a suckling pig, either just purchased or about to be sold. The pig peeks out from the bib like a baby. The man has a mole on his chin with a long whisker popping from it. This, evidentially, is a status symbol, for the barber doesn't trim it.

Behind the barber, blacksmiths hammer away at makeshift forges. Their assistants work portable bellows, fanning charcoal fires where the metal is beaten. The blacksmiths are of a lower caste, though they were once of the elite. They are said to be direct descendants of the god Indra, the pre-Hindu storm god, regulator of time, the god most often propitiated during drought. The tasks of these blacksmiths have always been associated with alchemy and transformation. Using fire, they pound metal into plows that turn the earth to receive the sun and rain. Some of these fire-blackened men are expert instrument makers, too. They shape metal into sonorous gongs and metallophone bars that let Indra's song ring through the universe. To create the keys for Tenganan's rare *gamelan selonding,* a blacksmith must understand the melting points of metals, know the textural aspects of sound, and know the alloys that produce sound. Ideally, the blacksmith should also be a gamelan musician.

In Bali, "art" is an unknown word. The farmer, woodworker, flower arranger, weaver, singer, musician, mask maker, quarryman, actor, tooth filer, dancer, and toddy gatherer often share overlapping disciplines. A woodcarver told me, "The best frogs are carved by artisans who are also farmers—they see frogs every day." A mask maker explained, "Because my father taught me, I know how to carve. Because I am a dancer, I know the gesture. Because I am a storyteller, I know the expression. Because I am a singer, I can accurately carve the mouth." For Westerners this overlap of disciplines seems unique. For the Balinese, the secular and sacred are inseparable. They blend continuously as Indra's wheel weaves them into a single design.

Just beyond town, I find the path that leads several kilometers to Tenganan. My ears fill with bawling cattle, crowing cocks, the rasp of ice grinders, voices of kids begging parents for colored drinks. Someone is playing a cassette of *gong kebyar* music, the multi-instrument gamelan noted for its quick changes in rhythm and ornamentation. It floats through the food stalls with brilliant textures, then explodes into bright flashes. *Kebyar,* "to burst open." Leaving the hubbub, I bargain hard for a handmade sickle, unfold my crumpled bills, hand them to the man at his forge.

> The blacksmith—
> his ear adorned with
> a red hibiscus.

After an hour's walk Tenganan appears. It sits in a narrow valley, a tidy village of stone dwellings, plank longhouses, granaries, and wooden shrines flanking two parallel, cobbled lanes. Thick rainforest rises on all sides. Hearth smoke mingles with mist. A lone satellite dish interrupts an otherwise traditional skyline of thatch and stone. Today's big feast—the culmination of the annual ceremony in honor of Indra—roughly corresponds to winter solstice in Bali: June, the onset of the dry season.

Two giant rotating wheels with swinging seats have been erected, fashioned entirely of pegged wood and operated by foot power. Historians have traced these wheels thousands of years back to Vedic festivals in India. They serve to entertain, but they are also a metaphor for Indra's great sun wheel turning the seasons, drawing water from earth to cloud, cycling it back as rain. By mid-day, the humidity is high. A farmer is busy cutting brambles in a patch of yams, his back shiny with sweat. In the early afternoon he'll put on a white shirt and wrap himself with his finest length of cloth for today's celebration. Women and girls will also halt their tasks—the cooking, plaiting of bamboo offerings, assembling pyramids of fruit and flowers—to bathe, arrange their hair, and wrap themselves with hand-woven *geringsing*, the earth-colored, double ikat cloth for which Tenganan is famous. Back home this rare style of weaving is found behind glass in museums, along with tap-estries from Gujurat and Okinawa, where the ikat tradition is also still alive.

In Bali art belongs not only to the daily round of work, but to a more ephemeral, meditative cycle that con-nects maker and deity. A shop owner explains: "*Geringsing* is gifted from the gods. When you weave you ask permis-sion from the gods to use their ideas. You ask if you can gather the plants they created for dye. You ask for consent to reproduce the designs they have invented to protect and bring good luck to the person who wears them. During the act of weaving, the artist does not pass time, but re-integrates with consecrated time. To create *geringsing* is to impregnate the cloth with the Beginning World, the original time of the gods."

In a sense it is a Delphic process, for as the weaver works, she is aided by a messaging from the deities to real-ize the creation. Woven into the *geringsing* are the talis-manic designs that safeguard one's being, keep the body unharmed, the mind pure, thoughts free from defilement. Preparing for a ceremony, adorned with symbols that can easily be read by the gods, a villager is incontestably marked as someone about to step from ordinary to non-ordinary reality, a mythical realm where one recovers the beginning world, the time of origin.

No ceremony in Bali is complete without the daz-zling music of the gamelan ensemble. More precisely, gamelan refers to the instruments themselves: gongs, drums, flutes, cymbals and metallophones—all of them living entities whose sound rearranges psychic configurations within the body, tunes the spirit, and keeps the village whole. Tenganan is famous for its *gamelan selonding,* the oldest and most sacred of all Balinese gamelans. Its vibratory flow is so imbued with purifying elixir that villagers dare not look at the instruments or musicians until after the first melody is played. Other Bali Aga villages are even more protective of their gamelans. They are direct copies of the originals bequeathed by Indra, so sacred that they are kept under lock and key in secret shrines, and never played.

The ritual cycle of time in Bali opens like a flower in all directions. Through dance, mime, music, and shadow puppetry the old stories are kept alive. Mythic times are returned, history is recaptured, harmony is maintained. The community is "kept round," as an elder musician put it. For those of us in a rush, feigning importance by being perpetually busy, village ritual in Bali is a welcome threshold to what Joseph Campbell termed "a still point of eternity," where transcendence reigns and one experiences the world with a renewed eye. Amid the *ke-pak ke-pum* of the drums, the liquid reverberation of the gongs, the impassioned dazzle of the metallophones, one is called into the melody like a bee to a flower. The music, cacophonous as it might seem to an untrained ear, gradually snares the listener into quiescence and realigns the body. Michael Tenzer, in his book *Balinese Music,* describes the *gamelan* as "full of insistent rhythms and elegant patterns . . . a complexity that make it one of the most rewarding musical experiences to be had on our planet."

While the rest of the Balinese adhere to a lunar calendar, the people of Tenganan follow a solar cycle, presided by the Vedic storm god, the millennia-old *soma*-drinking deity, Indra. The most important god of the Vedic era (1200-500 BC), his clock remains ablaze over Tenganan. In the beginning Indra used the sun to measure out space. He planted four corner posts and between them hung the walls of the world. He thatched clouds into a roof, opened one door, east, for the sun to enter; another west, for it to leave. To this day Tenganan retains its cosmological plan. It is superbly symmetrical, a microcosmic mirror of the macrocosm, a stone compass ringed by a wall with four openings facing the cardinal directions. When the Tengananese leave the village through these gates, they pass into "counted time," that of temporal duration. Reentering the gates, they reintegrate with sacred time.

Because Tenganan is oriented from a central point to the four directions via precisely-delineated directional paths, a villager is constantly reminded of the outward-expanding shape of the universe. Tenganan is, by its architectural plan, a temporal dimension of the cosmos. Within its dimension, mythical time is recovered, the village is an archetype of the time of creation. Ceremonies allow the villager to re-enact events that took place in what Mircea Eliade describes as "the time that was created and sanctified by the gods of which the festival is precisely a reactualization."

Indra's timepiece is a fiery sun wheel of song, exorcism, purification and trance through which his villagers assure fertility in their everyday world. Stewardship of the hills, woods, waters, and fields is Indra's gift to the villagers. *Semangat*, soul matter, is everywhere present: in wind, water, blood, and breath; in rocks, rice shoots, rainbows, and trees—especially ones of great age. Tengananese have preserved their animist beliefs, long ago rejecting Hinduism, the caste system, and cremation. They bury their dead face-down toward the ocean; their altars are aligned in the sea's direction, too. They have accepted television and telephones on a limited basis. Though cordial to tourists, no outsider is permitted to remain overnight.

I stroll, buy *es campur,* savoring the colorful mix of

shaved-ice, coconut, fruit, and tapioca pearls under a searing sky. I don't have to do any imagining to bring mythic past into modern time. Time itself is imbued with *semangat*. It circles through Indra's house like breath from the lips, blood through the body. With cyclic prediction, it delivers Indra's sky nymphs to bless the land. Today those nymphs are represented by young girls ready to pass into adulthood, adorned with mirrors and shining gold, wrapped in magically-charged *geringsing*. Riding the big wooden wheels, they swing in their seats, crest into the heavens, round the symbolic sun clock, and descend like raindrops—brilliant devas—to make potent the land.

Bali is eight degrees south of the equator. In June, winter solstice is a time for prayers and sacrifice to purify the village and assure fertility as the heat strengthens. Later the young devas riding the wheels will perform the *rejang*, a women's temple dance involving slow and solemn gestures to create a bodily rhythm that approaches about as close to the sacred time of the gods as humans can come. Transcending temporal time, they will inhabit the trans-human time of the gods when they created the various realities that constitute our world.

While the girls ride the wooden wheels, their male counterparts appease Indra by giving up their blood in ritual battle. A crowd gathers around a raised platform where young men challenge each other with thorny, yucca-like pandangus leaves bound into swords. Duels begin and end quickly. The challenged one holds up a handwoven rattan shield, but eventually suffers a scratched and bleeding back from his opponent's prickly sword. The young girls look on, whispering among themselves, checking out their favorites. All the while, the gamelan members, in their open-air longhouse, keep a steady, mesmerizing rhythm.

When the boys retreat from the battle platform, the loser's wounds are bathed with turmeric and vinegar. Only in the Western sense, though, is he a "loser." In Tenganan, where light and dark battle to renew the world in perpetual shadow play, the loser is the necessary participant in a ritual meant to keep things in balance. Between bouts, the boys laugh and kid each other, occasionally eyeing the girls, who turn inward in giggling groups, pretending not to notice. I catch two young warriors wearing batik T-shirts of Bob Marley over their *geringsing* wrap. A tourist notices them, too, and turns to his wife with a deliberately loud "Hummph! Tradition is disappearing." He's probably taken precious days off from work, spent lots of money to get here, and wants his worth. But why shouldn't these 20th-century youngsters include Marley with Indra? In their eyes, both are larger-than-life warrior heroes who brought light to darkness through deeds that have grown to a mythic proportion. In Tenganan, the wheel of time absorbs and recreates as it spins. Anomalies don't have to be resisted, they can be incorporated.

As trees turn gold and the final battles culminate, I feel as if my own muscles have been flayed, releasing another self from my skin. The gamelan reverberates, and now comes a group of women, not brightly jeweled or wrapped in magic cloth, but dressed in ordinary sarongs and long-sleeved, fitted *kebayas* of green and gold brocade. Stepping lightly, eyes glazed in trance, following a sunray to the village temple, they ascend a cobble stairway, duck through a cleft in a stone wall, and begin their dance in an open-air sanctuary. It is the hour of finality, of exaltation, a time when speech returns to gesture. The dancers raise urns of smoking incense above their heads and start to spin, abruptly changing direction, nearly colliding with one another as they fall into an off-center coma, a rhythmic tempo of involuntary stupor—the gamelan angularly play-ing off their erratic moves.

I observe them until a man approaches and asks me

if I want a drink. It is not good manners, on this auspicious day, to refuse. Discreetly, I slip away to join a circle of men outside the temple for a couple slugs of *arak,* and a puff or two on a *kretek,* a clove-flavored cigarette. Returning to the sanctuary, everything is aglow. The palm wine has kicked in, for sure, but so has the magnetic pull of the music, the heightened consciousness of the crowd, the loose-limbed swagger of the trance dancers—some whimpering or uttering low moans. The stone courtyard is radiant with a diaphanous luminosity as the sun's final rays blend into wavering hues of red, yellow, and lime. With hardly a notice, the *rejang* dancers have appeared. They have assembled near the trance dancers in two solemn, rippling rows—youngest girls up front, taller women behind, ascending in perfect order of height. Each dancer is wrapped with gold-painted heliotrope cloth, the hair beautifully coiled, laced with frangipani and crowned with tiaras of metallic leaves. Champa oil, incense, and sweat mingle into an erotic potion. Along with the *arak,* it has furthered my sense of distorted time.

Like flower petals set into motion by a gentle breath, the dancers begin to sway. A wand has been passed over them! Each lithe female has become a shimmering stalk potent with Indra's *soma,* the hallucinogenic drink that allows seer to become the seen. One breath, one life-blood, the girls lift their bodies up and out, as if from under the sea. This is not entertainment (although tourists pointing their cameras might believe so), but a dance of purification performed by unmarried girls, each a wavering flame, each burning with a light from Beyond. In extreme slow motion the girls fling their sashes, one side to the other, doing half turns as they lift them to Indra, who has by now ushered the sun out the western gate and rolled it over the hills toward the sea. The women rise and fall as one body, a choreographed prayer, a single breeze swelling and softening. A motion so smooth, so slow, with such a liquidity that one senses the many faces of the Goddess have been reflected from a stream so clear, that it is without beginning or end.

Tenganan begins to sink into a mingled whisper. Over the eyes-down faces of the *rejang* dancers, a pale moon is in the sky, the temple seems to float, all is dream-like. But wait! A man suddenly pinwheels out of nowhere, bounding past the dancers (their harmonious grace remains undisturbed) into the center of the trance dancers. He staggers, mimes, collapses into convulsive jerks, raises a *kris* (the sacred sword) and brings it to his chest. But the saber halts without piercing his skin, no matter how hard he pushes the blade. He shudders, then lapses into a slow wobble. His voice wanders, his words revert to jabber, pure sound—all power, no meaning. Time is a shattered clock, a mirror breaking with shrill laughter, angular rhythms, rippling gyrations. In heightened ecstasy the actor is a medium, the village a stage. In a concentrated, supernatural sense, everything is electric, fused, inseparable.

In Bali one never escapes the energetic, ever-present, reversible flow between noumenon and phenomenon. Immersed in this ritual, one dwells in the transparence between visible and invisible, an inebriated state of profound ecstasy. One is tempted to use the word magic, but the term doesn't fit. I sense that I've been part of an hallucination, that there has been a psychic shift, that a moment has swollen into an eternity, that an amorphous flower has opened, whose fragrance can never wear off.

Sticky and exhausted, I stare at the moon, its face green with the reflection of the hills. Turning toward the temple courtyard, I see that the gamelan has stopped, people are wandering away. I remove my sandals and let my feet absorb the warmth of the temple stone. In the courtyard, one performer remains.

> Flitting here, flitting there
> a dragonfly
> in pearl haze.

Ubud, 1996

SEARCHING FOR GHALIB'S HOUSE

Old Delhi, the courtly 17th-century Mughal city once known as Shahjahanabad, is but a shadow of its former self. Few tourists stay here, opting instead for the hotels of New Delhi, a brief cab ride away. For a hit of old Asia they day-trip to Old Delhi, explore the bazaars, the Red Fort, the Jain temple, the Jama Masjid and retreat to the air-conditioned beer parlors of the new city. A small, clean hotel in Old Delhi's bicycle bazaar suits me fine. It's at the end of a cul-de-sac, down a squeeze of an alley through a hubbub of porters strapped with frames, wheels, and handlebars. Monkeys prowl the balconies above parts and accessories shops, most of them family-operated. Fathers tally adding machines and spindle invoices, sons oversee orders and repairs, daughters bubble-wrap specialty items: Bollywood-star mud flaps, Blu Goddess brake lights, Breathable Soft Saddle bike seats.

In the tiny lobby of the Royal Palace Hotel—beyond the doorman, window cleaner, and elevator man—a courteous desk clerk smiles over an oversize register on the marble counter, one of the two brothers who expertly manage this twenty-room inn. He is the shorter, casually dressed brother—cheerful, outgoing, helpful beyond all expectations. A man in his heart. Ask and you shall receive. Directly behind him, in a hermetically sealed air-conditioned glass cubical, sits the older brother. He is the alter ego—tall, impeccably dressed, tightly wound, unsmiling. A man in his head. Whenever I deal with the brother out front, I deal with the one behind. They are two in one— the stern guy enclosed in glass, the jovial guy in open air. As the shorter brother happily draws me a map to Old Delhi's sights, the taller one frowns, eyes the wall clock, and begins his propitiations, waving incense around the oversize belly of Ganesha, lord of luck and finance, the god that keeps the hotel full.

Into the register book my passport is recorded. Visa, too. Along with veg or non-veg preference, origin of next destination, destination of next origin, visible marks: moles, ink stains, dribble blots. After the pertinent statistics are penned in their proper ledger boxes, I'm ushered to the 6 x 6 lift, the grate pulled open, the elevator man wedging himself in, his epaulets brushing my shoulders.

Thirty years ago I peered into Old Delhi's chaos from an upstairs room not far from here—a private mansion, one of those decrepit *havelis* once common in Old Delhi that doubled as a pilgrim's inn. It's long vanished, but I recall the quaint upstairs rooms looking over a courtyard shared by Indian families. From my street-side window, I peered into a chaos of humanity, everything unruly and strange. Spooked, I retreated from the view, stood at the mirror, examined my face as if it couldn't be mine. I was bearded, scrawny from travel, thirty-six years old—my father's age when he arrived in Delhi as an army conscript assigned to the India-Burma Theater. Now it was my turn for India, not as a conscript, but as a poet, foot-loose, albeit doing exactly what I'd be doing sitting still on a meditation cushion: "observing what comes up."

Mustering the courage, I shuffled down the stairway, dodged a ghost beggar on the lower step, elbowed into the horde, and found myself in a labyrinthine madhouse. Overloaded rickshaws jangled through lanes writhing like the tentacles of a giant anemone. A girl with liquid eyes sized up my pockets and blocked my path with her crutch. Labor-weary porters revived themselves in chai stalls where ragmen rubbed shoulders. From mirrored perfumeries, arms overhung the sidewalk with fragrance-dashed wrists to lure customers. Confectioners displayed mounds of milk sweets crowned with flies. Multistoried dwellings lurched and leaned, windows made up like women's eyes, doorways tall enough for elephant and driver. On a balcony, a man held out his false teeth, brushing them with a frayed twig. On the opposite parapet, a monkey did the same—with a toothbrush.

I shared a room with a Spaniard who felt suffocated by India. *Mucho mundo, mucho mundo!* he kept repeating. And buried his head in his pillow. I tried to explain what "coming unplugged" meant, the potential benefits of giving oneself over to chaos. He didn't buy it. The idea of losing his individuality to the multiplicity of the throng was out of the question. What he saw then is what is here now: an opaque jungle of stalls, kiosks, garish temples, vendors pushing hand-painted carts, yelling, "Refrigerated cold water! Animated healing juice! Black Cow tooth powder! Self-adhesive third eyes! Sleep-Soft earplugs!" Bells clanged, minarets blared, languages exchanged places in the ear. Imagination took second place to the apparitions filling the eye. A flute player sat in a nest of snakes. A magician swallowed a handful of glass. Veiled ladies left trails of bergamot, quickly subdued by the stench of an open-air urinal. A street artist sipped tea with his bear. A fakir puffed his checks and opened a mouthful of embers. A sadhu knotted his dreads into a tower. A sedated hippie imitated him. One big side show.

"The impossibility of India," I once wrote. I'd write the same today. India atom-bombs its way into the twenty-first century with its unshakeable bundle of castes, codes, karma, and an alarming birthrate. Concrete suburbs for the burgeoning middle class ooze into the packing-crate shanties of the poor. A beggar comes up like a praying mantis, his spindly arms rubbing his stomach. Above him Swissair and Cathay Pacific gain altitude with their caste of supersonic billionaires.

Arundhati Roy, William Dalrymple, Ryszard Kapuściński—they do a good job of sizing things up. I read them for that. But as a bard I take my cues from Bashō—a poet who moved through the world realizing its complexity, yet refusing to sabotage mystery by imposing analysis or intellect upon it. Not to say that Bashō shut out the devastation of the human imprint. In 1689, while visiting the site of a 12th-century battle in Mutsu Province, he was moved to tears as he wrote his famous haiku:

Summer grasses
all that remains of warriors'
dreams

To hear the rustling grasses, see their scorched tips, take note of their hardy roots: this was Bashō's occasion to reflect on history, feel the plight of human folly. Can I move with his lightness, yet deepness, though the plunder of our world? Where am I supposed to be while things get worse before they get better? In the garden, at the desk, on the cushion, tasting mountains, traveling the world building homes for the displaced? Is writing poetry enough? Do I continue to pay my taxes, give my nickels and dimes to an investor who'll put them toward the corporate rampage that so upsets me? Bashō again:

Over the moor
not attached to anything
a skylark sings

The Japanese have a term for what is subtle yet profound: *yugen*. Mystery, elegance, a single brush stroke to reveal the shadow of bamboo leaves on freshly fallen snow. Add a lone thatched hut and you evoke human fragility. As poet, monk, and teacher, Bashō moved between permanence and evanescence. His haiku sought to reveal what is overlooked in the ordinary, a certain dynamism in what seems inanimate. Perhaps haiku, that little chirp of a song, is my best resource for indicating something greater in life than the obvious. Bashō's poems are colored with mood—rich, deep, featherweight in tone. Bill Evans played his piano the way Bashō wrote his poems: a touch on the keys brought a single note to the furthest depths—rarified pictures, highly compressed. Listening to Evans play or reading Bashō is to hear with the eyes, see with the ears:

> *Hototogisu—*
> *the shriek lies stretched*
> *across the water*

On the eastern end of Chandni Chowk, Old Delhi's main street, is the imposing Lal Qila, the 17th-century Red Fort built by emperor Shah Jahan. At the western end is Fatehpuri Masjid, India's largest mosque. Between, are the *paratha* parlors dishing out savory flatbreads, and bazaars filled with spice, silks, books, sweets, and silver. You can get lost in the surrounding neighborhoods and never come out. Foreigners don't last long on the Chowk. It's as if a hundred projectors, each with a different movie, reels running wild, have spilled to the ground, mixing their images on a giant screen. The street is jammed with pursuers of costume jewelry, electronic toys, faux designer jeans, Hindu-goddess alarm clocks, plastic prayer mats, glossy posters of Guru Nanak, Marilyn Monroe, Einstein, and Sai Baba. A calendar vendor unrolls Muhammad Ali, then Jesus, then a Rajasthani farm girl with a clay jug on her head, her veil parted to reveal a coy smile, her eyes on a distant dune where her soldier husband waves from a camel, preening his mustache.

There is a shock of ammonia from the public latrine, a hit of crushed cardamom from a mortar, the sweat of the coolie, the oversweet drift of incense above the open drains. Along the route to the house of Mizra Ghalib, India's famous 19th-century Urdu poet, are Hindu, Jain, and Sikh temples. Wedged between them is a brick Baptist church, a padlock on the door. I skip the Hindu temple (the priest is already on the sidewalk waiting to snag his morning tourist quota) and visit the Jain temple. In the leafy courtyard it is mandatory to discard leather items before entering the inner sanctum. Shoes, wallets, messenger bags, purses, and belts are to be looked after by a shoe wallah. An immediate challenge to one's belief in trust.

Inside the temple, purity abounds. Everything is of vanilla-white marble, the altars freshly washed, set with quivering flames, sprinkled with pink petals. There are sculptures of Jain prophets and a profusion of mirrors. Women outnumber the men, their faces flare and dim as they congregate. In flowing cloth, they go icon to icon flicking rice, murmuring prayers, filling each room with a soft *hummm*. There is a trace of orange blossom and almond after they move on. The dominant figure in the temple is Mahavira, the prophet who laid out the core of Jain teachings in the sixth century BC. Buddha-like, he sits open-eyed in smiling repose, emanating utmost serenity, if not a removed austerity. The milky marble from which he is shaped radiates coolness, yet preserves the warmth of the mountain from which it was taken.

Back outside, two mendicants weave through the crowd. Stark naked, they adhere to the strict path of their forbears, the Digambar sect of Jainism—the naked faction, as opposed to the white-clothed sect. Chocolate skinned, penises flopping, they walk nonchalantly amid the frenzy of the Chowk. One of them carries a plastic bag filled with bananas and biscuits. Nobody seems to bat an eye. The mendicants are distinguishable from the crowd, but indistinguishable from nature, from how they first came into the world. If they cause a blush, I suppose it is linked to the fraudulence of our lives: the need to wrap ourselves, dress the part, state our role. We dress only to be undressed by others—the imagination always at work, wanting to rid the consciousness that separates, to remove the outerwear and uncover a universal naked-ness, a candor revealed only in the depths of dreams.

West of the Jain temple, the sidewalk becomes polished stone in front of the Sikh temple Sisgang Gu-rudwara, "Door to the Guru." Water laps over a trough where I remove shoes, wash feet, and wrap my head. A scarf is provided by an affable Sikh elder who, when he learns I am American, says: "Ah, Obama good. Friendly to people. All people. Mona Lisa smile." The prayer hall offers a cool relief from the heat of the streets. I sit on a carpet with other worshipers before three white-bearded musicians wearing snowy turbans and flowing robes. They play harmoniums and sing, while a priest, seated on a raised plinth behind them, turns the pages of the *Guru Granth Sahib,* the Sikh holy book. He whisks the printed word with a yak-tail wand. For a poet, the praise of the book—the fanning of perfumed air over poetry and prophecy—is worth a pause and a bow. The soothing vibes, however, betray the violence that took place here. In 1675 King Aurangzeb, Shah Jahan's ruth-less son, beheaded Teg Bahadur, the ninth Sikh Guru, for refusing to convert to Islam.

The Sikh holy book includes the poems of 15th-century Indian mystic Kabir, a low-caste weaver born in Benares, a bard especially significant to the Sikhs. A true rebel, he rejected the notion of caste, debunked idols, rebuffed the authority of the Vedas and Qur'an in exchange for the Bhakti path: songs of love to unite all beings. For Kabir a shout from the heart could lift consciousness into the Ineffable. Borrowing from Hindu and Muslim traditions and the Sanskrit and Persian languages, Kabir used everyday speech to popularize religious themes. He could be irreverent, humorous, rapturous, and romantic:

> *Friend, where*
> *have you been looking?*
> *in the temple, in the mosque*
> *circling the Ka'bah, bowing to Kailash?*
> *I'm not in rites and ceremonies*
> *or yoga or renunciation*
> *Open the door inside—*
> *The Guest of Love*
> *is within!*

He could be bold and up-front. Orthodox believers called him a heretic:

> *Pierce your tongue*
> *shake your dreads, shave your head?*
> *Kill your desires*
> *pour butter on stones*
> *read the Gita, learn to blabber?*
> *You want to die like this?*
> *Bound hand*
> *and foot!*

Following Kabir is the 16th-century poet, Mirabai—a revolutionary woman on the Bhakti path. Then comes Mirza Ghalib, born in Agra to a family of Turkish aristocrats in 1797, an age when the Mughal Empire was declining and the British were tightening their grip. Rebellions were on the rise, slaughter was in the air. At age eleven, Ghalib was composing verse in Persian, and six years later in Urdu. He was already a public figure when the family moved to Delhi in 1810. At age thirteen, he was married into an upper-class family and eventually gained privilege to an illustrious literary crowd, often butting heads with them in friendly dialogue. Ghalib and his wife had children, but none survived the first stages of infancy. By the time he died, at age seventy-two, he was best known for the ghazal, a demanding form of poetry whose themes of love, loss, and longing originated in ancient Arabic poetry. After medieval Persian poets fine-tuned the form, it arrived in India around the twelfth century. Basically the ghazal was a love poem to the Divine or to the earthly, written in couplets rich with rhyme, repetition, and fluctuating sound. Ghalib wrote in Urdu, using many Persian phrases and constructions that allow the reader to enjoy a provocative ambiguity, to ride several tracks of "color" at once, discover multiple layers of expression, and bring to life a poem within the poem: a collage of themes and images with unexpected connections: erotic, mystic, philosophic.

Ghalib's shifting moods are not always optimistic. "My heart is becoming uneasy again. That's why my fingernails are searching for my chest." His poems have never been easy to translate. He seems to toss a randomly plucked bouquet of imagery and experience into the air, letting the flowers fall where they may, asking the reader to pick them up and make a personal arrangement. Stating a point is not the essence; enjoying an uncertain mystery emanating from the final arrangement is.

Ghalib took pains to defend his style of writing, often enduring the ridicule of the literary elite. Criticized for writing obscure poems, Ghalib once replied:

"I've got to write what's difficult, if not it is difficult to write." Enduring the derision of the literary establishment was one thing, but it paled in comparison to surviving the cruelty and horrors of the ruthless British. "The prison of life and the bondage of grief are the same. Until death comes, how can one hope to be free?"

I honor Ghalib as a poet, an originator, and a rule breaker. Though raised a Muslim, he savored wine, gambling, and the company of courtesans. He favored spontaneous thinking, detached from prescribed religious or social codes. He shared affinities with Rumi and Hafiz but was more worldly, unafraid of sidetracks, forbidden alleys, dead ends. You've got to like him for his resistance, his rebellion, his craft, his outright counter-culture attitude.

> *Breaking rules is my religion.*
> *I've hocked my patched robe and prayer rug to buy wine.*
> *The pious praise the Garden of Paradise. But to the rapturous*
> *Paradise is a bouquet abandoned on a bed of forgetfulness.*
> *You won't find me circling the Ka'bah, my robe is already*
> *blighted by too many wine stains—*

Nearing Ghalib's historic neighborhood, I seek directions from a shopkeeper. "Go right, halfway down Meena Bazaar, one time more, right." He's been asked the way so often, he hardly looks up from the stilettos he's arranging on the rack outside his shoe shop. I follow into one of Shahjanabad's oldest quarters. Along the cramped lanes a few *havelis* have been restored, their façades rebricked and plastered, the foliated gateways repaired, one or two murals brightened to their original hue. During Ghalib's time these were well-kept homes of merchants. One by one he saw them razed by the British. Entire families were slaughtered, mutineers were hanged, the streets filled with rubble, the rats began their feast—and are still enjoying it today.

Buildings lean into one another, roofs rubbing. Gargoyles hunker and grimace as if constipated. Schoolboys amble by, bookbags balanced on their heads. A gnarl of electric wires is looped seriously low, post to post through hanging laundry. Caged birds, stray cats, flapping parakeets, the ever-present Indian crows create their own systems of caste and frenzy above the crowd. One alley rings with hammering urn makers; another with booksellers snapping hardbacks open and closed to rid them of dust. A curtained doorway reads: *Cataract Repair*; another: *Medical Master of Bunyons and Corn*; a third: *Mender of Dental Facilities, In and Out Surgical Removals*. (The mender's pliers, tweezers, and a bolt-cutter are laid out on a bench at the entrance.)

Everything changes around the corner. A few dusty trees, the creak of a hammock on a verandah—silence. No shoppers, no hawkers. A calf rests before a shrine marked with vermilion handprints. A brass bell dangles over a timeworn image of Parvati, bare-toed in a faded sari, her breasts naked. The shrine keeper is a teenage girl, busy braiding strings of marigolds, flicking water with her fingertips to cool them. The joss scent, the girl's perspiration, the pungent flowers freshly wetted send me elsewhere. "May she still want to, even if she can't," I hear Ghalib say.

Right turn, and another. Signs in Hindi give way to Arabic. Men wear knit caps, long white tunics. A goat rests in a doorway, a donkey is strapped with kindling. Women shape dung cakes and pat them on the walls to dry. Stone-paved alleys taper into a peaceful juncture marked by a compact green-and-white mosque, its stairway ascending into darkness, each step repeatedly advising the visitor: *Here Remove Shoes, Here Remove Shoes,*

Here Remove Shoes. "I am near Ghalib's house?" The man on his sidewalk chair is deaf, but he knows my question and points down the street, bending his finger to the left.

On Guli Qasim Jaan I arrive at Ghalib's house, what is left, anyway. No charge to enter. The Muslim doorkeeper hardly looks up from his scripture as I step into the open courtyard. How many rooms graced this patio? What melodies flowed from the balconies, what clang of cook pans, what snap of fire in the hearth? Only one brick wall of the original residence remains. Under it is the site's only display: a case of books, a few letters to Ghalib, a couple of envelopes posted by him, a rack of sun-faded postcards, and, mounted on the brick wall, a display of fragments from Ghalib's verse translated from the Urdu:

interested / displeased
knowledge / net - trap
sick of / angel faced beggar's words / amorous voice
hard work / tough life intuition/sword
half dream / arrow - pain speech / imprisonment
rare / world – universe lair / roasted
ring/circle on fire oath / determination
meeting with lover / trust – confidence
alas / one-sixteenth of a yard 100 colors
taste / wound collar / ashamed
naked / dagger eyelid / skill
canal of milk / nerve song / stone flash
difficult / possible weeping / wilderness
drown /delight

The doorkeeper gets up from his stool to check on me. When he sees me copying out the fragments, he watches curiously. No conversation, he doesn't speak English, but he's obviously pleased that I like Ghalib. After purchasing a copy of *Ghalib's Life and Poetry* I stroll the patio. It's been a worthy visit, if just for the reminder to look again at Ghalib's strangely-flavored work, his difficult life, his doubts and battles with earthly and Divine. Ghalib saw Delhi in turmoil, witnessed the Mughals' defeat and countless hangings of insurgents in the gallows opposite the Sikh temple. Some say he saw up to twenty thousand such executions.

> *People get a real sense of what the sun is like*
> *When I let the light reflect*
> *off one of my scars*

Ghalib worships the Omniscient, goes for the wine, gets lost in work-of-art faces, sees into women's dreams, falls over in love, gets put down by the literati, is chastised for being difficult. He sizes it all up from the point of view of a water-smoothed stone in a rushing stream. His lingo burns like a deep black wound, or soothes like a resinous pine in a breeze:

> *The hem of my robe is tied to a stone*
> *no dancer whirls on a carpet before me*
> *Why account for my deeds?*
> *the desperate can be irreverent and rude.*
> *Bowing before the worthless*
> *my head is covered with dust.*
> *Kissing the Threshold of the Mighty*
> *my lips are bruised.*

Best to read Ghalib without limits in the mind, for he unveils secrets that invite not "meaning" but quandary. And from quandary, significance. See more than what the eye lets in, he might advise. Let the poem be beyond you, a meaning not quite understood. Ghalib wants another part of the brain to work, the soul to renew its encounter with the word. You can almost hear him call from a window above the courtyard: Exit my home, see more than what the alleys appear to hold. Stumble into dead-end streets. Taste the uneasy secrets, the matted tangles, the oozing abrasions. Listen to the click of passing feet, the moan of human calamity, work your way through the madness into the Garden.

Outside Ghalib's house, shadows slip away like smoke, bodies drift into moveable thresholds. Pedestrians are no longer a jumbled montage of passing shapes, they all breathe in unison: Hindu, Sikh, Muslim, Jain, Christian—no divisive faiths, hostilities, battles. Voices unintelligible are not an affront, but an opening. In the scuffle comes a ricochet of gold from a woman's anklet. From a taxi's rear seat an eye looks into mine from a half-parted veil. On a doorstep sits an elderly couple, feeding each other from a bowl of rice. Dark, wrinkled, bone thin, they look up as I pass and smile. A smile of no teeth, no ego. A child rides by, pedaling her bike with feet of whirling fire. Her ribboned braids fly behind her like streamers from a mythic siren. Ghalib says:

> *There must be some sense*
> *to all this ecstasy!*
> *Is something hiding behind*
> *the curtain?*

Shahjahanabad, 2010

III.
Into the Dream Maze

Journeys, like artists, are born and not made. A thousand differing circumstances contribute to them, few of them willed or determined by the will—whatever we may think. They flower spontaneously out of the demands of our natures—and the best of them lead us not only outwards in space, but inwards as well.

Lawrence Durrell

There is no system to Perception. Its randomness is its secret.

Etel Adnan

BEAUTY ASKEW: THE HAIKU EYE

The spare, high-desert of New Mexico encourages one to write with an economy of words. The eye follows winding arroyos, lizard tracks, cloud shadows, and blowing seed. The breath gathers momentum along ridges, faults, and prehistoric waterlines. Fossils scatter at the feet, clay shards glisten after a sudden rain. On storm-washed chips of pottery, abstract designs come clear: a figure here, a zigzag there, a water ripple, an animal track, the pinch of an artisan's fingers. I am reminded of Sappho's poems, fragments mysterious and striking to the eye; missing something essential but somehow made more essential because of what's missing.

> suddenly
> in gold sandals
> dawn

New Mexico has been my home for more than fifty years. Within the bounty of its open skies, isolate canyons, ragged peaks, and knife-edged mesas, I have tended to my craft: at the desk, before the easel, in the garden, hiking the backcountry, writing poems, and practicing the art of haiku. Besides being a good way to observe and appreciate the beauty and function of our watersheds, haiku provides the perfect remedy against our full-throttle obsession with doing things quickly, getting answers fast. The practice demands that you slow down, become small, get down on your knees, bring your eyes to a caterpillar, your nose to crushed juniper berries after a hard rain, your ears to a beetle whittling out a nest in an adobe wall. Another function of haiku is that it brings us into the cyclic world of the seasons, the birth/death rounds of plants, insects, the backyard garden, the human who tends it.

My haiku eye opens whenever I relax into a state of "unreadiness"—no mind, no intellect in the way of what is present in any given moment. As I stop, breathe in, exhale, step away from the tangles of the mind—a past I am remembering, a future I am inventing—I may be awakened to a delicate surprise as I exit the door:

> yesterday's storm
> tipped from pear blossoms
> by the wind

On the other hand, I may open the door to something unexpected that intrudes on an otherwise serene evening. Even this interruption I must accept as part of the present moment; I must be totally there with it:

> spring evening—
> all the way down the mountain
> a car backfires

The late Raymond Carver told himself in a poem: "Put it all in, make use." This is what we do when we accept the world as is, no avoidance, no denial. Walt Whitman wrote "Bring all the art and science of the world and baffle and humble it with one spear of grass." And Matsuo Bashō, on his famous 1689 Japan walkabout, brushed this haiku into his notebook:

> *the beginning of art*
> *a rice-planting song*
> *in the north country*

Whitman and Bashō remind us that we are part of an intricately woven community of plants, soils, grasses, waters, and innumerable sentient creatures that inhabit watershed after watershed, knowing no political boundary. We belong to other peoples, too; ones who speak other languages on other continents who share the same human emotions. Often, though, it is not until a tragedy occurs that we are drawn together and realize the fragility of our existence. Who was it who wrote:

> if the world
> is so beautiful, why are we
> not beautiful in it?

One purpose of haiku is to convey beauty, but it is a beauty askew of the norm, less obvious to the eye. Haiku doesn't abide by standards of perfection. It isn't interested in the over-trimmed garden. It goes for rough edges, the wild tangle: a stray seed in the compost unfurling into a blossom, a spark from a shovel as it hits a stone, a cricket singing from the corner mop. In a passage from *Specimen Days*, Whitman conveys his love of overlooked beauty. Instead of places like Yellowstone or Niagara Falls that "afford the greatest natural shows," he is drawn to America's grasslands. "The prairies and plains, while less stunning at first sight, last longer, fill the esthetic sense fuller, precede all the rest."

For the artist or philosopher, beauty is to be rendered and discussed, but for those living in beauty, it is simply part of life. During my first years in New Mexico, I asked my neighbor Antonio if he thought his surroundings were beautiful. He gave me a bemused look and kept on shucking his harvest of blue corn. We were outside sitting on a tarp—his wife, her elder brother, and three children— all sharing the task. The sun had set and I was wondering how much shucking we could get done before dark. Suddenly, Antonio's twelve-year-old granddaughter stopped shucking. "Ohhh, look!" A full moon rising over the mesa was filling the lilac dusk with gold. The unspoken beauty of the moment bound all of us as we halted our task in silent appreciation. A haiku written by Bashō 300 years ago echoes this moment:

> *the farmer's child*
> *husking rice, stops*
> *and gazes at the moon*

At least once in a lifetime we are given an experience in the natural world that sets us back on our heels. Exiting the muted light of a Zen sitting room in the Jemez Mountains, I was astounded to find myself under a dome of sky so blue it was almost black. A chiming vibration passed through me. Perhaps it was sounding from the wind-bell under the eave. Or was it?

> around the bell
> blue sky
> ringing

Georgia O'Keeffe, Arthur Dove, and Emily Carr painted these ringing "energy fields" on their canvases. When it comes to language that replicates such energy fields, it is the haiku writer who paints a picture with words and compresses it into a poem. In addition to Bashō, the Japanese poets Chiyo-ni, Buson, and Issa are among the early haiku masters—excellent sources from which to begin. Here in New Mexico, the late poet Elizabeth Searle Lamb wrote many haiku that present the sudden jolt that transports us from the personal to the intimate to the universal.

> *pausing*

halfway up the stair—
white chrysanthemums

The clustered blooms cause her to halt, and, not ponder, but experience a moment of transcendence. She doesn't include herself in the poem, nor mention her own emotions. But we are aware that the incident has caused her to realize, during her busy day, that there is beauty in the world. The chrysanthemums have brought her outside her thinking, her doing, whatever she might have just heard on the news. The world is great and this greatness has been made known by the smallness of the flowers. Haiku present a significant moment amid everything transient; a split second in which things are profound, yet without meaning. A haiku by Renée Gregorio portrays another wake up:

not the 14,000-foot summit
but the breath
finding origin

I imagine her hiking a steep trail, focused on the destination. The switchbacks are exhausting, the talus unforgiving. Amid stress and distress, comes a surprise. The destination disappears. So does the self, and with it the mountain. What remains is "the breath finding origin." Very much akin to what one experiences on a cushion in a zendo, emptying all thoughts, becoming one with every inhalation/exhalation that originates in the *hara,* the center of the belly, the seat of our *ki,* our life force.

Several years ago I had the pleasure of walking the Sangre de Cristo Mountains with Nanao Sakaki, a true wanderer in the tradition of Bashō. We often hiked above timberline, sometimes taking a deliberately difficult route. Nanao's poem "Why?" ends with a stanza that replicates the surprise in Renée Gregorio's poem:

There is no mountain
nor myself.
Something
moves up and down
in the air.

A haiku poet lives for the unexpected turn, a sudden shift in reality when self is missing and an unexpected insight occurs:

now that fallen leaves
have buried the path
the trail is clear

Sometimes the moment is laughable: a gust carries the hat from your head, a hat you weren't wearing at all. Or, there is a whim not at all intended, but there on the page nevertheless:

wind took my head
but the hat
stayed on

It is a great joy when poems happen not at the desk, but while splitting wood, waiting for a bus, or searching the weeds for the missing bifocals (I once found mine on the hood of the car as I was pulling out of the driveway). One morning, after a severe windstorm, I was upset to spy a section of fence lying on the ground. Along with my toolbox, I carried my annoyance right out into the fields, only to find:

Between the rails

of the blown over fence
spring's first crocus

A few days later, I received a haiku on a postcard from fellow poet Steve Sanfield. The same storm had pounded his cabin in the California Sierras before heading across the desert to New Mexico:

wind shattered pines:
resin filling
the night air

During my late teens, long after my parents gave me enough early ventures into the natural world to set the background for haiku, I was browsing a shop in L.A.'s Chinatown when I found D. T. Suzuki's *Zen and Japanese Culture,* a substantial hardback enhanced with illustrations: a snow-laden peach tree, monkeys peering from bamboo, a cloud-hidden hermit shack, a solitary angler in mist. In the dim clutter of the shop, a cat napped under a lacquered altar set with a cup of tea and two tangerines. On the wall were antique photos of family elders. The world was suddenly very old, and very new. With eager adventure, I purchased the book, the most I'd ever spent on the printed word. As I drifted in and out of many striking passages, a poem by Masaoka Shiki (1869–1902) caught my eye:

among the grasses
an unknown flower
blooming white

As a boy, I had seen that flower in the sunlit grasses above the middle fork of the Kaweah River. It was insignificant, nameless. It was everything. As I pressed closer on hands and knees, it was every bit as large as a redwood.

Lost in its whiteness, I was inseparable from it. According to Suzuki, I had experienced the "suchness" of the flower, what he called *prajna* intuition (*pra*: before; *jna*: wisdom): a "quick knowing (sans) analytical thoughts, ideas, and concepts." A moment when observer is one with the observed, receiving it unhindered. No enquiry, no interpretation. No comparing the flower to a star, contrasting it with a redwood tree, or using the apparent loneliness of the flower (how can a flower be lonely?) as a metaphor for the emotional state of the perceiver. Mind isn't, flower is. Intellectual size-up is residue. Analysis can be done in a laboratory but it shouldn't happen down on all fours in a meadow. Nor should the fingers be busy counting syllables. Haiku has a beat of its own, already counted out before the hand picks up the pen.

Suzuki's take on the person who beholds a flower is that too often there is a gap between the eye and what the eye sees. The human mind relentlessly fills that gap with definition, categorization, empirical analysis—the need to make sense. Bashō told his poetry students:

> *Learn about the pine only from the pine, or about the bamboo only from the bamboo. When you see an object, leave your subjective preoccupation with yourself; otherwise you impose yourself on the object, and do not learn.*

As a college freshman, camped in coastal redwood canyons on a semester break, I tried a few haiku, but inevitably the dripping trees said it better. Counting syllables, worried whether the *kigo*—the seasonal word traditional to Japanese haiku—was there, I felt that my haiku were dictated by rules not my own. I was eighteen years old, exploring California's Big Sur coast, hiking the High Sierra, reading *Walden*, entranced by Hokusai's woodblock prints, and charmed by Gary Snyder's rough-cut translations of the 8th-century poet, Han Shan. The language was remarkably fresh. For a kid crazy about the wilderness, it drew me in:

> Clambering up the Cold Mountain path,
> The Cold Mountain trail goes on and on:
> The long gorge choked with scree and boulders,
> The wide creek, the mist-blurred grass.
> The moss is slippery, though there's been no rain
> The pine sings, but there's no wind.
> Who can leap the world's ties
> And sit with me among the white clouds?

Timidly, I handed my first few attempts at haiku to a writing professor, hoping for some feedback. The professor eventually returned my haiku, suggesting that instead of studying "an over-imitated Japanese pastime," I should consider the European sonnet, the sestina, the villanelle. He even suggested the limerick. I thought it odd that a California kid who got his kicks looking across the sea and imagining the mountains of Japan should be pointed toward Europe. From then on, I decided to hoe my own row and take my cues from non-academic poets writing from real life experience. Sad to say, that professor is still around—in the form of teachers who don't include haiku as a valid experience of poetry. A shame, because everything one should know about writing a long poem is inherent in haiku: brevity, silence, what to leave in, what to do without, the strength of singular imagery, the power of suggestion, the power of "what is" without modifiers or embroidery. One can also listen to *Kind of Blue*. Along with his music, Miles Davis offered his own advice, as wise and immediate as Bashō's dictums:

197

I always listen to what
I can leave out

Don't play what's there,
play what's not there

For awhile I gave up writing haiku, though I was aware that prose descriptions in my journal would often break off into three- or four-line snippets that floated on the page by themselves. As for reading haiku, I stuck with it, spurred by the discovery of R. H. Blyth's four-volume *Haiku* in the college library. I was especially drawn to the poets Yosa Buson (1716-1783) and Kobayashi Issa (1763-1827). The way they saw the world complemented my increasing forays out of Los Angeles, up the wind-blasted Big Sur coast. A primeval landscape, it was home to artists like Henry Miller, Robinson Jeffers, Jaime de Angulo, Edward Weston, and Emil White. Fog-shrouded cliffs were charged with the deep roll of Asian wind. Spring storms turned the air champagne. Sapphire coves glimmered under emerald hills mottled with blue ceanothus and orange poppies. The face of God, I thought. But almost immediately I heard a voice: Find that face in the flower!

One afternoon I was at the easel in the art department when a student stopped by and invited me to a poetry reading in the English Department. I wasn't keen on leaving my painting, but when I learned the poet lived in the Big Sur, I set down my brushes. The reading was in a featureless institution-green classroom, but when the poet entered I caught a waft of sea foam and wild fennel. The man, Eric Barker, asked if we were ready "for a walk through creation" and began to read his poems. I didn't quite understand them, but I felt them. I loved the wild imagery and the poet's salty presence: his sunburnt face, faded work shirt, sea-splashed cords, leather sandals. When he peppered his reading with stories between the poems, he spoke like a poet; images pulled from thin air matched his craft on the page. He described the work of the night tide, the hazards of solitude, a bath in a cold copper stream. His descriptions of how he lived and where his writing came from pumped my enthusiasm. A cabin in the cliffs above the sea? Getting up at midnight, running out naked to shoo wild peccaries from the cabbage patch? Standing beneath the Milky Way listening to waves pound the rocks, then returning to a lamplit cabin to write a poem? "*This* is a possibility!" I muttered to myself.

Eric Barker's effect was like a gospel ship rocking into a harbor with all the revelation I needed: that it was okay to come undone, go adrift, bump against sheer walls, drop the net into the unseen. The poet's voice—his cadence, his quavering lilt, his pauses—stayed with me. I felt like a novice musician at The Village Vanguard learning new licks from a master artist. Eric Barker's poems revealed how haiku imagery could work itself into longer poems. And, how a lifestyle embodying utmost simplicity could influence one's work. Henry Miller, who introduced Barker's New Direction's book, *A Ring of Willows,* noted his "Japanese sensibility":

> *Eric is of course not Japanese. Nor is his work modeled on Oriental lines. Perhaps I associate him with the masters of haiku because I see in him, the connection between the poet and poetry which is so markedly missing in most modern poets. Eric lives as a poet should live, that is, in a constant state of awareness of the animate and inanimate world about him. He makes no stir, he simply breathes . . . doing things effortlessly.*

Here indeed was an exception to the academic poet, a man fed by the natural world, living a spare life much like the early Chinese hermit poets who did away with social distractions, moved to the mountains, planted gardens, and prioritized a slow, reflective manner of being in the world. Solitude, for the most, but not without visits to others living similarly: studying the Tao, tilling the mind. In Japan this tradition would develop into the meditative sojourning embraced by Saigyō, Ryōkan, Bashō, Issa, and Santōka—poet monks who took to the road as an act of temporary renunciation, an exercise in solitude, a desire to wander "as helpless as the waves that beat on the shore, and fleeting like the froth that vanishes in a moment," wrote Issa.

Basic human curiosity played a big part in these journeys—the need to witness firsthand, to experience the "down low" reality of farmers, laborers, fisherwomen, merchants, street sweepers, even panhandlers, prostitutes, and thieves. There were literary implications too. Slinging a bundle over one's shoulder and walking into the world was almost certain to provide the sojourner with materials for his poetry. Moments of pause, moments of mystery, moments of doubt and reaffirmation led the poet deeper into introspection, yet trivial everyday events were not to be overlooked. Issa recorded an old woman blowing her nose into the petals of a moonflower. Saigyō, the cry of the first wild geese winging over the mountain. Santōka, the sound of a sad letter being dropped into a mailbox at twilight. Bashō, rolling a big snowball while his friend prepared tea. Ryōkan, sunning a few lice he plucked from his robe, then tucking them back in.

Returning from a journey, Bashō advised his students: "Seek always the truth of beauty but always return to the world of common experience." In the twentieth century, Kerouac followed up with: "Believe in the holy contour of life. Blow as deep as you want to blow. Submissive to everything, open, listening." Beat poets of the Fifties wrote of hitching a thousand miles to have a down-home conversation with a comrade. David Meltzer recalls the amity he shared with other poets in the Fifties and Sixties: "We didn't need awards or gigs or recompense. Things were cordial, non-competitive. We had each other. We just went out and read. We drank, we listened, we devoured!" Margaret Randall recounts the experience of "vibrant, many layered interactions . . . through person to person contact." Getting the latest, face to face, in times when word of mouth was paramount.

Probably ten years went by before I began writing haiku again. Two incidents rekindled the flame. First, reading the poems and journal entries of Santōka Taneda, I got to know the "unstructured structure" of his free-form haiku, poems that broke with traditional Japanese rules. I saw how he traveled, kept close to the unfettered lives of common people, and sought not so much to be informed by nature, as to be reformed by it. Second, I met the poet Steve Sanfield, who was living in the Sierra Nevada foothills and writing his own haiku. What was important, he reminded me, was to show the season of the heart, and to realize that haiku needn't clone Japanese predecessors in style or content—much like Whitman's disregarding European influences to embody the rhythms of his own continent.

The lid was off. I no longer had to be Japanese but could write from where I stood, wept, slept, exalted. I could pursue haiku as the spontaneous leap of nature into my consciousness. Or catch myself bumbling in awkward moments of human folly which, when penned, fell into the genre called *senryu*. Kobayashi Issa again became a favorite. Blyth called him "the poet of destiny who moved with the movement of fate." Issa wrote about fleas, mosquitoes, lice, polliwogs—and himself, the clumsy being who ambled among them. He opened up a democratic approach

201

to haiku, took it from literary circles, put it into the hands of the people. Anyone could write it. Priest, farmer, samurai, streetwalker, vagabond, child, grown-up. Caste, gender, age, background, schooling, no-schooling didn't weigh in. Two by Issa:

> how lovely
> through the torn paper window
> —the Milky Way

> it begins
> from the cicada's song
> the gentle breeze

There is a feeling of *sabi* in the first poem, a rustic unpretentiousness coupled with loneliness. The paper window is torn, but there is no complaint. Issa peers through the tear to the beauty of the Milky Way, and in so doing is transported from the poverty of his hut into the elegance of the universe. Small to big. Poor to rich.

The second poem is fascinating in its turn-around. The breeze does not carry the insect's song. Instead, it is borne from the song. It would take textbooks to explain the phenomenon of sound creating movement, not only in the ear, but in the universe. Issa, with only a few words, gives us the mystery and the science. Santōka Taneda (1882-1940) wrote poems in a spirit similar to Issa's:

> Finally
> both the futon and the night
> were long enough.

> in the grass
> trodden by the horse
> flowers in full bloom.

once again
no mail
dragonflies here and there.

The first poem brings a chuckle. Both the length of the night and the length of the bed are at last accommodating. After the chuckle, poignancy creeps in. The poem's bare details reveal much about Santōka's poverty. His life was unadorned, likewise his words. He enjoyed no permanent living quarters or conveniences. As a mendicant, he wandered, often sick and penniless, always between this world and that. Perpetually on the move, it is said that Santōka journeyed over 28,000 miles on foot. Who can be sure? He certainly didn't measure his steps with a pedometer!

Santōka's next two poems indicate season by using the *kigo* "flowers in full bloom" and "dragonflies." In the second poem the flowers endure despite the horse tramping the grass. In nature all goes on without blame. Strength, action, passivity, destruction, creation—they exist simultaneously. The third poem powerfully expresses a contrast between empty and full. There is an absence of mail, nothing to hold or read. Yet life is replete; the non-human world is alive and brimming. The poet sees the hovering dragonflies, and human emotion effervesces. The dragonflies are timeless, transient, transparent, and elusive—as in a *sumi-e* brush painting.

Another poet in the canon is Chiyo-ni (1703–1775), a student of two of Bashō's pupils. Painter, poet, and Buddhist nun, she remains Japan's most celebrated female haiku poet. As her premier translator, Patricia Donegan notes: "She lived the Way of Haikai, appreciating each moment, creating art as part of everyday life ... And she achieved fame during her lifetime through her intense devotion to her art in an age when women's freedom and creativity were restricted." All of her haiku are remarkable, her morning glory poem being the most famous:

> *morning glory*
> *wrapped around the well-bucket—*
> *I'll borrow water*

The poet wakes, brushes her hair, goes for water, and discovers the well bucket wrapped with a morning glory vine. Instead of removing it, she halts with a realization: this simple flower is an equal in her world. It has found an unexpected home around the bucket, and in her heart. Rather than disturb nature, Chiyo-ni inconveniences herself and borrows water from a neighbor. Her poem paints a picture with hardly a word said, and with no philosophic allusions. Everything is fragile in this transient world. Like the flower, we come, we go. A similar recognition of life's impermanence is expressed in an Aztec poem:

> *The body makes a few flowers*
> *then drops away withered*
> *somewhere.*

A student looking at modern haiku often asks: Why does haiku look like it does today? What happened to the rules? A simple answer, to quote Zen teacher Joko Beck, is: "a good practice is always undermining itself." Continent to continent, culture to culture, language to language, haiku makes itself new as practitioners part ways with rules that suited the Japanese landscape, its language, culture, and seasons. The core ideas of Bashō's time are with us, though. Keep it brief, let it jump, follow the natural world through its seasons, but do not forget the seasons of the heart. Harold Henderson and R.H. Blyth provided early translations of classical Japanese haiku into English. Henderson believed "Haiku should be starting points for trains of thoughts and emotions." Blyth saw haiku as a moment of living, sans emotions and subjectivity. Both approaches cause us to consider the haiku practice more deeply. Whichever school you identify with, it's worth remembering what Yogi Berra said about belonging to teams: "What difference does the uniform make? You don't hit with it."

In the West, most haiku writers don't adhere to the traditional Japanese form. A seventeen-syllable requirement rule can turn a simple image in English into a clumsy one. It encourages unnecessary adjectives. Descriptions become awkward. Added weight causes the picture to sag, the spark to dim. Seasons are there, as are moods in the psyche triggered during seasonal changes. This haiku by Steve Sanfield aptly stands on its own for exactly what it is, but it also reverberates with an inner cold, an ache found not in the bones, but in the heart:

> *The naked trees*
> *make it colder*
> *—this autumn moon*

A haiku by Penny Harter also stands complete as is; but on a second take it could also imply a personal rebirth after a season of hardship:

> *snowmelt—*
> *on the banks of the torrent*
> *small flowers*

The juxtaposition of delicate, upward sprouting flowers with the river's powerful, horizontal churn provides a provocative picture—nothing contrived or imagined, no clever, invented imagery. The flowers, the torrent, the melting snow are natural presences, there all the time, noticed or unnoticed—except that this time a poet happened along, senses tuned, receptive to the moment.

Whenever I experience a jolt that instantly triggers a flash of light, and with it a complete picture, I try to stay with it as long as possible, letting the details roll inside my mouth like smooth pebbles. As I walk into the world, I scribble a line or two and eventually my pocket pad brightens with haiku. Back home, in the realm of mundane practicalities—roof to repair, teeth to fix, bills to pay— these haiku offer calm direction: a trail of stepping-stones that gets me across the larger waters of tangled thoughts and emotional sidetracks. They bring me back to a slower moment, a transformative one. Haiku: so tiny, yet as footholds they provide enormous balance. Each stone shines like a mirror, triggering light into the larger, darker mind—one too filled with thought to notice, as did Moritake (1452-1540):

> *that fallen flower*
> *returning to the bough*
> *was a butterfly*

A deep surprise, a gong-rattling clonk, a giddy bafflement, a quiet revelation of the mysterious in the everyday—these zaps of primal, uninhibited delight are the seeds of haiku. Often frayed and threadbare, haiku are not concerned with lasting beauty, but with a significant moment amid everything transient—a split second in which things are profound, yet without meaning. Elizabeth Searle Lamb:

> *such small sounds . . .*
> *the silence of the night*
> *deepens*

Full of abandonment, precise in their communication, haiku are to be savored, as is the full moon on an empty belly. Living in the world with the haiku eye keeps the world new. Water seeps through stone as we sleep. Long after the raven flies, its shadow remains on the wall. Outside, the snow falls; inside, the nightgown on the chair is warm. What is familiar is suddenly renewed. The sameness and difference are one. Haiku expresses the ineffable magic of this unity. It captures and releases the light of a world that disappears as quickly as it arrives. I put down the pen, noticing the sky is bright and the wind has stopped. All that outside work I promised to do is still there, but, opening the door, I see I've had a little help.

   The unswept path
   swept clean
   by the breeze.

A LUMINOUS UPLIFT

One of my favorite sparsely settled arid uplifts in
the world is the Hopi heartland. Late July is a good time to
visit, when the Hopis observe the Niman ceremony, also
called the Home Dance. This is when the Kachinas leave
the Hopi villages for their homeland, Nuva'tukya'ovi—
known as the San Francisco Peaks on the Arizona map.
They have been present since mid-winter, animating the
mesas with singing and dancing, sending villagers' prayers
aloft to the ancestral spirits—the Cloud People—that they
may fill the summer sky with precious showers.

Every outsider has a different take on who the Kachinas are. Over the decades I've come to see them as spirit
beings who dwell above the world's turmoil. They come to
call the rain, a primary function. They also come to provide
pleasure, to assure the well-being of the villagers, and to
see that prayers and ceremonies are being conducted dutifully. As wisdom keepers, their roots lead back to the First
People: those who spoke the same language as the deer, the
eagles, the wind, the clouds. The Kachinas communicate
through songs, mime, footwork, symbolic choreography:
a constant dialogue between earth and sky, people and
habitat—one inseparable community. Their dance calls
power from the heavens, the rhythm of their footwork
shows us how to step lightly, move adeptly through the
world's disorder.

Despite the solemn departure of the Kachinas, this
is a happy time on the mesas—the high point of summer.
Moisture has come to the high desert, the stubby native
corn is bushing out. At the Home Dance children eagerly
await the gift-giving of the masked dancers. Villagers sprinkle the Kachinas with cornmeal, asking that their wishes be
conveyed to the higher spirits. The year's new brides, attired

in white home-spun cotton, make their first appearance. At the end of the dance, men and boys pluck spruce twigs from the Kachinas to plant in their fields to assure fertility.

"Dance," as used in relation with Pueblo, Hopi, and Zuni ceremonials is often misinterpreted by outsiders as something done for fun. I once wrote a friend in Los Angeles that I'd just returned from a dance at Ohkay Owingeh Pueblo and was feeling stoked. She wrote back, "I didn't know you knew those two-step jigs." In a follow-up letter, I tried to explain dance in terms of ritual drama: that these are restrained, carefully practiced ceremonial dances, much of their intent having to do with fertility and the calling of rain; that I had just returned from a nearby Tewa village where the Green Corn Dance was being observed; that it took place not in a dance hall, but outdoors in an earthen plaza surrounded by adobe dwellings; that it was one of many occasions during the year when Pueblo villagers don ritual attire, join in intricate choreography, and raise their voices to honor the natural world that sustains us. The dancer hears words of poetry sung by a chorus of men accompanied by drummers, shakes a rattle in response, lifts a fir sprig to the sky, and the body begins a slow, mesmerizing movement. It has become a musical instrument, shaking with ankle bells, pendants and seashells. The dancer has stepped into a sacred realm. The songs are poems to clouds, game animals and the cardinal directions, to the earth and sky, and especially to the mountains: the sacred water holders. The women step lightly, their softly pranced shuffle imitates "female rain," a gentle, steady soaking for the fields. The men step more fiercely, imitating "male rain," a harder downpour that replenishes springs, swells rivers, and washes clean the ego.

The letter to my friend closed with: "I've probably said too much, but I assure you when an entire community files out under the sun to dance—men, women, children,

five-year-olds, eighty-year-olds—they can dance themselves into a transcendent state. The energy is incredible.
As an observer you've been drawn in. You've been renewed.
You drive home, your hands not quite on the wheel. Everything's been transformed."

The Hopi village of Shungopavi on Second Mesa
will host tomorrow's Home Dance. From Santa Fe the
drive is five hours, heading west towards Four Corners,
where Utah, Colorado, Arizona, and New Mexico inter-
sect. Not that political boundaries define the region, but
that their intersection serves as quick reference. In essence
Four Corners is "red geography." The presence of Native
American languages, especially those spoken by the Diné
and Hopi, is the best indicator that you are within its
boundaries. So is the heat-varnished slickrock, the wind-
fluted buttes, the ocean-like plateau whose mineral-red soil
gives summer cloud-bottoms a tint of rouge.

For some, it's a monotonous land. When Mabel
Dodge Luhan drove D.H. Lawrence from Taos to Hopi in
1924, he eyed the landscape with resistance: "death-grey
mesas sticking up like broken pieces of ancient grey
bread." Lawrence was a fussy and impatient man, and the
journey (no air conditioning) over rutted roads was hot and
tiring. It still is. Many first-time visitors become edgy with
the ungodly stretch of space, the blinding metallic sky, the
"nothingness." They may take only superficial notice of the
topography, whereas one born from this land is out there
reading the topography as story lines from a tale many
times told.

When I worked as a poet in the Navajo Nation
schools, I watched teachers arrive from the corn-high Midwest and throw their arms up. Plunked in a treeless void,
they were often housed in drafty trailers subject to heat,
cold, and biting wind. "Absolutely nothing here!" a math
teacher complains. "Let's bail." But her husband is uncer-

tain over her suggestion to reapply elsewhere. Something's captured him. And the battle begins. She's looking up teaching positions in Vermont. He's reading Tony Hillerman, opening his mind to native mythology, checking topo maps, tracing out a jaw-rattling sidetrack into a lost canyon, ready to unroll a blanket, grill a steak over coals, and let his mind go. Lots of newcomers have ended their marriages out here.

Ed Abbey, an easterner who immediately fell in love with what he called Slickrock Country, rated this land among the "least inhabited, least inhibited, least developed, least improved, least civilized, least governed, least priest-ridden, most arid, most hostile, most lonesome, most grim bleak barren desolate and savage" territory in the Southwest. You bet. This isn't Wordsworth's sylvan Lake District, "the loveliest spot that man hath found." It belongs to the coyote, the prickly pear, the pack rat, the skinwalker. Too vast for a tank of gas, or for the mind to absorb. Pen your thoughts quickly, lest they vaporize in heatwaves or be carried aloft by carrion eaters.

In Gallup I pull off Interstate 40, old Highway 66, the road I traveled with my parents as a kid. Earl's Restaurant is a must. The door handles are a bit greasy but the inside is clean and bright. I find a booth, order a bowl of red chile, lean back and watch the show. A few tourists today. A gleaming Harley-Davidson parked near the front door newspaper racks; the usual Winnebago, Lazy Daze, and Prowler hogging the lot. Plenty of mud-splattered pickups parked between them, though. They've brought loads of Navajos in from the rez. The Diné language prevails. Extended families take their time at formica tables overflowing with mutton stew, sopaipillas, green chile cheeseburgers, Cokes, fry bread, big pots of coffee. Tall Navajo men in Levis, Western shirts, black cowboy hats, pointed leather boots. Grandmas in wide, pleated moss-green velveteen skirts, puffy burgundy blouses, balled-up money pouches tucked inside. Their sneakers are well worn, copious turquoise adorns their necks, bracelets of silver and coral wrap their wrists. Not so, their daughters who sport butt-hugging designer jeans, sleeveless tops, midriff tunics, short shorts, and Nike running shoes. Their crow-black hair, freshly shampooed, trails a bubble-gum scent. One item worn by grandma that they don't forsake: the protective jewelry. Turquoise pendants. Crystal talismans. Malachite hairpieces. Pumpkin shell earrings.

The unhurried pace of Earl's is a good pacifier for the mad-eyed, cross-country Americans hellbent on getting from Boston to Las Vegas in thirty-six hours. They usually happen upon the restaurant by chance. Having missed the exit for Taco Bell and McDonald's, they find themselves cruising old Route 66 along the railroad, craning their necks at the pawneries, the smoke shops, the barred-window trading posts. Suddenly, Earl's. In they come, gaggles of them barking and honking, hoping for rapid service, military efficiency. But one look around, and they begin to slow down to fit the scene: a trucker at the counter over coconut cream pie; the itinerant salesman stirring another cup of coffee; slow-talking cowboys whiling away time under the clock; a pair of tribal police on a lunch break; and, well-settled into their booths, Native American families sipping iced teas, waiting for their orders of steak and potatoes, baked chicken, Frito pie, iceberg salad topped with squirts of pink, tostadas piled with shredded beef, refried beans, and sliced jalapeños.

The meals, the talk, have no time frame. The core of a conversation must be approached by a slow circling towards center—details of weather, livestock, price of hay, last Friday's basketball game—until the focal point is reached: a son at war, a daughter's graduation, an upcoming sing at Hat Rock. The circling is very measured, much in contrast to the harr-harr, slap-me-on-the-back at a far table where horsy guffaws erupt from a carload of Texans who've fallen into a booth, immediately waved away a jewelry vendor, and asked for the air-conditioning to be turned up.

Meanwhile, Earl's continues to fill: everyone from the disabled uranium miner to a rodeo queen in metallic-green Wranglers, to local politicos adjusting their bolo ties, to a war vet in sleeveless tee, his hatband full of feathers, to a copper-skinned beauty wearing "Pinnacle Savings" on her lapel, her rare looks that of a princess from the Mongolian steppes. Likely, there's a crystal gazer, sandpainter, or a hand trembler in the mix, too.

Around the tables, the gift bearers scout customers, holding out strings of juniper beads, opening trays of *heishe*, macaw feathers, and sterling silver. A girl, maybe twelve—pitch black eyes, ponytail gathered under a beaded barrette—quietly approaches me: a deer from the woods. She extends a tray of jewelry. Why not? You don't dismiss a gift bearer. A pair of hand-crafted beaded earrings for ten dollars? Sure, I'll take two. Which garners me a souvenir gift of a tiny turquoise earring. "No charge to you." The little vendor then tucks my ten and two fives under a rubber band around her wrist. *Ahéhee'* —and prances away as softly as she arrived.

At the wheel again, I plug a Nigerian Highlife tape into the deck, leave the interstate, and swing northwest on reservation roads: Yah-Ta-Hey, Window Rock, Kin-li-chee. Deep stands of ponderosa on the backbone of the Chuska mountains, followed by a long downshift into the golden light of Navajoland, which opens out not as "scenery" but as living skin, a great ashen puma doing a cat stretch. The feeling is ancient, like the Australian bush country, far from the idea of wilderness held by most North Americans. What makes this country truly wild is that people live out here. That and the geologic oddities that fool the eye as you dip and rise over the baked plain: a ziggurat, a stone rainbow, a phallic pillar politely called "Standing Rock" on the map.

There are plenty of resting places for spirits, too—ones borne into existence by the actions of the supernaturals. Shaped by Changing Woman, smoothed by the Colored Winds. Hidden shrines mark places where people emerged, where they ended up, where they moved on from. Glyph drawings carved into stone portray ancestral spirits, migration routes, solar events. An anthropomorphic boulder may signify a "breathing" or "speaking" place where the wind changes form as it cuts through the hogbacks. A jag of lightning or a plumed serpent may indicate special ceremonial areas. A student at Shiprock High once wrote about a healing place in the cliffs above Lukachukai. "Whenever my head hurts, my uncle takes me there to listen and to sing." He wasn't talking about a headache, something to go to the medicine cabinet for. He was describing a psychological pain, and the uncle, a healer learned in the ceremonial chants, knew the cure.

The road climbs onto a ragged spur. Space opens into a 360-degree mandala, an immense ceramic plate fired in the sun's kiln. On one horizon obsidian tailfeathers protrude from the sand where a mythical bird plunged from the sky; on another, Abalone Shell Mountain floats in desert haze. To the north is Naatsis'áán, a huge laccolithic head rising from the horizon to get a better look at you. Hundreds of wind-whorled geologic oddities figure into this space. The Hopis, Zunis, and Navajos each have their own names for them. There is history apart from myth out here, too. Poignant history. American wars on the Indian. Broken treaties. Bloody massacres. Impromptu carnages of rage and anger. In 1864 the Diné were forced onto The Long Walk after Kit Carson razed their crops, burnt the orchards, and killed the livestock—the same scorched-earth tactic the government tried on Vietnam. But the Vietnamese go forward, as do the Diné, their language and customs alive, their land reclaimed—though not without ongoing legal battles with coal and uranium corporations over the poisoned wells, spoiled waterholes, radioactive rivers, cancer-ridden workers.

Above Jeddito Wash there's a wind-gouged overlook studded with juniper. I remember this place. A friend and I pulled off to sleep here one February night after the Hopi Powamu ceremonies. We pushed back the seats and pulled up a blanket. Sometime before dawn my friend got up to pee, but quickly returned and locked the door. "Something's walking toward the car." At the window appeared a silhouette in a man's overcoat. "I'm trying to get back home." It was a stifled, high-pitched voice. Afraid, I replied: "Go down the road to Keams and get some help from the tribal police." The shadow vanished without a sound. Next morning, I walked around the car in search of footprints, but there were none.

Recounting this story to both Hopis and Navajos, I received various comments but no explanation. Older ones simply nodded and smiled. Younger ones talked of skinwalkers or asked what I had been smoking. A Hopi elder gave me this to think about: "When you come to this country you must learn to see with eyes that are not your own. Whatever you think is a dream or a vision may not be. Because out here whatever you imagine you can reach right out and touch." Again, that wild feeling. A land inhabited by tricksters, bogeys, and phantoms who slip from shadows with their own tales of search, whimsy, and woe.

After a stop at the Keams Trading Post for gas, I enter the Hopi tribal lands. It is late July, the season of terraced clouds, and chocolate-brown puddles line the road. Mud smell, a tangy drift of *artemisia tridentata*. Low bunches of Hopi corn are miraculously maturing in the dunes. If you are a farmer in the high desert, rain is never far from your thoughts. You look to the sky, ask it down. For the Hopis, the Kachinas are the intermediaries between tiller and deity. Their petition initiates the transformation of tiny cloud puffs into swollen thunderheads.

Fifty miles on, the road begins to skirt First Mesa. Up high, to the right, a keen eye can discern the outline of stone dwellings: Walpi, "Place of the Notch," a classic sky village, one of the oldest continuously inhabited villages in North America. A few more miles and the road climbs onto Second Mesa where, like Walpi, the villages of Sipaulovi and Mishongnovi grow right out of the rock. Lower down is Shungopavi, site of tomorrow's dance. At the Hopi Cultural Center, I order a mutton stew with corn bread and salad, fill my water jugs, and head onto a dirt track for a night's rest.

The stars are bright by the time I rake the sand, stake my tent, kindle a small brushwood fire, and finish a beer. The Milky Way weaves a luminous trail across the zenith, like the line of sacred cornmeal the kiva priests sift to guide the Kachinas into the villages. Lying on my back, feeling the earth's curve, I hear my heart thump, feel my body lift into the constellations. The mile-high uplift where I sleep stretches into limitless space, blipped with sawed-off buttes, fractured by gullies. A satellite view reveals the Colorado Plateau to be a great heart-shaped blush of mineral sand raised above the Río Colorado, the Little Colorado, the Río San Juan, and the Río Grande. It is a heartland into which I easily fit, a luminous uplift that can be read as a metaphor for poetry in its purest state: a raised moment where language reveals itself as an energy force, a flash from the subconscious or a spark from daily life when a mystery beneath the obvious is suddenly exposed.

As sleep approaches, I look straight up, no artificial light to distract from the startlingly near stars. I follow into their connect-the-dots map, recounting past travels into similar arid uplifts: Bolivia's altiplano, Ladakh's moonscape: geographies that reduce one's stature to an insignificant speck. Here people dwell at the sky's edge, sow their seeds, guard their prophecies, beautify the world through art, prayer, and ritual observance. Here, the voice of the mountains and the cries of the wind are manifest through occult entities who enliven the dry summers and harsh winters with a blaze of color and sound. Ongoing celebrations of song, poetry and masked dance keep the world turning. Bolivia's indigenous villages and Ladakh's monastic ones overlook infinite space edged with crystal peaks, cardinal points of consciousness humming on the horizon. Physical geography is in constant metamorphosis. Mountains struggle up, gravity tugs them down. Plates shift, granite snaps. A double-finned fishtail summit is thrust into the stars; an apron of ice collapses into an avalanche. Plateaus broken by snowcapped spurs, jagged horns, and labyrinthine pockets expose a shifting core where, upon entering, one's own shape shifts. Such lands, as Federico García Lorca expressed, "raise the poet to a sharp-edged throne."

Dawn. A blue-edged lemon light flares from the horizon. I boil coffee, nibble a muffin, pack the gear, drive the switchbacks up through a mosaic of sunburnt sandstone to Shungopavi. A familiar road, yet after parking the car and stretching to stand, I'm amazed to find myself here again. Each time seems the first. At this hour the village is hushed, activity largely confined to the tiny kitchens in the flat-roofed contiguous dwellings—their interiors plastered smooth, ceilings low with exposed beams, their fitted-stone exteriors darkened at the doorways with decades of finger touch. The porches have been freshly sprinkled and swept. Each reveals a still-life: a hoe handle topped with a rubber doll's head guarding a pair of fluffy-bear slippers washed and set to dry on an overturned wash-tub; a broken Batman kite resting on a pile of axed juniper; a cactus in a Folgers Coffee can on a blue metal chair; a yellow mop and a red plastic bucket propped against an "Urban Girl" bicycle, an ear of corn dangling from each handle grip. Most of these porches line a sheer cliff. You exit a Hopi house and find yourself in eternity. "A balance of solid and void," observed the architect Vincent Scully. What better place for the otherworldly Kachinas to appear.

In a doorway stands an elder. He's dressed for today's Home Dance, silver hair pulled into a ponytail, tied with a woven band that matches his turquoise shirt and red pants. His hands are braced on his walker, his head upright ready to receive the sun. Behind him, a girl arranges coffee cups on a table, a woman lifts a pressure cooker onto a wood-burning stove. A stone stairway climbs the outside wall to a roof where children, just waking, giggle inside their blankets. A grandmother wearing a patterned dress and a bright calico apron ascends, bucket in hand, and proceeds bandy-legged across the roof to feed an eagle tethered to a post, soon to be sacrificed, its feathers plucked for ritual use. The eagle extends its wings over the woman's offering of meat scraps, bows its head and begins to eat.

Sunrise. A bronze glow bathes Shungopavi. I close my eyes and give thanks, grateful for another day, for the opportunity to be here. A distant clatter of shells and rattles sounds from below the mesa. The Kachinas! Without warning, never by any discernable clockwork, they are here. Masked and feathered, backlit by solar rays, they advance over the rimrock in a long file. The Kachina Father, bare bodied save for his snow-white kilt, leads them on. His long black hair bobs with a single eagle feather as he walks barefoot, sifting a cornmeal trail into Shungopavi's plaza. The Kachinas carry armfuls of corn stalks, set them in the center of the plaza and line up to be blessed with sprinkles of cornmeal. These are the stately Hemis Kachinas, the Far Away Kachinas who will return to their distant mountain at the close of day.

The Kachina Father speaks a few words, followed by a long pause, after which the lead Kachina gives a pronounced shake to his rattle. In unison, the group begins a soft mesmerizing murmur. A gentle stamping of feet keeps time, aided by the turtle-shell rattles strapped under the right knees. The Kachinas, singing and moving in unison, all in identical attire, masks and headdresses bobbing, undulate into a long rolling line—a perfect synchronization of visual and aural. Word made flesh, music rising from flesh. What impresses the beholder is the pulsating texture of the whole. Individual dancers have become inseparable from one another. Within the physics of sound and movement, a forgotten language has been reinstated. The hypnotic chant rises: elemental, dreamlike, poetic. At intervals, the Kachina at the head of the line begins a 180-degree turn. The rest of the dancers follow, one after another, precisely turning until they all face the Hopi families seated along the plaza walls.

Concentrating on the dancers, I shut my eyes to listen more fully—and fall into another world. Neon soundwaves shimmer across my eyelids. There is a snake-like melody of spirals. A prance of bighorns. A paper-doll string of hunters. Bursts of ultraviolet dots and circles. Opening my eyes, I count at least three dozen Hemis Kachinas dancing with ten Kachina Manas, Hopi "women" impersonated by men, masked and dressed in long black mantas, their shoulders draped with white and red capes. Each carries a painted gourd and a wooden rasp. The Hemis Kachinas are tall and elegant, they seem to have been swept in on waves of sun. Their masks—half turquoise, half yellow-ochre—have narrow eye-slits with spotted cloud humps painted above them. Tiny white circles descend down the center of the masks to meet spruce-branch ruffs ringing the necks. The Kachinas are crowned by thin wooden headboards painted with thunderheads whose descending rain shafts—black and ultramarine against turquoise blue—can also be read as ascending phalli, returning energy to the universe. Eagle, turkey, parrot, and macaw feathers adorn the headboards, whose rear sides are carved with fertility images: pollywogs, frogs, rainbows, butterflies, corn and squash blossoms. The headboards are like painted altars extending the body heavenward, giving it "sky-elegance."

A Hopi man invites me up a ladder to see it all from above. The roof is packed with Hopis, a couple reservation teachers, three tribal police, and a sprinkle of visitors from afar, including a Tibetan monk in maroon and gold. The weight of the crowd is enough to sag the underlying ceiling beams—each time someone moves, the roof ripples. From here I can absorb the overall dance pattern and focus on a single Kachina—a lot to take in, a real test of observation and memory. No photos are allowed, no sketching, recording, or note-taking. A visitor is forced to simply "be," to renew the eyes and ears; the nostrils too: a waft of boiling stew from the rooms below, a curl of juniper smoke from a stovepipe, a tang of far-off rain.

Excluding their masks and headboards, the Hemis Kachinas are bare from the waist up, though you don't notice this at first. Their chests and backs are darkened with earth and painted with interlocking crescent designs—a handclasp symbol of friendship. There is a lot of regalia, too: blue leather armbands, silver bracelets, black and white rope bandoliers looped over the shoulders, and, from the waist down, handwoven white kilts embroidered with red, green and black geometric designs. Spruce sprigs are tucked into the sashes, bobbing as the dancers gently stamp their moccasined feet, turn, reverse step, turn again.

Sprigs are also held in the left hand, while the right bears a gourd rattle. The right leg—tied with a turtle-shell rattle, deer hoofs inside—gives a resounding clatter.

It is tiring, almost, to take it all in. The eye focuses and blurs, relieves itself in the pale backdrop of sky, then loses itself to the low murmur of the trance-evoking chant that vibrates not only from the dancers' masks, but from the whole of their bodies. At intervals the song is punctuated with shakes of the hand rattles as the Kachinas rotate to receive blessings from their Father. All day long the ritual goes on, hardly a pause. Three lengthy rounds in the morning, three in the afternoon. Enough to fully envelop any spectator. Bring me in, bring me in farther, I find myself saying—as in the act of lovemaking.

One cannot fail to be transfixed. A *force vitale* goes straight into the body, the psyche. And plenty of artistic craft goes into making this force visible. Call it theater, but if so, theater of the transcendent—meant to awaken, to invoke awe. As spectator one becomes an essential biological part of the "performance," which is in no way entertainment. It is a phenomenon where sacred is inseparable from secular, a ritual which carries us into the "holy." Wholeness. The sky is no longer backdrop, it has come forward to occupy tangible space between the dancers' bodies. The chamois-colored plateau scrolls out below the mesa as a rippling soundwave, an extension of the Kachinas' song.

It is relaxing, for a moment, to observe the simpler attire of the Kachina Manas: yellow-orange masks with red hairs falling past the eye slits towards a collar of feathers; black hairpieces whorled into the traditional hairdos of unmarried Hopi women. There is a pause in the dance, while two priests spread out a line of cushions, onto which the Manas kneel, turn their gourds—painted with cloud, lightning, and frog designs—upside down, and place notched sticks over them. The Hemis Kachinas stand above them, bowing with their rattles. The Manas, in corn-grinding mime, begin to rasp their sticks with sheep scapulae to produce a loud, rising crescendo of frog-croak. Frogs are the sure symbol of rain, their sound especially auspicious when paired with the turtle-shell leg rattles. The turtle, like the frog, is a both-worlds creature associated with water. Almost all of these Kachina dances have to do with petitioning moisture for the crops, as well as good health for the entire Hopi community. Rain, snow—let it come!

After the interlude, the cushions, gourds, and rasps are collected and put aside. The Kachinas exit the plaza and re-enter bearing armloads of bundled corn plants and cat-tails tied with hand-carved kachina dolls for the girls, small handmade bows and arrows for the boys, handwoven plaques for their mothers. And more! Plastic laundry tubs with cantaloupes and watermelons, baskets of zucchini and squash, trays of piki bread and store-bought cakes, cartons of grapes and nectarines, bowls of peaches and apricots, bags of beans and flour. An apron, a shawl, a baking pan. Cans of coffee, packets of Jell-O and Kool Aid. The plaza has been transformed into a cornucopia.

After a long round of resumed dancing, the Kachinas begin to give away the goodies, straining to see through their eye slits to find who they are meant for. It feels like Christmas, yet without the round-the-tree brouhaha. Instead, only a hushed gratitude. All is quiet save for the clacking of the Kachinas' leg rattles as they move in and out of families seated along the plaza walls. The kids eagerly await—huddled between grannies and young mothers—until a giant masked figure steps forward and points a finger. The youngster, excited but shy, must be coaxed to receive the gift. After the gift-giving, the Kachinas line up for more dancing.

When I look again, the plaza is entirely clear, just bare earth. But its perimeters have become a garden. Each seated Hopi holds a cornstalk or a cattail upright, and the effect, the multiplicity of numbers, creates an eruption of green. Fruit, painted dolls, ceremonial carvings are in the hands of young and old. Everyone's lap is overflowing. Like the miracle of the loaves and fish, there is delight in sudden abundance.

Far into the afternoon the chanting continues. High on the mesa, the Kachinas are backed only by sky. On the rooftop, we too are in the altitudes, consciousness raised, heavens reverberating with song. Nowhere else on the North American continent does one come so close to the idea of immortality in the real world. The Hemis Kachinas slowly turn, lifting and bringing their feet down, shaking their rattles, while their Father calls out subtle shifts in position and encourages them to step up their energy. It is amazing how the long spell of singing has drawn the clouds. By late afternoon the wind is up, the blistering heat has cooled, the air is dark. The smell of rain has reached Shungopavi, excitement ripples through the crowd. "Don't look at the rain or it won't come," a Hopi woman next to me warns. Not long, and here it is. Thunder lets loose. Glassy drops ping-pong down, pocking the dust, sending odors of wet earth, wool, leather, hot tin, musty stone, and spruce needles into the air.

The Hemis Kachinas hold to their rhythm, unbroken in trance. The downpour smears their body paint as they uncoil into a long, glistening serpent. The tourists, wide-eyed, are exhilarated. Like children thrilled by a summer rain, they make no attempt to take cover. Instead, they submit to the deluge and enjoy a rare communal ecstasy. Hopis pull plastic garbage bags over their heads, couples laugh while battling with inside-out umbrellas, teenage lovers use the occasion to cozy up to one another. A visitor lifts her arms to the sky, and, in an accent I detect as French, exclaims: "You don't have to do anything but be here. Hopi does it all to you!"

In this wild, cloud-joined moment—Kachinas moving horizontally across the plaza, rain vertically descending—one is stopped in a vortex. No clock, no compass. Present are the ancestors (my father's face in that of the old Hopi man keeping time on the sidelines), present are the gods (there are no impersonators behind those masks!), present are the yet to be born (in the Hopi brides solemnly sprinkling the Kachinas with pinches of corn-meal), present is the union of right thought, right action, right harmony between gods and humans.

At sunset the rhythm halts, the desert is storm darkened, the sky has gone from chamomile to wild rose. Nearly twelve hours of uninterrupted ceremony and I am intoxicated, cleansed by wave after wave of sound washing over the body. The acoustics of the plaza—a sound box amplifying the chant with a slightly out-of-synch echo—has mesmerized everyone. Soon the plaza clears, as do the rooftops. People hurry to gather at a tamped-earth square by the kiva, where the priests are praying inside. Suddenly, out from the smoke hole emerge the male and female clan leaders who have not been seen since the first dance of the day.

Now comes the final dance to end the Home-going ceremony. The blessing rite by the clan leaders that began the day is repeated: tobacco smoke from a clay pipe, water sprinkled from a ceremonial bowl with an eagle feather, a sift of cornmeal from a leather pouch. The Hemis Kachinas raise their voices into a final song above the Manas kneeling and rasping their painted gourds. When the song has finished, silence falls. The Kachina Father recites a lengthy and noble farewell, which is acknowledged with the shake of the lead Kachina's rattle. Twilight has deepened, the Hopi men walk briskly up to the masked gods and pluck spruce boughs from their sashes. And then it is done. Like a poet finishes a verse. Like a cloud completes its action. Like lovers breaking from the spell of their bond.

The Kachinas depart—a melancholy sight for visitors, but from the Hopis no gesture of mourning. Most have ambled off before the Hemis Kachinas have fully disappeared over the rim of Shungopavi's mesa. No time for sentimentality, only for ongoing beautification. As the spirit beings file over the mesa toward Nuva'tukya'ovi, my body burns with an afterglow—as if filled with warm crystal.

I am unsure of what the villagers pray for during that last dance, but as a visitor I am filled with thanks. I ask the Kachinas to care for this village that has welcomed me, to restore world peace, to bless the gardens and orchards, the tenders of the land, the families, elders, newborn, the work of the mothers, the passing on of tradition by the wisdom keepers. Moisture and benevolence, yes. Renewal and revitalization for all sentient beings. Healthy earth, healthy sky.

Again, I cross the wide mesa to bed down.

Every pinpoint of starlight shimmers with song. The great indigo drum of the heavens softly beats. Today I was in a place where my eyes opened wide, as if seeing the world for the first time. That is what Hopi allows us. The essence of transport. The discovery that we are a song of multiplicity in which the gods exchange place with humans. And humans, like them, do a dance in which the body steps beyond itself, becomes one with a greater body—a body waiting to be filled, there inside us all the time.

SOUTHWEST SKETCHES

INTO THE DREAM MAZE

If I pick apart the reasons for loading up an old pickup and moving to New Mexico fifty years ago, logical ones like wanting to live where the air is bright and the space wide open, my mind strays. There is a deeper stratum where logic falls away into the honeycomb of the psyche and reasons vanish. I'm here because the land matches an interior one, something dreamed, a place very alive, one that appears whether I shut my eyes or open them: a warp of sand dotted with piñon and juniper, a weft of blue sky fringed with gold chamisa, an unlikely arrangement of lop-sided buttes and razor-sharp mesas backed by snow-dusted peaks. Sleep on any off-the-map canyon rim and upon waking dreams unroll into a convergence of physical and psychic worlds. In rippling heat waves, in ghost imagery of shifting mirages, the mind halts, body becomes still, unnecessary baggage evaporates. With lightness the eye takes hold. A sparse and elegant bounty reveals something personal in the remote, a reflection of a raw and wild self.

Starlit chill
warm slickrock
tonight's bed.

ENCHANTMENT

At age ten I flew over the Southwest in a Lockheed Constellation, a sleek and powerful plane manufactured in the city where I grew up. While my mother nervously prayed the rosary, I peered through a curtained porthole into a great unrolling scroll. The Grand Canyon, a tapestry of blazing shadows. The Painted Desert, eddies of pale fluorescence. Gallup, vertebras of sunlit hogbacks in evening lilac. As a grown man I've re-crossed this childhood trail many times. In the desert I begin to grasp a part of me that remains hidden in other environs. Something of one's personality is in the shape and color of the land, the brilliant solitude, the sharpness of edge meeting edge, sky cutting apart earth. A psychic, magnetic, or emotional schematic might well accompany the geographer's map, for this is a place where heart, mind, rock, and mirage overlap. Quiet yourself and you hear a pulse, a ripple, a long pull of wind rearranging dry river pebbles, a hypnotic cadence lodged so deep you might have heard it before you were born. In the eloquent warning of a rattlesnake you hear it again, as you do when Pueblo dancers shake their rattles and call the rain. The desert speaks with a charged sparsity. Alive with surprise, bathed in rarefied light, christened with sudden shadows, it undulates with unpredictable music, the power to sing you into it—rouse you to ecstatic awe.

Sunrise—
in every alcove
the echo of a rain song.

A CEREMONIAL THREAD

In places like Bisti, Kasha Katuwe, or the scribbled canyons north of Ka'waika, the high desert resembles those crazy topographic contours I squiggled as a child: intricate drawings of nonexistent places happily mapped on squares of newsprint with thick-lead Dixon Beginners pencils. In moments of trance, all cares hushed, no intellect in the way, I floated high on life's current, a master cartographer shaping continents of every imaginable climate and geography, a quizzical reality unknown to any explorer but me. My language was the line, a ceremonial thread extending from body to page, a singular alphabet that spoke in a silent passage, procreating as it went, bestowing dimension to the flat surface over which it rolled—a sonorous filament intimate with the pronouncement of my dreams. To be hushed, attuned, thoroughly present, living in the euphoric crossroads where imagination, reverie, and the everyday blend, was to inhabit a circular flow—no divide between dream and waking. It is a thread that continues to uncoil, a magic lifeline that steadies me through the world's chaos, the human wobble, the madness of our times.

> Mountains grow
> shadows swell from this
> little bamboo pen.

AHSHISLEPAH

Wake in moonless blue indigo, three a.m. Slow whistle of wind funneling through burnished stone, sharpening cliff edges, sliding down fluted coves. Breath of the cosmos, gossamer-fine nebulae spinning above slant-rhyme hoodoos and half-melted ziggurats banded with carbonized fern. Lift the head, let the eyes roam over seismographic jolts and tumbles, a mapmaker's hand gone crazy. Ahshislepah: Gray Salt Place. It reads like a lunar surface bumped and knobbed, smoothed by heat, pock-marked by storm, gullied with elephant-skin wrinkles. Stars reverberate under the eyelids, heart thrums with solar configurations. Shapeless, shifting exploded matter reconfigures inside the body. Marine skeletons crumble from wind-scalloped sandstone. Fossilized stumps jut from layers of shale. Molecules ping and zap, do an ultraviolet dance in the head. A spooky cobalt glow bathes each roost, nipple, and curve. Primeval consciousness, a ceaseless rave. Pearled arabesques of agate and carnelian. The ocean's roar in a petrified dune. A river of stars in a seam of quartz. The taste of Creation expanding, contracting, around the still center of time.

> Immense sky
> filled with the fragrance
> of a single moon flower.

WIJIJI

The trail follows out into the center of the world. Each step over the land is a step inside. While tiny lemon-colored composites underfoot talk to each other, I roll a pebble around with my tongue, speak to stone, imitate the calls of rock wren and thrush. A cliff edge rises before me, breathes with electrons, ebbs with tidal waltz. What is solid isn't stone, only a severed window of sky where we find hold. Body is brittle air, sunlight, and blood. Universe a fragile empire dissolved on the tongue, a petroglyph carved in mineral-varnished stone. Spiral, dot inside circle, solar flare, river-rippled memory path, a game animal traveling beyond the limits of our imagination. We wander through geography that beckons with symbols for another reality. Past and future don't work so well out here. The land, the shape of ourselves in it, are of this moment. Circular, time-less. That's what the rocks say. With the ranger's map in hand, I appear to be walking a straight line toward the an-cient site of Wijiji, but no, this is a diaphanous trail, woven into the zodiac. Breathe it all in, breathe it out. A thousand years ago, the brochures don't tell you, is today.

> Disappearing
>   into heatwaves
> a white rainbow.

A SEE-THROUGH GARDEN

Sunlight spins through filigree silhouettes of cliff rose, wild tansy, Apache plume. Hummingbird drinks from trumpet vine, damselfly plays in rice grass as I fashion tiny chert lean-tos for centipedes, then go to work arranging stepping stones that begin anywhere, lead nowhere. Nothing symbolic, no hidden meaning. The stones simply "are," inert and quiet, save for the movement inside their fractures. Thunderheads mount as I putter. A sudden downdraft and a pile of scrap wood dances, an empty pail spins a rag-band tune. I take to the porch, tighten my cap, hold onto the chair. Rain thrashes, wind sweeps it off, out comes the sun. I study an upright slab of granite and see "mountain." I ponder an arrangement of white pebbles and see "river." Garden is not the right word. This is merely a patch, a state of mind, things half finished, a world in transition. A composed dynamism of fallen twigs, unruly tangles, rusting wheelbarrow, coils of hair left for the warbler building her nest. A place that draws in the wild, holds it for awhile, then exhales it again.

Evening breeze
over a plum branch, my glove
lifts a finger.

CALLING THE RAIN

On a hot afternoon at seven thousand feet, I clank my hoe between rows of struggling corn. In the distance a thundercloud swells over Tsicomo peak. In its shadow are the Tewa-speaking Pueblos Ohkay Owingeh and Kha P'o. Decades living here and I'm still beginning to know the land and its people, the abrupt temper of wind, the severity of drought. On Pueblo feast days I come to realize how ceremonies call rain from the sky, give life to the corn. Poems set to choral chant, mime, and intricate footwork keep the seasons turning, the soul in balance. I follow this cycle of ritual drama as an observer with deep appreciation for the beauty and power of song. Today, with no thought to that, something inside me gets my feet tapping. Torrid weather, dearth of rain, garden wilted. Desperate to call that swelling thundercloud my way, I grab my gourd rattle and give it a shake. Not enough. I must form some words, sing them into action, lose myself entirely to the calling of rain. No trite imitation of someone else's ritual, I must make it my own, sing for however long it takes to move that cloud over my backyard. Half hour passes, I keep it up. Step toward Tsicomo, turn to the garden. Float, become cloud. Drop, become rain. Let words become dance, until Yo! The cloud moves slowly overhead—step step step, a little closer, until thick poker-chip splats begin to pelt.

> A raindrop—
> inside it, another
> has fallen.

CALDERA

Across the fields, beyond ragged coves of juniper, rising behind the dark anvil of Mesa Prieta, the rounded peaks of the Jemez float like islands. Two summits form the edges of what was once a 20,000-foot volcano. A million years ago it blew, leaving a caldera that cooled and filled with grassy swales and fumaroles. Or so I thought. Recently a geologist set me straight. Those summits weren't much higher than they are now: 12,000 feet. The caldera wasn't formed by a blown-off crown, but by multiple eruptions that emptied a cavity of magma from the mountain, causing it to collapse. Despite the facts, my volcano shines quite believably thirty miles west, scintillating in thin air. I often end the day observing its perfect symmetry through a glass of Chardonnay, its honeyed tint blending with the mountain's faded amethyst into a most delectable hue. Does the volcano correspond to Mount Analogue, René Daumal's mythical peak occasionally glimpsed through the mist of one's personal quest? A metaphor for the unreachable pinnacle? A symbol for the very core of the psyche, a molten tension just under the skin that erupts as fire, or sometimes cools and congeals as it rises? As the sun sets behind the volcano, its rays fan into silver twilight. As dusk cools, to the east a white orb peeks above a low ridgeline.

> Without a sound
> summer hills
> fill with moonlight.

BORROWED SCENERY

The garden has no fixed boundary. Wild grasses edge in from the fields. Primrose spread out beyond the gate. Our view from the front porch looks over chest-high sunflowers, wild rose, sky-blue morning glories—east, toward a row of chalky hills spotted with low pine and juniper. Framed by the porch posts, the hills rivel into the fields, through the split-rail fence, adding their colors—fiery paintbrush, yellow clusters of snakeweed—to the purple columbine and golden yarrow at our feet. Distance is brought near, background and foreground are one, perspective flattened as in a Hiroshige woodblock print. The hills have become part of the garden, what Japanese landscape artists call *shakkei*: borrowed scenery. Twentieth-century poet-painter Kodōjin wrote a haiku about the close-by going astray to include the far-away: "pumpkin vines/stretching out/to the borders of the province." Three-hundred years earlier, Matsuo Bashō offered a reverse image:

> *Letting the mountain*
> *move into the garden—*
> *a summer room.*

TWO MEN, ONE HOE

Settle into a rusty metal lawn chair, take a rest from the garden. Scatter seed to the grosbeaks, offer a quartered orange to the oriole, toss a few crumbs to the scrub jay tap-dancing along the fence. Planting, pruning, setting stone, yes, but mostly I like to amble the tangles, get low, pluck a weed, open the acequia, watch snowmelt bubble through the plums into the newly-sprouted kitchen greens. The sandstone paths don't need water, but I give a spray from the hose just to bring out the patterns of fossilized fern. Between the stones crickets sing, answered by frogs chanting in Mr. Martinez's alfalfa field behind our house. That square of green is his garden, tame and ordered, but no less meditative than mine. Shovel in hand, he's out there at dawn, wrapped in stillness, directing water, watching clouds scuttle over the mesas into the silver-clear sky. "All day long we work," he says, "without pay—me until the hay's cut, you until your book's out." He runs another furrow with his hoe. I go back upstairs to the page. End of day, I'm still at it, and he is too.

> Two men
> one hoe, heaven above
> earth below.

WHISKERED INTELLIGENCE

From a water-carved hollow comes a three-dimensional howl, a reverberating blip, a rhapsodic vocal blaze. Daybreak, and old Mr. Cool is heralding it in, his voice revved to greet the first quivering light on the cottonwoods. His is a cacophonous laugh, a wheel of concentric sound textures—electric circuitry of Shiva's ancient dance pulling matter from nothingness, recycling it through the universe, sending it back into the ever-regenerative void. I put down my coffee as the lone crooner goes backstage, then reappears, family in tow, trotting a quick-rhyme choreograph of gone-crazy barks, operatic laughs, bubbled free verse—a scrambled time-signature, a vacant pause, a fresh rise of chortled wheeze—all for free in the grand ole desert opry. With whiskered intelligence, coyotes loop through ravines, eyes flashing, laughter hounding reality with praise. They bark to warm the soul, follow musical ridgelines with sovereign impulse, imitate passing clouds with soprano hops, amplify silence with sonorous color brushed from the palette of their canyon labyrinth. A down-home gospel choir belting it out in a Mississippi chapel rocks me out of my seat, but it's old Mr. Cool who converts me.

Dandelions bobbing
to coyote's Charlie Parker
impromptu.

PONDERING A CLEAR TAOS STREAM

I look into a cold Taos stream, see warm colors of shimmering stones under satin eddies. The stones stand still, but, as the sun moves, back and forth they go, shifting shape and color as shadows warp and weave. Where do we go with our last breath? What happens after we pass? Pundits, scientists, troubadours, butterflies, terns, and hummingbirds haven't come back with an answer. Humans wouldn't listen to a cicada's report anyway. Too busy riding the teeter-totter of the market, loading gun barrels, ducking rockets. Think I'll take a walk upstream, cool my ears at the source, work my way back through the willows, hitch a ride to Dori's Bakery, see if she's got something hot in the oven. Why not let the dead be dead, stones be stones, the water flow? Sometimes as a kid I'd pretend dying. Flat on my back in spurs and chaps, eyes to sky, I'd leave the human realm, fade into a larger sphere—nothingness at the core. No matter how tall I once stood, when down in the dust I was "out," small enough to fit into the universe again. Today I watch the stream course around smooth boulders, curl into itself, and regain shape. Into the reeds it carries my reflection, while steady in the current,

> facing the water's flow
> a silver minnow
> perfectly still.

MORITZ THOMSEN, LIVING POOR

Something has me recalling a long-gone amigo today. Perhaps it's the rarity of a truly muggy day in our normally bone-dry New Mexico high desert that brings his apparition forward. Isn't that him just outside my window as I sharpen pencils in my adobe study? A scarecrow peeking between the scraggly tomato vines, furrowed face, wry smile, keen blue eyes ever alert in a half-cocked head about to clarify some aspect of boondock living: a loneliness, a fellowship, a rivalry, a trial. Years, decades, centuries have passed since I first met him. Time has wrinkled into the air and blown off as dust, only to return as a thick humidity drifting north from the Gulf of Mexico, and from even farther south—the equatorial rainforests.

Moritz Thomsen was fifty-two years old, "a wizened elder" I thought, when I met him as a rebellious twenty-three-year-old in Ecuador. Despite the generation gap, we both shared common ground as Peace Corps Volunteers, the first of a new breed involved in positive, one-on-one human exchange overseas, while bombs exploded in Vietnam. I was an idealist fresh out of college, my senses ajar with the poverty and beauty of the high Andes—working for peace, yes, but paradoxically ready to fight for the cause of the Quechua people with whom I lived: landless serfs strapped under the yoke of iron-fisted landlords who ruled a feudal hacienda system. Moritz, meanwhile, practiced a profoundly centered pragmatism, living and working with impoverished Black farmers on the swampy Ecuadorian coast. In 1966 he had already served two years in the village of Río Verde, busy with the woes of an agricultural co-op, and busy tying up a book that would eventually become a classic: *Living Poor*.

I soon came to know Moritz as an exception to his

generation—and as an exceptional man, period. Only lastly did he admit to being a writer, yet his writings were those of a master seer: sizzling, passionate, filled with re-markable insight and bone-rattling truths. He would be immensely influential on my life as a writer—a young man whose senses had already been rearranged by the unavoid-able challenges life in a new country delivers. Every worldly experience could "find record," Moritz said, "become a seismograph of one's parallel inner journey." Ideas like this enlivened me with chiropractic shocks—almost too much for a tenderfoot fresh out of the L.A. suburbs to digest.

His clownish yet whimsically deadpan balancing act between wisdom and folly combined with his outright vulnerability was a surprise; as was his anarchistic ap-proach to the Peace Corps mentality of "what needed to be done" (according to the government) vs. the reality of "what might be possible to do" (by rookie dreamers like me). This unrestrained energy was an inspiration and a challenge at a time when all cultural, religious, and social footholds had slipped out from under me. The Peace Corps I regarded as a kind of self-imposed exile—just the right answer to my need to withdraw from the cast of characters I'd been brought up with: the commanding elders, the playground bullies, the high school peers who gave me weird looks whenever my "loner aspect" exposed itself, or when I described a far-off place I longed to visit. "Doesn't sound like my neighborhood" was a typical classmate brush off.

Moritz set me straight—that is, he placed me on a crooked and tumultuous path of chance-taking and per-sonal inquiry in every aspect of life, work, and writing. At times he seemed harsh. "Get off your romanticism!" he'd beef when my stories waxed dreamy. "You're a well-off kid here for a couple years sizing up others' poverty who'll probably leave the ilk of resentment when you return home. You are a foreigner and you live above the ones you work with—ones who struggle without hope. You can't throw that off, but you can drop down a couple tiers and listen and observe and move more slowly, no plan to fix things or upgrade people's lives. After all, you've come from a slick, frenetic get-ahead culture to the realities of peasantry: knuckle-busting labor, betrayals of the weather, bad harvest, the fight to stay alive. These people are at the end of their tether, strapped with prejudice and uncertainty, wanting to gain the power to make a new world."

Though I sometimes saw Moritz as a hardened World War II vet who suffered from escalated cynicism, I would soon place a rusty halo over him, for in him I recognized the reincarnate rebel monk, Ikkyu, always ready to pull the rug out from under my quick-to-judge attitude. Once when I spouted off about people living too comfortably to live deeply, Moritz screwed up his face. "Watch your mind, you might drive a potential friend away."

In Quito, we usually met at a bistro specializing in French cuisine. I would grab a bus north from Riobamba, a small market and administrative town at the base of 20,500-foot Chimborazo. Moritz would take a break from the coastal heat and the rising temperatures of the squabbling farmers he had encouraged into a cooperative marketing venture. Switchbacking up from the rainforest in a battered banana truck, he arrived haggard but ready to roll into animated talk.

We sat at a table adorned with a cold ray of Andean light and broke bread over endless rounds of onion soup. After serving us, our waiter, dressed in a soiled white jacket, retreated to a corner and stacked classical long-play records on a vintage phonograph. Between commonplace gripes and surreal war stories that life in a foreign legion brings, we held real conversations. Moritz suggested that reality might be more interesting than anything the imagination might deliver. He urged me to write the truth of the immediate situation: "Pull from the evolving moment, what comes to you in the everyday. Learn the forms, then forget literary rules. Come up with your own. Ditto literary trend or artsy fashions that hold to already-established traditions. Break through! Take a chance with new territory."

He was particularly helpful to me, a kid who was not only waking to the sufferings of Ecuador's indigenous population kept uneducated and landless by the ruling elite—but also waking to the possibility of writing the details ("mind-cleansing insights" Moritz called them) of the changing tide of the indigenous: their demands for civil liberties in a top-heavy system of money and law and social hierarchy. I was beginning to write poems, stories, and short vignettes on a battered Hermes war correspondent's typewriter, which I kept a close eye on. "If it's not banged up enough, bang it up some more," Moritz advised. "More wrecked it looks, less likely it'll be stolen." The little machine was a boon. I could finally write as fast as my mind unleashed the particulars of the lives around me, the mood inside me, the fraught situation of the farmers, the stark landscape of the high Andean *páramo*.

What did Moritz recommend? Live your life, write from the core of it, tell the non-embellished truth. Sort the grain from the chaff. Don't overcook. Keep dashes, hyphens, and quotation marks sparse (I never did get that down), and for godsakes, read. A well-crafted, truly original, deep-from-down-under passage by a committed writer will "take the top of your head off," he said, paraphrasing Emily Dickinson. "Worth a whole semester of classroom prattle." At the time he was reading Conrad and Nabokov. Over the years he had me look at: Steinbeck, B. Traven, Alejo Carpentier, Peter Matthiessen, V.S. Naipul, Bruce Chatwin—and Proust, to name a few. Now and then he'd throw me a quote. "The best way, according to Tolstoy, is that writing come from a full life, sort of like the foam on a glass of beer."

Moritz could write from the center of his reality, yet step far above, fluttering like a mad angel sizing it all up with proper overview. I had no clue to this kind of discipline and constantly stumbled in the way of myself. During these times, in person or via letter, Moritz never helped me up with a soft hand. Instead, he provided a swift kick with a broken-soled shoe and laughingly set me reeling. "Don't smooth it out! Keep it raw, sensitive." Or, "So what if you write all day and don't make a dime. Have courage!" Or, "Never fail your journal. It's your record of existence, who you are, who you are becoming. Any fragment, anything that happens along the way, especially what you don't think is important, can yield gold."

After two years in the Peace Corps and a third about to begin, I was deeply immersed in Ecuador's agrarian reform and the quest of Quechua serfs to liberate themselves from a church and state that insisted they were lesser citizens—children whose karma did not guarantee social or political equality. I was also deep into my own writing—scratching out poems, scribbling quick-flash pictures, listening hard, never without my pocket pad. A journal entry from that period: "Two men that have shaped me toward liberated thinking: Moritz Thomsen, isolated in coastal rainforests, & Johnny Lovewisdom, hermit iconoclast in the crinkled hills of southern Ecuador. One continues in seemingly fruitless hard labor, from which grows his writing like a stem from his head. The other writes provocative newsletters filled with Eastern thought and alternative lifestyle, and has offered to print my poems on his old-timey mimeo machine. He's at least as poor as Moritz, though 'poor' isn't the right word. What these guys are up to is more in the category of inspired simplicity. Of the two, Moritz is more approachable. Terse, yes, but always redeemed by a charming, understated mix of humor and integrity. A soul shineth beneath his cloak of cynicism—a bright keen eye."

As a writer, Moritz held only modest faith in big publishers. His book *Living Poor,* originally published by the University of Washington Press, had a catchy dust jacket bearing all the playfulness and color of an Ecuadorian fiesta. Not long after, the book was picked up by a mainstream publisher who paid Moritz for the rights to reissue it as a mass-market paperback. Moritz submitted one of his drawings for the cover, but it was rejected. To his bitter dismay, the new version of his book was issued with a cover having absolutely nothing to with the coastal Blacks he lived and worked with. Instead, it pictured a gringo in khaki examining a wilted radish, backed by a Quechua Indian and a volcano. "You can't trust New York. They're provincials, they can't see beyond their own borders!"

Moritz would get his revenge years later when his second book, *The Farm on the River of Emeralds,* was published. On its cover was a stunning pen-and-ink drawing—his own. The book highlighted a forgotten pocket of Afro-Ecuadorian people where Moritz, a white North American, had carved out a farm in the rainforest with a black South American, twenty years his junior. A masterpiece of storytelling, it was an intensely personal account filled with hilarious if not horrifying episodes involving a convoluted network of neighbors—thieves, dreamers, peanut pickers, feisty women, drunken visionaries, scheming desperados. In the mix, Moritz and his partner, Ramón, were often at odds, slowed by their prejudices, stuck in their habits, suffering continuous bouts with hunger, sickness, and despair.

In 1972, three years after I left the Peace Corps, a brief collection of my Ecuador stories, *Desde AlIa,* was published. *The San Francisco Chronicle* sent me an unexpected review of the book, written by none other than Moritz Thomsen. I hadn't heard from him in months and was thrilled. "A Poetic Vision of Ecuador" he titled the review, noting: "The book was written, I would imagine, under the molten pressure of the moment as it was revealed . . . for it sustains an unbelievable amount of creative tension almost as though the writer were changed into some sort of divine receptacle for receiving a thousand elusive impressions. It is probably the best and most profound description of Ecuador that has yet been written."

Shortly after he received my aerogram of thanks, Moritz wrote me from his farm. "For months now we've been so heavily involved in trying to save 'the situation' that I've written practically no letters. The 'situation' we've been trying to save is the result of a year of steady rain. Living here more and more makes Macondo, Marquez' surrealist town in *Cien Años de Soledad,* sheer realism. Remember the guy who was always surrounded with butterflies? Well, I have a guy here who is always surrounded with bees." His main reason for writing, however, was to welcome me back to Ecuador should I ever decide to return. "I may even be able to offer you a tower house in patch of jungle that theoretically will make your creative juices boil."

It would be nearly five years before I'd take him up on the offer. I knew from his letters that he had become increasingly broke, tired, dissatisfied, and hungry. "We have been trying to work our asses off farming, with many days coming up when there was literally nothing to eat in the house. It's resulted in malnutrition, night blindness, creepy skin, falling hair and a mind which reels uncontrollably into rage and hopelessness. In four months I've turned into an old man."

During this time, my friend Jeff Ashe, accompanied by his new bride, paid a visit to Moritz. He reported that Moritz's "tower house"—which I envisioned as a kind of

Robinson Jeffers Tor House—was finally built, "only more in the form of a tumble-down hut. All night drunks stumbled past in the dark keeping us awake. All we had to cover us was a very short sheet. Sarah wanted to be sure her feet were covered, afraid vampire bats would suck blood out of her toes. I wanted to cover my head because we were being eaten alive by mosquitoes. Moritz was pretty much living on eggs from his chicken farm, the hut virtually rotting before our eyes with mold and termites."

In many of his letters, Moritz rambled from topic to topic, never without clarity and precision. But a head-on crash from which he never fully recovered, unhealthy conditions on the farm, and dire lack of food all took their toll. "Jesus, what a shitty letter; if you didn't believe my first remarks about malnutrition—do you believe me now? Mind skittering helplessly, fingers hitting the wrong keys, the author limping from typer to bed to chair to the book to the typer for a pissy thought???"

On hindsight, it was rare to hear Moritz go on about his deteriorating health. He was usually full of cutting humor, and quick with advice, suggesting agents and constantly reiterating: "Your job is to write a book as concisely as you know how, without any excess fat. As to publishing, if you don't blow your own fucking horn nobody's going to blow it for you . . . I've been trying to blow my own horn for years, but I get these terrible pains in my neck and spine."

When I finally got to Ecuador, Moritz was living in the Andes. He had been kicked off his coastal farm by his partner Ramón and had moved into a little apartment in Quito. The day we met I found him on the lawn behind our favorite owner-managed bookstore, the compact and eclectic Libri Mundi. Moritz was hunkered over his precious collection of LPs—Bach, Orf, Rachmaninoff, Copland, Ives—meticulously washing each vinyl with soap and water and placing it on the lawn to dry, desperately trying to rid the grooves of years of jungle mold. Moritz himself was terribly sick from the same mold, and "from forty Marlboros a day." Nobody who visited him could get him to quit.

Death was looking over his shoulder. He refused to do much of anything except flatly accept the situation. The solitude of the farm he fought so hard to carve out of the jungle—a metaphor for the new life he wanted to carve from his life as a young man suffering the tyranny of a cruel and egocentric father—was missing in Quito. With all the English-speaking friends, international cuisine, bookstores, newspapers and telephones, Moritz was undergoing culture shock. He began as a man who wanted to cut distractions, live simply, embrace "decent poverty," and "have human relationships with the poor farmers who lived up and down the river." Now he was juggling his relief to be free of the failed farm with his feeling of displacement amid the civilized sidewalks around him. His refrain: "True sustained happiness begins a moment after death."

Moritz would often mock getting old. I could easily picture him stark naked in pouring rain, waving a machete, cranking up Copland or the soaring music of Roy Harris, defying the Grim Reaper with foul threats. His primary wish was to write well, tell an honest, uncensored tale in his own voice—no matter how raw it might seem to his well-mannered contemporaries. Ex-Peace Corpsman, Paul Theroux, put it this way: "He would rather say something truthful in a clumsy way than lie elegantly." On one of our French bistro meetings, Moritz recounted how the unceasing rain in *One Hundred Years of Solitude* accurately described his experience in Río Verde, one of the world's most sultry places. "On the farm it began raining in 1970, and, let's see . . . it didn't quit until late '73."

Decades later, when Renée and I visited Cuba's hurricane-wracked town of Gibara, I reflected on Moritz's stories of rain, "the tides, the winter storms, the fight to stay alive," and his rap on magic realism, "the ordinary as miraculous and the miraculous as ordinary." We had paused on a sidewalk next to a peeling façade when a man walking down the middle of the street stopped. "You mustn't stand there. Dangerous," he warned. "Always something falling." We looked up. Hurricanes, mold, and mildew had bubbled the plaster, cracked the wall, and melted the ornamentation below the parapets. Among the debris on the sidewalk was a winged creature staring up at me. No hallucination, it was simply a gargoyle loosened from the eaves by the yearly monsoon.

Moritz would have enjoyed such a story, beaming a broad smile while dipping his baguette into another round of French onion soup. A tough-minded hardscrabble guy, he was a good listener, a superb wordsmith, and a splendid storyteller—capable of making your eyes roll from their sockets with his amusing yet tragic tales of the twisted events that led to his leaving the farm he worked so hard to establish. And other stories, too—deeply reflective, bitingly honest—about his battles with Germany in World War II, and battles with his wealthy, overbearing father who berated him at every turn: from boyhood, to his pig-raising attempts in California, and into his Peace Corps years. All of this he would later weave into *The Saddest Pleasure,* and once more—fully fleshed out—into *My Two Wars.*

Moritz said he wanted to go back to Río Verde, say adios to the farm, build a choza on the other side of the river, clear a meadow and blast Bartok and Stravinsky across the jungle—at all those people "who had given me a thousand sleepless nights with their country music." Later he wrote me: "Ah, writing, what a racket. Why do we get so much pleasure out of publicly disrobing?" He spoke of quitting writing to paint, but added that when he tried to draw "Ecuadorian boys standing in tall grass, I could only draw the heads sort of sticking out." A moment of self-effacement, for sure. Moritz was in fact a very gifted pen-and-ink draftsman, as proven by the delicate drawings that graced the pages of *Living Poor*.

In the midst of his plot to liberate himself from the tractor seat and relocate across the river, listen to music, and study such masters as "van Gogh, Picasso, and old Mike Angelo," Moritz also thought about travel. "There is so little time left before the whole fucking planet is homogenized into one little package of margarine that I suppose we should be hysterically looking for spots that still retain something of their own essence. Peru, maybe the Amazon, Bahia maybe, though that is almost lost . . ."

Like the old Japanese poet-wanderers, Moritz wanted to take to the road as a way to stay tuned to the lives and struggles of others. The solitude of the pilgrimage would also provide an opportunity to reflect and size up his own life. In a letter spelling out a possible trip to Brazil, Moritz proposed that I return to South America and make a reconnaissance. "Go by bus to Lima, to Cuzco, to Iquitos, and by boat to Belém with some stopovers in dismal little river towns . . . then to Bahia to recover. Do this first, send me a report, and I will ponder the feasibility of following you."

None of this came to pass. By this time, I'd gone through a divorce, traveled to India, met the Dalai Lama in Dharamsala, and was caught up in the struggle to publish a new book, *A Question of Journey*. My last record of correspondence from Moritz was dated February 1986, when Moritz had written a sympathetic response to one of the numerous rejection letters I shared with him regarding *A Question of Journey*: "Your enclosed letter of rejection was quite disgusting. Gave me the idea of satirizing those jerks—an article in the form a letter to Rabbi Moses rejecting the Bible for publication. At times like this it is comforting to contemplate the 64 rejections of Beckett's first novel. On the other hand there is the possibility that both of us are suffering from the same vice—this debatable premise that what we feel is interesting to others. This subjective approach is certainly the most delicate and dangerous approach."

With one book going the rounds (*The Saddest Pleasure*), Moritz was deep into another, "about combat—combat with my father, combat against Germany." Life in Quito didn't work out; the city had grown enormous since the old Peace Corps days, so Moritz had returned to the coast. "Bought 20 acres, built a shack, settled down to die. No luck. Almost stopped writing but not quite. Smoking one cigarette a day! Well, sometimes two. On my 70th birthday I received a gift from God: fell out of my house and broke my wrist and shoulder. Still can't type with two hands, though I never could with much style."

Years later, largely due to my repeated travels in Southeast Asia, our exchange of letters had fallen off. I learned of Moritz's death through a fellow writer in New Mexico who visited him during his final days in Guayaquil. I had just finished reading *The Saddest Pleasure*, Moritz's account of his Lima-Cuzco-Brazil travels, released by Graywolf Press in 1991, one of the great travel books in the English language. Unsentimental, nakedly illuminating, rich with geographical observations, social insight, and riveting personal reflections, it is an absolutely frank self-portrait of a sixty-three-year-old man undergoing total transformation, frail and candid, swinging between monumental darkness and a stripped-bare bliss where dream, memory, present-tense travel, and personal awakening all converge.

Moritz Thomsen was one of the most honest and generous persons I have known, an enormously talented individual who made my life richer as a man, a friend, and a writer. He was a maverick extraordinaire, living far outside literary circles, keeping true to his own vision, hands in the earth, fingers calloused from plow and typewriter. The jungle, the river, the farm, the road—these were links that bound him more closely to other human beings. The loneliness that Moritz experienced—as an ex-pat in Ecuador and as a solitary traveler on the road—came to represent a fundamental loneliness shared by all humans.

With so much praise in the wind, Moritz is undoubtedly shuddering. I can hear him bellowing, "Enough! Get back to your work." Okay, compadre, I will. Not, however, without raising a toast to your soul searching, your uncompromising passion, your sharp observations and terrific insight, your indefatigable courage to immerse yourself in a life few of us would risk.

Salud!

PLANET PILGRIM, NANAO SAKAKI

Nanao Sakaki, a true counter-culture exemplar, lived in a school bus parked under Taos Mountain for most of the 1980s. Those who never met him often heard rumors about a strange "Japanese beatnik" tramping the outback of New Mexico's northern peaks. Over time Nanao did gain notoriety as the "quintessential Japanese Beat poet," mostly in literary circles. But he wasn't just a roving "Beat" drifting wherever the winds took him. He was a very focused traveler, a cross-cultural pilgrim, foot-sure with personal direction, avidly recording the details of each geography he walked.

Nanao Sakaki was a friend, a fellow wanderer, a planetary pilgrim and a staunch defender of mountains and rivers. As an environmental activist he was keenly in-terested in the particulars of whatever geography he was drawn to: the mountains of China, the reefs of Okinawa, the Aboriginal Dream Lands of Australia, the forests of Tasmania, the Hopi sky villages, the hidden clefts of the Sangre de Cristos. He was much more than the "Japa-nese hippie" so many Americans and Japanese judged him to be.

Nanao was born in 1923 in Kyushu, Japan's southernmost province. His father, in the cloth-dying business, went bankrupt when Nanao was eight: "My first lesson—never trust money." The family practiced Buddhism, though religion always roused suspicion in Nanao. I once asked what sect of Buddhism he favored. With a frown, then a twinkle, he replied: "Maybe white-water sect."

As a twenty-two-year-old draftee during World War II, he was stationed 100 miles south of Nagasaki, where, on one ill-omened day, he picked up a B-29 on the radar screen. Three minutes later a mushroom cloud appeared and the world was no longer the same. After the war, Nanao gave up on mainstream society and dropped out. He took to the streets of Tokyo, lived with friends, read, studied English, held odd jobs and wandered. Exploring mountains, rivers, seashores and city labyrinths, he began to report on his observations through poetry.

From 1955 on, Nanao walked Japan extensively. His wanderings inspired others to quit the competitive neck-break up the corporate ladder, abandon the money struggle, rejoin the natural world, learn the faces of flowers, eat from tide pools, study the soil with farmers. "But one thing," he warned those who might follow his trail, "no matter how many kilometers you have walked, no matter how much knowledge and experience you have returned with, if you can't make a good cup of tea, then you must go back, walk again!"

In the 1960s Nanao founded The Bum Academy, later called Buzoku, or the Tribe. Nanao encouraged members to become intimate with Japan by traveling on foot, as did 17th-century haiku master Bashō on his famous trek, recorded as *Oku no Hosomichi, Narrow Road to the Interior*. The Tribe eventually left Tokyo for the backcountry, set up a communal farm and later extended their experiment to Suwanose, a tiny island in Japan's southernmost archipelago. Subtropical, volcanic, vulnerable to cyclones, the island was sparsely occupied: just a few hardy families eking out a living on the volcanic terrain. Here, the Tribe founded Banyan Ashram and furthered its self-sustaining lifestyle—one of cooperation, mutual aid, "fishing in the ocean ... Building a shelter in mountains ... Farming the ancient way ... Singing against nuclear war."

Around this time Nanao crossed paths with poets Gary Snyder and Allen Ginsberg, with whom he would maintain a lifelong friendship. In 1969 he made his first trip to North America. Mountains, deserts, native peoples and back-to-the-land communities were his focus. In 1971, shortly after I moved to New Mexico, I was introduced to Nanao by Gary Snyder at his home in the California Sierra Nevada mountains—my old stomping grounds. Soon enough, Nanao would be knocking at my door in New Mexico.

It was not just the unusual topography—wind-sheared mesas backed by lofty peaks—that brought him to New Mexico. It was the indigenous cultures and their colorful cycle of ritual-dramas. It was the pioneering spirit of the evolving counter-culture that took root in the Sixties. It was the rich assortment of independent thinkers, especially artists, who had come to live in Santa Fe, Taos and—in the case of Georgia O'Keeffe—in the rugged isolation of the Río Chama Valley. Another draw was the anarchist spirit of northern New Mexico, people with a history of standing up to protect their land, water, language and lifestyles.

Nanao was the very embodiment of crazy wisdom and spirited non-conformism—a proper heir to the old Tang Dynasty poet Li Bo, as well as to the legendary Taoist, Lao Tzu. You might find Nanao talking to a columbine on the slopes of Truchas Peak, or lifting his deep, resonant voice into an impromptu folk song, singing his way along an ancient Chacoan trail. His reputation grew not through a promotional website, beefed up bio, or extensive publication list, but by walking the world, meeting its inhabitants face to face, creating dialogue with the likes of bears, humans, dragonflies and fiddlehead ferns.

Nanao was also heir to the Japanese outrider poets: Saigyō, Ikkyu, Ryōkan and Issa—all who were creative rule-breakers regarding secular or monastic protocol. Their priorities were to get down low, see the world through the eyes of common people, embrace the interconnectedness of all beings. Bashō summed it up: "Keep the mind high in the world of true understanding, yet do not forget the value of that which is low. Seek always the truth of beauty, but always return to the world of common experience."

What Nanao passed on to us was the karma that he inherited: the Japanese idea of a poet taking to the road not for escape or diversion, but as a means of knowing the natural world and its human inhabitants—their plights and struggles—more intimately. As one walked, inspiration for poetry would evolve through humility and curiosity. Nanao rarely commented on the craft of poetry, but once, following a long, dry arroyo toward a prehistoric ruin, he advised: "Keep it simple. What you can't remember doesn't belong." He said he began with a thought, an image, a little story. While walking he fine-tuned its rhythm to breath counts, a circling hawk, the weave of lizard tracks in the sand.

> *Every footprint is a song*
> *the song of life*
> *painted on the sand*
> *painted in the air ...*

A favorite poet of Nanao's was Kobayashi Issa (1763-1827), one of Japan's best-loved haiku masters. Issa's use of the vernacular, his playful juxtapositions of comic and tragic, his focus on the humble and commonplace, his use of lowly images to create striking poetry— these are trademarks that Nanao carried forward in his own poems. In Issa's *Oraga Haru, the Year of My Life*, there is a passage where Issa throws a bundle over his shoulder and hits the trail, writing: "To my great surprise, I noticed that my shadow was the very image of Saigyō, the famous poet-priest of times gone by." When Nanao threw a pack on his back and hit the trail, it was Issa's shadow that followed.

Though Nanao never pretended to be intentionally trying to follow in Issa's footsteps, he did admit that "We live in the same language, but maybe a little different way of expression." A big difference between Nanao and his forebears is that he took an active interest in not just walking watersheds, but in saving them. And saving coral reefs, too. In 1982 he stood up with an environmental coalition against the Japanese government and its plans to increase tourism in southern Okinawa by building an airport over the world's last great blue coral reef. Protests escalated without result until, in 1988, while in San Francisco, Nanao organized poetry readings to raise money for the cause. News of the situation traveled worldwide through the media, and the airport was eventually scrapped.

Around this time, while touring central Australia with Gary Snyder, Nanao became aware of the desecration of sacred Aboriginal sites by American and Japanese multi-national companies. Subsequently, both Nanao and Gary spread the word through their writings and public appearances. In the early Nineties, Nanao was invited to Tasmania to read his poetry and help save virgin forests threatened by a Japanese pulp-paper corporation. Returning to Japan, he stood with poets, scientists, and environmentalists against the damming of the Nagara River. He also demonstrated against Japan's plan for more nuclear power reactors. One can only imagine what role Nanao would have taken as a major figure in counter-culture work had he lived to see the Fukushima disaster, or the proposed fracking of watersheds surrounding his beloved Taos retreat.

Despite his ever-active role in campaigns against

nuclear proliferation, military expansion, the destruction of forests, the damming of rivers, the control of water by industrialists and political embargos preventing free movement of world citizens, Nanao never lost his humor, nor his gift for chanting goodness into the lives of those around him. Perpetually curious, nimble of foot and spirit, he took a crooked walking stick to the straight path and opened a gnarly trail for others to follow.

Wind for mind / Just enough.

On his world itineraries, Nanao would repeatedly visit the American Southwest. I was fortunate to be on his list of people to call on. At that time my little house on the Rio Grande north of Albuquerque served as a good base. One summer I was sitting at my desk when a crack of thunder shook my chair. At the door was Nanao, wearing a big smile: "Time for spine alignment!"

Usually we would bird watch in the bosque along the river. Or head into the high desert: Chaco Canyon, Ashislepah, the Hopi villages, Monument Valley, Cañon de Chelly. Or to the mountains: the Sandias, Jemez, Sangre de Cristos, and further north, along the spine of the Rockies. We would set camp, tell stories, climb a peak, explore a canyon, pick mushrooms, swim, slap mosquitoes, watch a moonflower slowly unspiral at dusk and fall asleep under shooting stars.

In the early 1980s I published *Real Play*, Nanao's first comprehensive book of poems and sketches. We finalized the production under Taos Mountain, sipping a mild hallucinogenic tea. In his introduction to the poems, Gary Snyder wrote: "the subtropical East China Sea carpenter and spear fisherman found himself equally at home in the desert, so much so that on one occasion when an eminent Buddhist priest once boasted to Nanao of his lineage, Nanao responded: 'I need no lineage, I am desert rat.'"

Nanao affectionately described the arid, light-emblazoned Taos highlands as one of his favorite places on earth. "Huge desert meeting high mountain. Same feeling as wide ocean meeting volcano." Once, bedding down in a thin blanket under a scraggly juniper, Nanao peered out at the star-blanketed high desert and exclaimed: "Part dream, but at the same time, part real—very solid."

In his school-bus abode above Taos, Nanao prepared excellent Japanese cuisine over an outdoor wood fire, often supplemented by mushrooms gathered in wet ravines. He wasn't keen on book-learned Westerners' romantic admiration for things Japanese, especially the tea ceremony. His own ceremony consisted of hand-raking a mat of spruce needles around an outdoor fire for his guests to sit on (preferably not in the lotus position) while he boiled water in a banged-up pot dangling from a blackened tripod. Fine quality *sencha* was briefly steeped in a bamboo strainer and poured into whatever mug, cup, or bowl was on hand. The rest followed naturally: slurp in silence, sharpen the senses, listen to a chattering squirrel fight off the jays. Make merry.

Once, Nanao presented me with a Japanese *fundoshi*, a simple, one-piece loincloth. He showed me how to tie it and how to wear it. A few weeks later he asked if I remembered how to tie it. I didn't, so he had me strip and re-learn the art of wrapping. Laughingly, he suggested I wear it to the market next time I went shopping. "No need for air conditioning," he added. "Wearing only *fundoshi*, summer breeze goes right through you!" Leaving Nanao's bus that afternoon, I started down the path, when—like the ghost of the old Chinese hermit-poet, Han Shan—Nanao stuck his head from the door and waved me back. "You forgot your footprint!"

One autumn, Nanao and I were invited to join a Navajo guide for a three-day horseback ride into Monument Valley. Nanao had never ridden a horse. Rising and falling on the back of his Indian pony—pointed beard, knit cap, wool scarf, binocs, canvas jacket and backpack—Nanao looked like an ancient mariner. He compared galloping over the sand to skimming Japan's reefs on a small boat. As the wind became a fierce gale, our guide sniffed the air, buttoned his collar and eyed Nanao with amusement. "Okay, cowboy, let's see how well you take the wind! Let me see you roll a Bull Durham one-handed on a bronc in a blizzard!" Nanao didn't understand a word. He just rode straight into the blowing sand, saying: "I don't mind wind. Wind feeds earth, wind feeds fish. Wind feeds my bones!"

The sun quickly became a rusty blur, and Nanao became a phantom lost in swirling dust. As his horse spooked and whinnied, his comical silhouette tilted to and fro above the saddle. Like a Mongolian shaman disappearing between worlds on his spirit journey, Nanao had become exactly what he often said of himself: "just a shadow."

Later, sipping tea at the campfire he described the feeling of that moment. "I felt my spirit being carried away. A good reason to travel! On horse, on foot, down on knees, you get away from self, you evolve. So many people just looking at magazines, dreaming about a future, never making a change. Just interested in self. No society, no universe."

In 1985 Nanao opened a folder of Kobayashi Issa's haiku that he had been translating into English. Eventually, we selected forty-five of them for publication. Nanao rendered the Japanese characters and his English versions in his own hand. We titled the book *Inch by Inch*, xeroxed 300 copies and sewed them into covers with a group of friends, everybody singing and passing cups of sake. Nanao compared the event to "midwife bringing a child into the world." A favorite haiku in the book:

> *Just as he is*
> *he goes to bed and gets up*
> *—the snail*

Did the snail show Issa how simple life could be lived—no possessions, no unnecessary baggage, no fashions to worry about? "Yes, that's a good understanding," Nanao chuckled. "But maybe Issa also wondered, Why? Why the snail is that way and I am this way? Such a moment makes life wide. Most humans miss the snail. They are too busy filling themselves, going to schools, thinking about money, getting caught in relationships. No need to be slave of each other. Or self, or money, or experience. Always we can jump over experience. When we are separated from our experience we wake up."

On his last visit to New Mexico, in 1998, Nanao seemed fit as ever. His beard had thinned a bit; his white hair, as custom, was pulled into a ponytail under a floppy fisherman's hat. He wore his usual double-stitched walking shorts, from which his sinewy legs found their way into a pair of second-hand Italian hiking boots. His lean but strong frame was clad in a Grateful Dead t-shirt half-exposed under a nylon windbreaker, over which his day-pack was strapped. Knife, binoculars, notebook, fountain pen, plum extract, water bottle, a field guide, and dried fruit—"enough." His eyes twinkled beneath bushy black eyebrows, his walnut-colored face displayed good cheer, smooth and unwrinkled. Not bad for a man nearing eighty who had roughed it around the world!

On that occasion, Renée and I hiked fourteen miles with Nanao into the Sandia Mountains on a trail that gained 3,500 feet as it ascended a 10,000-foot ridge. The altitude bothered him only a little. I asked him why some feel better as they get older. He said age settles us in. "You see more deeply, feel more deeply. So you are lighter. When you are young you are too busy escaping, holding yourself too tightly. When you are old you are not trying to run, not rebelling. You are quieter, you listen. Everything talks to you, all is alive."

We passed clusters of Apache Plume, silvery pink among gnome-like boulders. "Rocks dreaming, maybe of becoming flowers? Me dreaming, maybe of becoming rocks!" Following a tough upgrade through flowering cactus and mountain mahogany, soon turning to thickets of oak and deep stands of ponderosa, Nanao bent low to a patch of wildflowers. "Hello, I know you. But I forget your name. So sorry. Will you tell me who you are?"

Climbing steadily, adjusting the breath, finding pace, Nanao talked about climbing Sakurajima as a boy, an active volcano behind Kagoshima City. He talked about tangling with octopus in the East China Sea, about the bombed landscapes of Japan, unemployment, the postwar times when he survived off of food left on shrines as he wandered. Cresting a final ridge, we met a group of hikers eating their sack lunches. Silently they munched, not knowing what to make of this strange apparition before them. Nanao—wiry, tanned, his beard wisping in the wind—paused and looked far into the horizon over the cloud-dappled eastern plains. "Oh wow! I see New York City. I can see Wall Street. I can see Atlantic!"

A few days later, Nanao and I joined a friend for a meal of shaved daikon, salad and grilled tuna. After a few rounds of stout ale, Nanao suddenly broke out with a wild idea for "completely new language." What he proposed was a minimalist international lingo composed of no more than a thousand words; word clusters, to be exact, like the heads of wild yarrow. Each cluster would consist of "the best, most original expressions to be found in languages like Quechua, Icelandic, Tewa, English, Japanese, French, Tibetan." Nanao proposed that the first word in this new language be taken from the Indonesian: *sama sama*.

"Same same, and at the same time thank you, too. We are all same people. Shakespeare's time. Lao Tzu's time. Chaplin's time. Anasazi's time. You are my face I am your body, *sama sama*. I thank you, you thank me. That is the first word."

This idea of sameness was not just a whim. It was deeply imbedded in Nanao's wartime experience. Before the bombing of Hiroshima, he was a young man at a navy base sending off kamikaze pilots, realizing "this friend is going to die. It's nonsense! No meaning. It's just wasting life. After the war, so many people homeless. My own family moving place to place. But maybe everybody happier because no rich, no poor. Everybody same level. Everybody hungry. Everybody has no house. Everybody same starting line."

Years have passed now. In the June heat, I guide irrigation water into the wells around tomatoes and pole beans. Pink hollyhocks spire between silver chamisa. Tufts of seed float through the air. Grasshoppers buzz through the air, too, the same endlessly hungry critters that Nanao once suggested eating. As I reread my time with him—moments of work and play, nights of silence and song, road trips full of revelation and wisdom—I wonder what closure I could possibly offer? Punctuation doesn't quite fit this pilgrim of sand and sea who compares old age to "sky blue turquoise."

Perhaps the most fitting closure, other than a flake of jasper or a splinter of dinosaur bone, is a poem by Nanao written twenty-some years ago; a reminder that what we see, what we name, how we suppose reality to be, might just as well not be. What is a mountain? How far away? Is it all just illusory suspension of mist and sand, riptide fossilized in the mind's eye?

WHY

Why climb a mountain?
Look, a mountain there.

I don't climb mountain.
Mountain climbs me.
Mountain is myself.
I climb myself.

There is no mountain
nor myself.
Something
moves up and down
in the air.

On the night of the Winter Solstice, 2008, Nanao Sakaki took to the Star Path. He was living simply, as always, in a mountain cabin in Nagano Prefecture, Japan. In just a few days he would have completed his 86th birthday. As reported by friends, he had been of clear mind and good physical shape. He apparently died of heart failure after he lost balance and fell on his way to the outhouse near his cabin. Lots of snow up there. My hunch is that he slipped on ice while having a look at the pre-dawn constellations.

265

He wasn't just headed out to relieve himself, he was already on the trail to the Milky Way.

In his cabin a backpack leaned against the wall—like always, ready to go. His binocs were handy, too. On a shelf were a few books, a field guide, a pair of deer antlers. Above them a chart was pinned to the wall: "Jurassic fossils of Japan." For all of us, Nanao left a beautiful presence, an inspiring body of work, big laughter and song, and exemplary courage to stand up to those who'd rather raze than preserve our planet. Among Nanao's dictums: "Spare eater the wisdom of belly / Jolly worker the wisdom of mind." Add to these: "Coral sand beach as a bed / "Southern Cross as a pillow." Wonder where Nanao sleeps tonight—!

THE COMING OF THE DEER

On the hour's drive from our home in El Rito to Taos—over piñon-dotted hills, down along the Ojo Caliente River, east across the llano—Renée and I meet only a couple of cars. The Sangre de Cristo range, purple in the shadow of the rising sun, graces the eastern sky: a choppy snow-crowned corridor that never tires the eye. To the far north, the iceberg tip of 14,400-foot Mt. Blanca juts above the horizon. Called Tsisnaajin by the Diné, it is one of several sacred peaks that marks the extremes of their homeland. Closer in, the perfect curve of San Antonio Mountain peeks from the plain like a half-risen moon. Southeast, twenty miles as the crow flies, is the horned summit of Ku Sehn Pin, a cardinal peak for the Tewa people.

Just outside Taos, the pale wind-worn llano is cut by the 800-foot-deep Río Grande Gorge. We cross it on a steel bridge where tourists park their cars and stare into the black depths. Selfie sticks, not walking sticks, are the rule. Everyone needs a shot of themselves standing above the hellish chasm of eternity, which will be blocked by their huge smiling faces.

Shortly after crossing the gorge, we leave the main road for a narrow strip of asphalt that curves through the fields toward Taos Pueblo. Here the plain meets the mountains, the grass becomes tall, its shiny tufts washing the steeply-rising foothills. One crest, Taos Mountain, sacred to the Tiwa people who live beneath it, looms conspicuously. It walks slightly forward from the summits and leans to inspect our presence. Satisfied, it retreats with a nod, its solid shape becoming indistinct as it vanishes into the blur of a lowering snow cloud.

The Tiwa village of Taos, along with the Keresan village of Acoma and the Hopi village of Oraibi, is one of the oldest continuously inhabited settlements in the United States—a thousand years or more. Like a sculpted earth altar, its mud walls and flat roofs step tier by tier into the sky. A few turquoise-outlined windows and doors mark the austere façade; a couple of clay-pot chimneys issue curls of smoke. Three stories up, two blanket-wrapped figures sit at the sky's edge, issuing ceremonious calls. At the eastern edge of the village, a low adobe wall divides the human world from the wild. Behind the wall a canyon narrows into clefts of gray stone and jagged fir. This is the Beyond World, an enchanted darkness where bear, lion, elk, and wildcat abide, where sacred Blue Lake shines like an earth-eye in the folds of Taos Mountain.

That mountain—iconic, bold, yet with a softness in its curve—dominates the pueblo. A snow-dusted buffalo's hump, a wave of solidified music, no artist has quite caught it. Marsden Hartley, John Marin, Georgia O'Keeffe came close. But the mountain's charisma, its transcendent presence—a song stilled in midair—continues to elude the science of paint, the sentiment of the painter. Every prayer, every chant offered by the Tiwa villagers during their unbroken cycle of ritual drama has settled in up there, greening the spruce, frosting the cliffs, swirling the mists, energizing the wind, melting the snow to feed the fields. The mountain, spoken to, returns its voice, breathes it back into us individually and collectively. In his book *Mountain Dialogues*, Frank Waters, a dweller under the mountain for decades, equates that voice with *prana*, "a subtle vital energy . . . manifested as the breath of life . . . a microcosmic manifestation of the macrocosmic rhythm to which the whole universe moves."

From the mountain, into the willows, and out under a small wooden bridge, a stream courses through a deliberately left-bare expanse that bisects Taos Pueblo into two ceremonial halves. The space is like a huge baked-earth drumhead stretched taught. Stepping into it you enter a topographical silence. The ground rises, the sky comes down. You hear the drumming of your mind, the tangled thoughts that need be shed to stand quietly and imbibe the rhythm of the mountain: the "vital effluence, vibration, chemical exhalation" described by D. H. Lawrence in *The Spirit of Place*.

Today, Christmas day, the bitingly cold afternoon goes hazy with flickers of mica, snowflakes, blowing cinders, a stray feather. A vortex of air swirls around the fading sun and into the psyche. A pause occurs, a gap, a mental blankness—as if a phonograph needle has been raised from a record. When it is lowered again, I am in a different groove. Out of nowhere comes a tatty group of underworld beings, the sacred clowns. Soot-dark and corn-tasseled, their half-naked bodies are smeared with stripes, their faces given mask-like designs. Except for their protective body paint, they wear only breechcloths. In today's single-digit temperatures, they've thrown blankets over their shoulders, and, with raucous shouts and playful banter, scamper house to house with their mysterious bundles. Always entertaining, they can assume a menacing character, too. At one doorway they persistently rev up their calls until a man appears. Solemnly they usher him to the icy creek, and demand that he strip and bathe. Obligingly, the man disrobes. With a grimace and plenty of fortitude he takes the plunge. The outsider is horrified. Was this a punishment? Baptism? Initiation? The insider shrugs off these interpretations. No explanation is offered to the puzzled visitor.

As quickly as they appeared, the clowns vanish—to where? How did they manage to trick the eye? In their absence I notice a dozen scars of blackened earth where bonfires burned for last night's Christmas Eve celebration, the

Catholic rite where the Blessed Lady is taken from the village chapel of San Geronimo and paraded under the stars. To gunfire, drums, and clanging bells she is carried between towers of flame, wobbling on her palanquin. Stumbling through the darkness follow the torchbearers, musicians, priest, acolytes, dogs, villagers, and tourists.

Today the rite is all Indian. Out of nowhere the clowns reappear, seemingly even darker with clay and carbon than they were before they vanished. There is no question to ask, nothing to figure out at these ceremonies. One accepts, or else suffers the drudgery of mental conjecturing. At a Zuni night-ritual years ago, an Indian man noting my astonishment at what I was witnessing, bent toward my ear: "Pretty good show, eh? It's just an old Indian trick." He was giving the white man a little chuckle and something to think about. He wasn't implying that what I was seeing—a surreal before-dawn appearance of the masked gods wrapped in twenty-below vapors on the roof of a ceremonial house—was a manifestation achieved with sleight of hand. It was the medicine way of the Ancients passed on through generations.

The Taos Deer Dance commences with the assembling of male and female dancers at the pueblo's north end. All takes place in the open. The men wear ribboned shirts, scarves, kilts, trousers; some wear braids and are wrapped with blankets. The women are in long traditional dresses, bare at one shoulder, their backs draped with bright scarves and shawls. Some wear velveteen blouses and skirts; all are adorned with native jewelry and hold evergreen sprigs in their hands. Soon, the clowns are circling them, trying to disrupt their solemn focus. As the dancers gently lift and lower their moccasined feet, the clowns go about their feisty yells. The dancers, about sixty of them, move in two snaking rows in front of a group of male singers. They pay no attention to the pranks of the ritual buffoons—even when they lift a woman's braids and offer a wise crack or tease the men by forcing cigarettes into their mouths. The singers, too, eight or nine of them, remain centered. They clap their hands softly as they chant. Wrapped in blankets, they hunker low to the ground around a man gently keeping time on a hand drum.

The bawdy clowns are far from Barnum & Bailey comedians. They are teachers who test the people's worth, to see if they can maintain focus and unruffled calm when faced with adversity. It's a good lesson for all of us. Soon the clowns fall in line. Instead of dancing out of step and interrupting the dancers, they dance in step and mind their business. They even help readjust the dancers' attire as it loosens. They police the spectators, too, making sure they don't get too close to the ritual participants or to the sacred kivas, or that they don't bear any concealed cameras or phones. From place to place the dance moves around the village. Then, suddenly, it stops.

Dozens of animals are beginning to emerge from their ceremonial chambers. Not only from the smoky far end of the village do the deer, buffalo, and elk appear, but from the "far end" of a supernatural past. In slow file they march west through the pueblo, toward the red smudge of sun lowering over the whitewashed chapel of San Geronimo. The deer antlers are "snow-dusted" with puffs of eagle down fluttering in the mist. The impersonators—boys and men—are bent and blackened, faces hardly visible under the still-bloody skins of the freshly-slaughtered deer. They are not actors, but "gone beyond" inhabitants of the animal spirit stepping ahead on all fours, their hands braced on sticks held out from the hides to represent the animal's front legs. They are one with the deer whose abode is the heart of the forest, the dark temple of the mountain, the inner imprint of the body's nomadic past.

All of this carries forward a cyclic calendar whose

fertility rites survive from millennia-old rituals meant to keep the world in balance. The animals have stepped from the mountains, answered the calls of the villagers, availed themselves to the hunt. Voices high-pitched and thin, they bear the sound of a woody inner sanctum, a resting place of psychic energy, the breath of the gods—a place devoid of the unpredictable violent actions of human beings.

As the animals pass, there is a powerful smell from the raw skins. The open eyes in the deer and buffalo heads are glassy with a spooky outward stare. A few eyes are missing, leaving only haunted begrimed holes in the heads. A few tongues, still freshly pink, loll from blackened lips. Some of the mouths are stuffed with fir sprigs. The deer walk lightly; the buffalos lumber, nodding their heavy heads. The observer watches, brought into the realm of the Great Hunt. This is no boisterous herd charging forward; it is a solemn array of beasts—wild meat, sacred heat—slowly parading forward to meet the slayer with his spearpoints. Only with acute attention does the observer, thoroughly drawn into the ritual, realize the shaggy buffalo heads are propped upon men, sweating and grunting, clumsily trying to maintain balance as they trudge into the circle of villagers gathered at the San Geronimo chapel. The church is hardly important. Nothing Spanish or Christian dominates this ceremony. The only god watching is Taos Mountain.

The clowns, meanwhile, have ignited a signal fire of resinous pine, fanned it into a blaze, and smothered it with evergreen branches. A pall of incense rolls through the pueblo. As the Deer Dance gathers energy, one is transported into a mytho-magic realm. Inside the circle of villagers, two Deer Mothers, wrapped in white buckskin, move slowly, elegantly, through the raucous clowns who've become Paleo-hunters, ochre-darkened, eyes circled with black. They aim tiny symbolic bows and arrows at the deer, uttering weird ghost-animal cries that add a shiver to the spectator already suffering the piercing cold.

The Deer Mothers are crowned with parrot and eagle feathers, their cheeks painted with circles from which lines extend toward their chins. Trancelike, they move through the chaos of the hunt, arms bent at the elbows, raised to the sky, one hand with a small gourd rattle, the other holding a pair of eagle feathers. Poised so, they replicate the figures in the 800-year-old petroglyphs on the bluffs along the Río Grande. They also evoke the Siberian Animal Mothers carved by archaic hunters: potent half-woman, half-deer fertility figures; apt symbols for birth and regeneration.

An occasional shake of the Deer Mother's rattle over the animals energizes their movement, although the design of their choreography is hard to discern in a circle so tightly packed. Among the deer and buffalo a shaggy-skinned creature appears from the chaos, moving directly toward me—and only me, it seems. I avert my eyes. Coyote? Puma? The skin is chafed and warped. The impersonator—knobby-kneed, darkened with grease—hobbles under it, either an old man or a gangly adolescent. He leans on his foreleg sticks, shaking side to side as he comes forward, eyes spinning vacantly into another world. I resume my focus on the Deer Mothers—a dignified counterpoint to this eerie ghost, and to the yowling clown-hunters who scuffle and change direction erratically. They aim their arrows, make an occasional kill, sling the deer over their shoulders, and try to escape with their prey through the spectators. They often fail, halted by two Deer Captains standing at the edge of the circle who recapture the deer and release them back into the ring.

All the while, wavering ripples of Tiwa song reverberate from the chorus of singers and their drummer. Two files of men and women are dancing to the side of the deer and Paleo-hunters, the same ones who danced earlier at the pueblo's north end before the deer appeared. The tone of the singers' chant is soft, at times just a whisper oscillating from their bodies—*uumm uuummm uuummmm*—a mountain mantra slithering from a cliff hollow, the voice of timeless antiquity, beast and human inseparable. As the hunt comes to a close, many animals have been "killed," carried across the river, back into the folds of Taos Mountain to replenish the wild. Inside the circle enough deer remain unharmed to assure plentiful meat for the winter.

"This dance . . . is as ancient as the earliest human efforts at sympathetic magic," wrote Erna Fergusson in *Dancing Gods*. Ninety years later it goes on. A thousand years ago, 10,000 years ago, 40,000 years ago it perhaps came to be. The deer taken are "given" for sustenance; the deer allowed to remain are regenerative presences inside the circle of life. As the ritual begins to close, two hunters break rank and place bits of raw venison into the open mouths of the assembled villagers. This primal rite of communion is punctuated by a nod from the Deer Mother's rattle, at which the animals bend to their knees, then rise to a similar shake of the rattle—a genuflection to the life-giving forces of mountain, cloud, wind, and sun.

After the dance, a Taos villager waves us into her house. "Get warm!" There is only a sleeping room and a tiny kitchen. Piñon logs glow in a fireplace molded into a corner of the earthen walls. She turns up the wick of her lantern, fetches two enamelware bowls, and ladles up a steaming meal of stew. "Venison," she smiles. At the table is another guest who has been quiet except for the occasional movement of a cane poking out from her shawl. She is the woman's mother, and when she finally speaks she tells us she danced the Deer Dance as a young woman. "Now I am too old, but no matter, it has been passed on. There are more dancers than ever today. More deer, too, and more buffalo."

When Renée and I exit, we do so with warm good-byes and warm stomachs. Beginning our drive home, we pass a buffalo herd grazing the snowy pastures north of the pueblo, a vast grassland sweeping into the deep forests that rise to meet the misty tundra below the high peaks. Among them, Taos Mountain wears a tiara of suspended snow crystals. This is Indian land, the unspoiled land of centuries ago. And centuries ago is now. Today's ceremony is the center point where we all dance as one. "It gets in, doesn't it," Renée contemplates.

And then our voices blend: People travel to the other side of the world to see such ceremonies, but here we have just stepped from a place unlike anywhere else in the world. This is the other side. This is home.

El Rito, 2020

IV.
Uncommon Country: an afterword

Imagination goes with us on our journey, a thrilling and often beautiful companion. Modern purposefulness gives place to plurality of sensation; explanation is shamed—if not always silenced—by mystery. The traveler simultaneously sheds and receives. Those who have never arrived in the unknown without credentials, without introductions to the right people, or the wrong ones—have missed an exigent luxury.

Shirley Hazzard

FINDING NEW MEXICO, 1971

New Mexico's outback—remote, eccentric, idiosyncratic—isn't a place you can easily set out for and make your own. One can relocate and live a lifetime in the state as a non-native and hardly make a blip on the screen compared to the scope of history shared by the Pueblos and their ancestors, or the four hundred years of Hispanic presence. One does not purposefully "adjust" to this reality, but instead settles in and gradually becomes part of the flow. The Río Grande is somewhat of a metaphor for this merge. Depending on the season, the river may be running chocolate, Mars red, or blue green, revealing both the mix of soils feeding it and the temperament of intersecting weather patterns that nourish it.

What strikes me, after living fifty years in New Mexico, is how truly magical it is when a place—after a certain amount of courting goes on—finally accepts you, allows you in, not on your terms, but under its own conditions. For this to happen you have to be open, submissive, unafraid, free of expectations, and ready to receive. When the courting is over and the knot has been tied, you realize: this is a marriage; I am bound to a relationship, to this Other that has embraced me. Resilience and respect are key—a certain flexibility to bend with the wind, ride the volatile storms, step aside of the flashfloods. Adaptability is called for, a non-reactive bounce that assures no blame for what doesn't go right, and plenty of humor for what goes wrong.

In 2017, in preparation for the "Voices of Counterculture in the Southwest" exhibit at the New Mexico History Museum, participants were asked: What, exactly, drew you and others of the Sixties Generation to New Mexico? The request led me to investigate where, precisely, the momentum began—not an easy task, given that a true journey usually has its origins in the mists shrouding the less-obvious sources. Retracing my personal history, I see a not-quite-definable uplift, a place apart from the rest of the United States, that drew me, much in the same way a mythic center compels one to migrate. Circling that center, one eventually zeros in, only to have it become real: a psychic as well as physical place aloof from the commons, off radar, above the dust.

In spring 1971, friend and fellow poet Ed Kissam sold me his vintage 1953 Chevy pickup for the grand sum of $150. A gift, really, a steal—one that got me on the road from California to New Mexico. Fifty years later, on a classic northern New Mexico autumn afternoon, Ed and I popped the cork of a California cabernet and sat down to mull over the era I refer to as "The Great Unloosening," otherwise known as the Sixties—how our poetic wanderings were part of a bigger, broader shift of social consciousness. As we set out to explore places where old and new cultures mingled, it became evident that poetry, politics, and history were intertwined. As poets we had been turned on to a new language, one central to understanding the direction our lives were taking. As Ed summarized: "Allen Ginsberg's blockbuster *Howl* repositioned personal anguish as part of 20th-century real-world life; Gary Snyder's sharp-eyed, deeply grounded travels through his trans-Pacific world opened our view to China and Japan; and Michael McClure had a wild, elegant, graceful way of linking human passions not just to planet earth, but to the Milky Way, the galaxy."

Young people were leaving the cities for rural callings: the Sierra foothills, the Vermont woods, the Colorado Plateau, the Maine coast, the Cascades; any roost, inlet, vale, or mountain that afforded a view into a world much wider than one imagined—realistically, metaphorically. If you were a poet, such an all-encompassing view couldn't be matched by rhymed couplets or a mannered classroom approach to wordsmithing. Open lives, open landscape required open verse. Why not allow topographic features—a cinder cone, sea-washed stack, slickrock dome; even silos, tombstones, highway markers—to become typographic projections on the page? Each landscape had a certain speech, twang, susurration. As did the characters who inhabited the landscape. Old-school metric conventions couldn't hold the rough-cut lingo of a bronc rider. The cloud-like joining of fingertips as Indians greeted each other and began a soft exchange in their native tongues—you had to find a new form for that. A blowing tumbleweed hopped and crackled, paused, then jumped into the sky with a twist of wind. The suck of a mudhole after a thunderstorm had its cadence. So did the ghost voices of Pawnee ponies clattering through the mountains from the plains. Trance songs of the peyote cult, drummers chanting a buffalo stomp, the rasp of wooden matracas from a darkened Penitente morada during Holy Week; you listened and the sound kept you present, moved the rest of the world out of sight.

In the cities protestors filled the streets, universities were in chaos. Powerful revolutionary language was needed to confront the escalating war in Vietnam, the outrage over Nixon's secret bombing of Cambodia, the cracked-open heads, the napalmed children, the mangled soldiers, the burning ghettos, the vengeful madmen in government meeting rooms. Dylan described them in "Masters of War"; Shelley in his preface to "Alastor": "Men who are morally dead, neither friends, nor lovers, nor fathers, nor citizens of the world, nor benefactors of their country."

In 1969 half a million people marched on Washington. In 1970 four student protestors at Kent State were killed by National Guardsmen, and two more at Jackson State. The shootings galvanized the country against the war, but four more years would pass before the Fall of Saigon. The outspoken poets of the Beat Generation shone brightly during these times, as did the voices of Denise Levertov, Robert Duncan, and Robert Creeley with their idiosyncratic ways of explaining the world. At the headwaters was Ezra Pound, the modernist who overturned poetic meter and genteel literary style with his dictum: *Make it New!*

I set out for the American Southwest in 1971, but I've decided to turn back a few pages and write from a period slightly previous. Really, this account began as a story for my children, now in their fifties, and for their children. The "Voices of Counterculture" exhibit in Santa Fe was a big inspiration, but the real boost happened during a phone conversation with Gary Snyder just before he came to speak at the exhibit. When I mentioned that my grandchildren hadn't ever asked about how I got to New Mexico or what the times were like, he answered: "Well, sometimes you don't wait for the question. You just have to begin telling the story."

Here, then, is a bit of that tale.

❧

In 1968, three years before packing up the little blue Chevy pickup and heading east from the Sonoma County wine country to New Mexico's high desert, I was a Peace Corps Volunteer beginning my third year in the Andes, despite the hassles of a draft board thousands of miles away, one that protestors had bombed the day after the U.S. bombed the outskirts of Saigon. Vietnam was out of control, President Johnson was ordering all draft-eligible males to fight. To abandon the peace work I entered by choice for a war I didn't believe in was unacceptable. A few volunteers in my situation had already escaped into South American cities. One fed-up amigo hiked up a hill in Ecuador and shot his trigger finger off. Attorneys assigned to draft-eligible volunteers made scant headway in battling for our rights. The C.I.A. had come on the scene, infiltrating our work, our parties, our personal lives. Shady characters posing as hippies, evangelists, and geologists were scoping out war dissidents and pro-Cuba, pro-Allende leftists.

Tired of the harassment, I opted to use my accrued vacation days and take a month's breather: bus, taxi, and hitch the Andean corridor to Machu Picchu, cross the Bolivian altiplano by rail, catch a lorry to the Atacama Desert, head south to the Chilean archipelago. I was just beginning to read Pablo Neruda, and it was a privilege to have his poems in hand while traveling the geography that so deeply permeated them. Nathaniel Tarn's translation of *Alturas de Macchu Picchu* was in my pack as I hiked from the Río Urubamba up to the 15th-century Incan city. In those days, one could actually get away with sleeping in the ruins. At the top, I broke bread with an Argentine couple who had already laid out their bedrolls. They offered cheese and wine, I added a baguette and hard salami. By firelight we read Neruda's poetry under the stars, a fitting dessert for our modest feast.

In the morning Machu Picchu was all mist and gliding raptors, silvered stone and towering thrones. "Green stardust, crowned solitudes, a new level of silence," wrote Neruda. Indeed, I was in "the condor's shadow, between cliffs and rushing waters," trembling not from the morning chill, but from the joy of a journey that was already beginning to yield personal inquiries, chance meetings with strangers, and a romance with a woman who embraced the open road with enthusiasm that matched my own. When the journey ended in southern Chile, I stared into an open sea and thought: I could live here, quit the country that raised me on perpetual war. Follow Neruda's example, craft a home, celebrate the hidden connections between conscious and unconscious landscapes, allow my poetry to take its course. It was a dream not to be realized in Chile, but it would eventually mature in New Mexico.

Returning to Ecuador, I opened my postal box to yet another Selective Service notice: ORDER TO REPORT FOR ARMED FORCES PHYSICAL EXAMINATION. I would be flown, at taxpayers' expense, to a U.S. base in Panama for the exam. I boarded the plane in a white shirt, pressed jeans, and polished oxfords. My satchel, however, held unlaundered clothes. My arrival in Panama City coincided with one of the country's many political uprisings, this time a coup d'état to overthrow the president, who had been given refuge at the base where I was to have my physical. Panama City was sweltering and tense. I ducked bottles and rocks to get to my hotel. The U.S. military base was also tense. I walked in—unshowered, wearing frayed sweatpants, a sweat-ringed T-shirt, and flip-flops—and defiantly bared my half-burnt draft card. None of this roused any attention, not even purposely flunking the intelligence tests. Officers younger than me smirked. "Brandi, you're a sorry son of a bitch. Get your ass back to Quito and wait for your orders!"

In Ecuador, I wanted time to consider my situation. A sympathetic Peace Corps rep met my needs and allowed me a transfer to the rainforests east of the Andes. I'd work with the Jívaro (Shuar) people along the Río Zamora as a liaison between the tribe and the Ecuadorian government to help negotiate a community school. The opportunity offered isolation and contemplation. The Jívaros still maintained their traditional lifestyle, lived in pole-frame longhouses, hunted, trapped fish, and enjoyed the use of *banisteriopsis caapi*, a medicinal plant locally known as *yagé* or *ayahuasca*. But all was on the brink. Christian missionaries were offering a new god, free concrete-block homes for the converted, a hoe, and a cow. Once given their prize, most of the converted left the hoe to rust, moved the cow into the house, and slept and cooked outside.

A few weeks into my stay, Taisha, a young shaman, approached me and asked if I would like to "dream" with a small circle of his people. With hidden excitement and a fair amount of apprehension, I agreed. Taisha's invitation to a healing ceremony incorporating *ayahuasca* came as a complete surprise. I was in my early twenties, wasn't much of a marijuana smoker, and had yet to try LSD. Taisha told me to fast, remain quiet for the day, and come to his longhouse at dusk.

I entered to a half-dozen men and women sitting around a man who was to be cured of chest and leg spasms. Rain pattered the thatch, the only sound save for the movement of two shadows tending coals at either end of the hut. The embers were to be kept tamped so as not to allow even the slightest flicker to disturb the trance flight of the participants. After ingesting the *ayahuasca,* a lull followed. The patient, wearing only a breechcloth, then stood to allow two female attendants to massage the "poison" down his body and out. The participants circling him were attendants, too, sending him energy while looking into themselves. Before the ritual, Taisha had asked me who I wanted to visit. I thought of my mother. But she did not appear. Instead, came a violet-green supernova that faded into a gaseous vortex from which emerged a perfect earth shape. My mother, after all?

A few months later, I scrapped my thinking of going deeper into the rainforest to escape the draft. I was already ill from skin infections, anemia, sores that wouldn't heal, and a repetitive diet of starchy cassava. One morning a care package for the village arrived by canoe, sent by the Bishop of Zamora. When the crate was opened, it revealed not the expected tins of tuna and bags of rice, but hundreds of plastic squeeze-strips of restaurant ketchup. The Jívaros unhappily divvied them up. Halfway back to my quarters, jittery with low blood sugar, I opened my share, pressed the ketchup onto my palm, and licked it up like a mad animal.

My stay along the Río Zamora was pleasurably cut short when I met Gioia Tama Gianni, a native of Buenos Aires who was visiting her father in Guayaquil. She had come to see a friend in the mountain town of Loja where I kept an apartment as a retreat from the rainforest. One afternoon she knocked at my door and introduced herself. With a twinkle in her eye, she said she hoped I might have information on the Galapagos Islands, and a contact for marijuana. I told her I might be able to help her with the grass, but not the Galapagos. She suggested we talk further and asked if I wanted to have dinner with her and her friend, Gerard, who taught French at the Alianza Francesa. *"Con gusto,"* I said, but added that I already had a date with someone who had knocked on my door earlier. Lynette, a Columbia University anthropology student who grew up in Toulouse, was doing research in Ecuador, and was "looking for something to do" that evening. *"Pues, bring her, too,"* Gioia smiled.

The meal was a classic *steak au poivre*, flambéed with cognac, served with asparagus and fresh bread. When I remarked how Ecuador's lousy beef never tasted so good, Gerard raised a glass. "That's because it's Argentine. The French Embassy flies it in from Buenos Aires." To which Gioia raised another glass. "And the wine is flown in from France." Several empty bottles lay on the floor at the end of the night. Lovely Lynette lay in Gerard's arms, Gioia in mine. After a brief courtship we were married in a civil court in Loja. We had a long rambling plan to travel South America, but when I learned that the $75 monthly Peace Corps stipend for my years of service wouldn't be paid until I returned to the U.S., practicalities began to weigh. With only $400 between us, we bagged South America for the north.

Our flight to L.A. on a lime-green Braniff Airlines DC-8 was routed through Mexico City where there was a plane change. In typical Sixties fashion, when spontaneity ruled, we devised a new travel plan. At the airport we approached the Mexican staff at the Braniff counter—everything painted hot pink, one of the featured colors that year. The all-women staff wore hot pink shorts, blouses, boots, and eyeliner to match. Everybody was friendly and with a little persuasion we got a refund for the Mexico-L.A. leg. With computers absent and human personalities at the forefront, congenial exchange seemed easier in those days. Our refund afforded us two bus tickets, plus meal and hotel money to sightsee northern Mexico. A slow entry to the States was preferable to banging down on a runway and having to do a quick biological reset. The bus would allow us to enjoy the gradual change from the subtropics to the Sierra Madre to the Sonoran Desert to the green California coast.

My parents welcomed us warmly. When I announced our plan to drive my old VW bug north to Alaska, my father sanctioned the idea and bought four new tires for the car. As a World War II vet, he held no animosity toward his draft-defiant son. Vietnam was a dead end, it bore no relation to the Allied effort he participated in to save the world from fascism. My mother, though, was uneasy. She fretted over my notion to visit the parish priest to have him sign my request for Conscientious Objector status: a last resort in my obligatory draft protest. "This isn't a seventh-grade revolt against a teacher," she cried, "you're a grown man defying the government!" What would the church-goers say, and the flag-flying neighbors! Determined, I called on the priest, anyway. The rectory door was opened by a pimply man I recognized as a sanctimonious kid from early school days. Father O'Brien appeared, sat me down, gave me a glass of water, and instantly denied my request: "The Church has no history of support for conscientious objectors. The Vatican won't authorize me to sign this."

In Juneau, Alaska, we holed up for seven months. Gioia was pregnant, working in a bakery; I went from car-pentry to truck driving to cannery work. When that ran out, I shoveled snow until the Welfare Department found me a job. I was to work in Nome as a probation officer with Inupiat authorities to supervise offenders arrested for sell-ing contraband liquor to Native Americans. Uh? The Wel-fare Department must have tallied some far-fetched equation relating my work with Native peoples of Ecuador to what I might accomplish with Native peoples of Alaska. The salary would be considerable. My parents celebrated. They insisted on sending me the only formal attire I ever owned, my high school graduation suit. When it arrived, I tried it on for size. It wasn't only the suit that didn't fit, it was the job.

The continuing draft harassment didn't fit either. A lawyer provided by the American Friends Service Commit-tee said I had no legitimate case as an ex-Peace Corps Vol-unteer to refuse induction. We paid our rent, packed the bug, and headed south on the Alcan Highway. Ice crept up the inside of the windshield, the heater barely got the car above freezing—my fault for not installing the de-rigor auxiliary heater native Alaskans had suggested. It was 55-below our first night in the Yukon. In the morning, the car wouldn't start. When I tried to engage the gear shift, it broke. The brakes were frozen, the steering wheel, too. The car had to be towed to a garage, thawed, and repaired.

Blowing snow followed us south, not a patch of soil visible for 2,400 miles until we got to Redding, California, where Gioia, seven months pregnant, announced "I want to have my baby in Spanish. Let's go to Mexico."

Two thousand miles later we found refuge in the temperate surrounds of Lake Chapala where D.H. Lawrence arrived in 1923 and began writing *The Plumed Serpent*. Somerset Maugham and Tennessee Williams followed. In Ajijic, a lakeside village of cobbled streets, there was a long-established Bohemian scene. A *casita* could be had for $25 a month. Farmers worked the fields, families netted fish, a street market sold fresh produce, meat, spices, edible cactus, medicinal herbs, and occasional bundles of *lophophora williamsii*, its tapered, carrot-like roots nestled between dried oregano and fresh cilantro. An art gallery put up my drawings; Gioia crocheted apparel for Puerto Vallarta tourists. Our daughter Giovanna was born strong and healthy, with dual citizenry, in a Guadalajara hospital.

To supplement my meager art sales, I worked in an expat community as a gardener (until I pruned an orange tree too close), then delivering oxygen to an invalid (until he died). Finally I got a job as a translator. A retiree relocating to Chapala needed someone to deal with the Mexican *aduana* to retrieve her belongings, crated and shipped separately. Among them was her prized Karmann Ghia. It had been dispatched from Los Angeles to Guadalajara in a boxcar, but got lost along the way and the rail officials couldn't find it. A mess for my employer, but it would mean extra hours and pay for me. Each visit to the railway was a time-consuming bureaucratic tangle, until the car was finally located and rerouted to Guadalajara. After signing papers we were escorted to the boxcar. The door was pulled open, and there stood the precious Ghia, front and rear crumpled like an accordion. The wheels hadn't been blocked and the car had been slamming back and forth for

2,000 miles. The owner let out a wail. I steadied her with an arm. For the next month, I dealt with claims adjusters, found a body shop, and paint to match the car's Neptune Blue. It was good money, right up until our tourist visas ran out, which meant a return to the U.S.

In California, I was a step ahead of the draft board which had yet to process my change of address from Alaska to Mexico. I would now submit a new address from the northern Sierras where we landed a job caretaking a one-room cabin on a ridge above the Yuba River, part of an 1800's gold dig called the Grizzly Mine. A $55 monthly stipend helped with groceries and propane to run the fridge and stove. Around us, the woods were filling with emigrants, including Gary Snyder, who had recently returned from Japan and was building an off-the-grid house with his wife, Masa.

There was good chemistry among a young, divergent set of freethinking newcomers, everybody eager for dialogue and the hard work of homesteading. The sound of hammers and saws filled the woods. Political and environmental discussions were shared over collaborative meals. Music, poetry, and sessions of Zen sitting offset mental musings. Snyder put Gioia and me in touch with Steve Sanfield, poet and storyteller, and Jacquie Bellon, a talented French-Vietnamese artist and buoyant conversationalist. Both would remain vital companions. Those who could afford it bought land. My Peace Corps stipend gave us enough to make an offer on a meadow with a small house. When we were outbid by $1,000 and a kilo of grass, I began to rethink things. Something was pulling me outward from the circle, a psychic shift that often haunted me as a teenager: to simply pick up and go, no established reason.

My shelf was filling with books on the American Southwest: John Wesley Powell's *Exploration of the Colorado*

River and Its Canyons; Ed Abbey's *Desert Solitaire;* Frank Waters' *People of the Valley* and *The Man Who Killed the Deer,* both set in northern New Mexico. At the 3R's bookstore in Grass Valley, I bought Adam Clark Vroman's *Southwest Photographs,* Erna Fergusson's *Dancing Gods,* and *Sun Chief: The Autobiography of a Hopi Indian.* One lucky day, I found volume nine of the Smithsonian *Handbook of North American Indians*—600 pages of text and photos devoted to the tribes of the Southwest. Driving home, we stopped for gas in North San Juan when a Willys jeep pulled up with a New Mexico license plate. The driver, Steve Beckwitt, was returning to California with his family from a canyon east of Taos. When I mentioned our plans for a Southwest exploration, he suggested we visit the canyon. "Beautiful land, plenty of water, National Forest all around. But it was too remote for us."

We soon left the Sierras for the Sonoma coast, a place called Dry Creek, where I found work in the vineyards and a free house to live in. We'd now have extra funds for travel. At this time I decided to legally declare my opposition to the Vietnam War and refuse induction. Plenty of men were doing the same; the courts were jammed, so were the jails. Months would pass before I would have to appear in court. Then came the unthinkable. The court date was set for December, a month after my twenty-sixth birthday, the age in the pre-lottery draft when men were automatically exempt from service. Karma had stepped through the door. I was a free man.

One day, returning to Dry Creek with groceries, we noticed something on our doorstep. Steve Beckwitt, now living in the Sierras, had stopped by with Gary Snyder, who had tucked two tickets under a rock, with a note: "a stone from the White Mountains." We had been invited to a poetry reading he was giving in San Francisco with David Monongye, a Hopi elder. The event was a perfect sendoff for our Southwest journey. Two days later, we headed east in our pickup, now outfitted with a tin-topped wooden camper. In the White Mountains we halted and placed Gary's stone under a 4,000-year-old bristlecone pine. A thank you and an homage. Our Southwest journey had officially commenced.

❧

The engine drums, but silence echoes inside my head. The trees pass, the rocks pass, a deer leaps, thoughts rise. "Each day is a journey, and the journey itself is home," to quote Bashō's famous opening of *Oku No Hosomichi*. The big steering wheel of our compact truck steadies my hand. Gioia is at my side, our two-year-old daughter, Giovanna, asleep on her lap. We've slowly crested the Sierra Nevada and dropped into Basin and Range country, a wind-hammered expanse of mountains and playas. The straight-six engine is efficient on gas and wastes nary a drop of oil. A sane unhurried way to go, it has us overnighting not at stops planned by AAA travel agents for speed-thirsty V8s, but between such stops. Places unheard of: Ubehebe, Pahrump, Orson's Well, Paradox.

In a jagged, rust-colored upthrust of mineral hills—one of dozens of transverse ranges chiseled into Nevada's chrome-blue sky—we halt, pull out the bedrolls, and set camp. The afternoon cools, low-moving clouds pattern the sand. A swig of spring water dashed with psilocybin mushrooms, and shapes and colors begin to heighten. The clouds, cartoon-like at first, morph into ominous atomic clouds: dark, boiling hallucinogenic reminders of the 1950's nuclear tests staged in this desert. Ones that spelled infection and death for thousands of military personal ordered to witness the inferno up close, and radioactive contamination for millions of civilians as the fallout blew east, all the way to the Atlantic.

We spend days camped among islands of naked slickrock. As the past slips away, a new imprint takes its place: a pale vacuum of sky, a bounteous expanse of quicksilver earth, a spare desert rubbed by wind, tufted by a long vanished sea. With the heat beating right through them, the mountains are see-through, a pinkish-bronze champagne. Whenever we cross one range into the next, the brink of something irregular is exposed: an edge where the mind drops off into a physiological collision of planes, a tortoise-shell mosaic, its timelines dark crystal, its bloodstreams garnet. The horizon is pure, no charts left by those gone before; only wild stretching sand, the chinked walls of a cliff dwelling, maybe a shaman's painted notation on the underside of an overhang. Breath of song in stone. A toe print in mudrock becoming fossilized.

After crossing the Colorado River, we loop up onto the Hopi mesas. The bone-dry sky has the *tinng* of a metal wand on a triangle. A lone buzzard rides a thermal, not a wingbeat to break its glide. We pass villages that need a strain of the eye to detect them: Moenkopi, Hotevilla, Oraibi—flat stone rooflines shelved into gold sandstone. Three more villages—Mishongnovi, Sipaulovi, and Walpi—grow right out of the bluffs, their cubical rock-and-clay dwellings, ceremonial plazas, and sacred kivas held outward into pure space as if in the palm of a hand.

The desert unfurls like a Chinese scroll, but instead of mossy green peaks with a zigzag trail vanishing into mist, gray volcanic cones rise from a baked brown platter scarred with a thin line of pavement fading into dust. Whatever awaits beyond this raw expanse of silence, it has already begun to fill me. Not as an unknown, but as something conversant. I take out paper, brush, a tin of watercolors. The desert breathes, blinks, and trembles. All that moves out there—synclines, anticlines, hoodoos, laccoliths—moves inside me. The land defines the seer, makes a verb of the brush, bends light into melody, loosens color from turrets of stone. As I sketch, a far-off glimmer reveals itself in the haze: a triangular façade of snow. It must be Nuva'tukya'ovi, the mountain home of the Hopi gods. Fervor and resolve is what I feel; that I can give myself over to the unsteady horizon glinting in the heatwaves.

In southern Colorado, a June blizzard—red dust and corn snow—pelts us as we hurriedly set camp southeast of Durango, on the edge of the Ute Reservation. The land is owned by a friend who has offered us unlimited stay. After a week of local forays, we decide Colorado doesn't fit the bill. With its big barns, white-railed fences, and plush ranches backed by calendar-worthy mountains, it is too picture-perfect. Gated communities for the well-to-do, A-frame second homes, faux log cabins, mining towns remaking themselves for tourists and ski buffs, and the biggest town, Durango, already wired for a population explosion. What I had in mind was the tough beauty Ed Abbey described in *Desert Solitaire:* the "bare bones of existence, the elemental and fundamental bedrock which sustains us."

We thanked our host, drove east following the San Juan Mountains to Pagosa Springs, took a hard right south, crossed a forested summit, and descended into New Mexico. A rustic sign announced LAND OF ENCHANTMENT. "Enchant," according to my Webster's: *to charm, sing one closer, rouse to ecstatic admiration.* The territory was spunky. Green at first, but as we descended the asphalt got rough, cows nibbled weeds in the potholes, road signs didn't make sense: PASS, when you were about to crest a hill; DO NOT PASS when the horizon was empty. The land— dark, timeworn, boulder strewn—had taken a break from evolution to conduct its own dissonant symphony. Knife-edged mesas leaned and fell into one another as if gravity couldn't make up its mind. Unlike the vertical rise of Colorado, New Mexico stretched horizontally. It roiled and buckled into a weave of sienna and ochre streaked with violet: a Navajo eye-dazzler, ridges and valleys pulled taut into zigzag threads of time.

Rubbing my eyes, opening them fully, my pulse slowed to a different tempo. To the east, a brow of snow peaks above dark anvil-shaped mesas. To the west, a flint-edged butte and a blown-out volcano. I ran my fingers over the topography—sandy yellow, umber, chalk-gray—as if tracing the papery skin of a horned lizard. Shifting out of gear, I let the truck coast around a long bend of sandstone cliffs. Rain and wind softened, they exposed bright, over-saturated Kodachrome hues like those in the Santa Fe Railway brochures I collected as a boy.

We passed villages not there. You didn't see them from the color of the earth until a sunbeam shot from a tin roof and a clutch of low adobes appeared, circling a mud-block church. Little details came into focus as we drove near: flaps of drying laundry, flits of mountain bluebirds, a magpie's hop and skuttle, red geraniums in a turquoise window, swallow nests lining an empty steeple. Swooned by each sidetrack, we spent a week driving what we could have done in a few hours: the Río Chamita, the Brazos, Mesa de los Viejos, and a track of coral dust that petered out in the creamy bluffs surrounding the Monastery of Christ in the Desert.

Here, a fledgling community of Benedictine Trappists had raised a communal hall, kitchen, library, and monks' quarters with the help of nearby villagers. An earthen chapel, humble yet eye-catching in its modern design, blended into the terra-cotta cliffs. Even its sharp-lined bell tower—dusty brown, outlined by a sky so blue it seemed flaked from obsidian—was not out of place. To the eye it was a wedge of cliff that had broken away from a weathered bluff. Inside, the space was Zen-simple. A rough-edged stone on a pedestal served as an altar. Its handwoven cloth held a pottery chalice and two candles. In a corner was a Pueblo drum hollowed from a cottonwood trunk, deer hide stretched over its two heads. On a side wall hung a primitive Christ who seemed to have floated off his cross, his withered arms two limbs of a desert tree raised heavenward. Above him the sky stepped in through ceiling-high windows. The cliffs stepped in too, and with them a soft amber warmth of heat and mineral absorbed by the plain walls and floor. An austere beauty, quiet, refined, conducive to meditation.

Three years ago, the poet-monk and theologian, Thomas Merton, had stopped here on his way to India to meet Hindu teachers, Buddhist monks, and the Dalai Lama. He thought the canyon to be the perfect place to carry on the true practice of the early Christian hermits. His journal describes "Snowless, arid mountains. Clean long shapes stretching for miles under pure light. Mesas, full rivers, cottonwoods, sagebrush, high red cliffs, piñon pines . . . miles of emptiness. Perfect silence." Here one could seek the purity of heart he described in *The Wisdom of the Desert:* "the death of our own being" required to take on "the full difficulty and magnitude of the task of loving others."

Exiting the chapel, we found ourselves in a changed atmosphere. The air pollen colored, a thunderhead mushrooming into the sky—its frilled underside reflecting the dusty-orange canyon stone. A few monks in cassocks were bent to the ground, hoeing their garden. Silhouetted against the 200-million-year-old cliffs, they became Byzantine saints, dark umber painted on a panel of rubbed gold.

Back on the highway, we came to a village with a

house under construction. Earth and timber raised in the old cooperative style, sun-hardened mud bricks handed from one worker to another, field to building site. No contractor, blueprint, or inspector. No sound of power tools. Only the hammer, two-person saw, adze, draw-shave, squeak of an awl, *uumph* of men lifting a freshly peeled roof beam into place. Off to the side, women heated posole, beans, and tortillas. Uphill, the village church stood in a courtyard where the dead slept under mounds of earth decorated with synthetic roses. One mound had a cross tied with a toy car: "Please Give Geraldo a Place in Heaven." Miniature whirlwinds kicked up wilted petals and chewing gum wrappers. A gravedigger leaned on his shovel, listening to a transistor radio looped over an iron fence. His horse stood in the willows against a yellow sun. I felt I had stepped into one of Lorca's poems.

> *Caballito negro.*
> *Donde llevas tu jinete muerto?*

For most Americans, New Mexico was ambivalent territory: over the border, off the radar. A not-quite-on-the-map place that had so escaped time and defied assimilation that outsiders had little clue as to where it was or how it fit into America's history. The only other place I could summon that was so wrapped in its own lingo, topography, and time warp, and so thoroughly imbued with attitude, fiesta, and unpredictability, was New Orleans, where the metronome of life plinked day by day without tomorrow.

Northern New Mexico had that spirit. It was where you left the America of money and speed for slow living. A place not having the same names for things, the same music, language, or thought patterns as the place from where you came. Here the sacred dramas in Tewa, Spanish,

Towa, and Keres were fused into one vibrating Center: a plaza filled with all-night singing set inside a great amphitheater of heat and rainbows ringed by guardian mountains. Many stories, an abundance of myths. Over there, that pink hill, a breast where the spirit beings drink. Up high, that cliff split in two, the Wind God's door. Thomas Merton noted the "Crows in New Mexico seem to be flying at a greater psychic altitude, in a different realm."

In Los Ojos, the road circled a pine-clad hill where Our Lady of Lourdes smiled from a stone grotto. It then approached Tierra Amarilla where a billboard painted with the Mexican revolutionary Emiliano Zapata read TIERRA O MUERTE! Locals hadn't quelled their ire over property confiscated after the U.S. conquest of New Mexico in 1848. Land grants awarded by the Spanish and Mexican governments (protected by the Treaty of Guadalupe Hidalgo) were manipulated by the chicanery of U.S. lawyers, declared public domain, sold to the government, given to the U.S. Forest Service, or became corporate or privately owned real estate.

In 1967 Tierra Amarilla made international headlines when protestors led by Reies Tijerina raised their banners—*Vivan Los Pueblos Libres de Nuevo Mexico!*—and marched to Santa Fe. When peaceful venues went unheard, armed protestors attacked the Tierra Amarilla courthouse to free jailed protestors—one of the feistier events in the long struggle by Hispanos to reclaim their terrenos. When the National Guard stepped in with an army tank, the revolution folded, but not without awakening the American public to the Chicano land rights movement.

The pavement now took a crazy swagger into the Piedra Lumbre. Asymmetry defined this land, an off-center beauty. Fence lines wavered trying to stay with the dips and ruffles in the hardpan. The road did a raggedy waltz into a cleft of dusty maroon hills. A rusty windmill clanked. Weeds poked through the floorboards of a collapsed dance hall. Abandoned houses bore handprints of their makers in the mud plaster. We crossed a flimsy bridge over a water ditch, into a stand of cottonwoods, onto a backroad into Abiquiu. A barn was undergoing repair with pieces recycled from an older one: oxidized tin, weathered planks, nails pried from boards and hammered straight. Everything had a patina: hay rakes, plows, a broken swing set, a faded Desoto rusting in nodding bluebells. A feast of scraps, it seemed—traces of optimism, hints of tragedy. A poem by Antonio Machado caught it:

> *Our life amounts to time.*
> *Dying coals, smoke in the west.*
> *Ladders over the stars, altarpieces*
> *of hopes and memories.*

On the banks of the Río Chama, we spread our sleeping bags. Warm pine needles scented the mile-high chill. The stars gave a blue tint to the canyon walls. Our little truck also shone blue. Its zinc-roofed camper held tools, tarps, cooking gear, jars of rice and lentils, extra clothes, and one very special item: a 1903 hand-operated mimeograph protected by a bell-shaped metal case—the one I had been printing poetry books on in California. Sewn into wrappers, they were sold at San Francisco's City Lights bookstore, generously received by Lawrence Ferlinghetti who displayed them face out on the small-press rack downstairs. I asked $1.50, he sold them for $3.00. Even after his cut, I had enough money for a bowl of noodles at Sam Wo's with a round of friends. Now the mimeo was asleep, padded with blankets, waiting to be cranked into action wherever the road might lead.

Next morning we stopped for breakfast at a roadside café. The screen-door pull bar announced "Rainbow

Bread is Good Bread." It was the kind of place thick with cooking where all heads turn when strangers enter—and the men warming their feet at the stove did exactly that. Resting their boots on the chrome bar ringing the cast-iron belly, they shot us a modest glance and returned to the high art of banter. Their Spanish had a lilting cadence that fit the land. The men fit the land too: leathered faces, knobby knuckles, sweat-ringed hats. They sipped coffee from enameled metal cups, and smoked hand-rolled cigarettes whose tobacco soured the air. The girl who brought our food had braids tucked into a halo around the back of her head. She wore an apron stitched with rosebuds, and bore the warmth of the kitchen—the kind of kitchen written in folktales where an elfin person stirs bubbling pots on a giant stove. Our blue-corn cheese enchiladas were smothered with *chile rojo* and came with a side of lettuce and tomato dashed with lemon and oregano. The waitress returned with two coffees and a basket of *sopaipillas*, puffed fry-bread served with honey. The meal was a sensory liftoff, prelude to a lifelong addiction.

Before resuming our drive, I took Ed Abbey's latest novel, *Black Sun,* from the camper. I had dog-eared a page the night before, the reply a grizzled fire lookout gave to his young lover when she asked why he chose to live in the Southwest: "I like the simplicity of the landscape . . . I like the men and women who have lived out here long enough to acquire some of the character of the country . . . men of pride and independence with the look of great distances in their eyes." It was a look I wanted to have in my eyes. I considered the stumps on newly-cleared land, the careful contours of the plow, hayfields running between eroded hills, ten-foot piles of firewood, homes with roofs made of flattened lard cans. What would it take to eke out a living here?

We headed east over a lava-strewn *llano* toward Taos. A gnarl of black boulders. Miles of wind-worn table-land. Sage, globemallow, saltbush, and thistle. Flocks of horned larks rising and falling along the road shoulder. All was empty save for a distant canvas tent with a crooked stovepipe, a sheepherder's camp plunked among rocky fissures. His itinerant world, geared to the turn of the seasons, seemed light, a weightless refuge compared to my need for permanence. It was an interpretation, though. Had I walked up to him, would I have been greeted with cheer, or cast aside by a hardened loneliness, a life shorn to self-loyalty and habit?

Driving the plateau, we were lifted skyward on a swelling ocean of sage leading east to a snowy citadel of peaks. The uplift, ringed by mountains, was an expression of the gods: a shining mandala sliced by a dark cicatriz, an ingress to the Underworld carved by the Río Grande. The Tewas called it *P'osoge*, Big River, but its sacred implications were in the word *Avanyu,* the Plumed Serpent, the Tewa guardian of water whose river-like designs were painted on Pueblo pottery, carved on canyon walls, embroidered on dancers' kilts, or revealed in the sinuous, collective motion of dancers coiling and uncoiling during open-air ceremonies in the Pueblo plazas.

The road took us across that force of water, hidden deep between layers of basalt, to Taos, where we gassed up, and headed into the Sangre de Cristos, following the old trade route shared by the Taos Indians and the plains tribes. Apache plume decorated the rocky slopes, giving way to pine, spruce, and alpine fir. Far above, summits of bare tundra rumbled with dark clouds. Down below, streamers of rain brushed the desert pastels with feathery gray.

In 1923 D.H. Lawrence wrote of the Sangre de Cristos: "Savage, heartless wildness of the mountains." He was staying at the wealthy art patroness Mabel Dodge Luhan's ranch, invited with hopes that he might rouse new dialogue among the artists living there. Mabel's husband, a Taos Indian, pointed to the guardian peak behind his pueblo and reminded Lawrence that mountains were not savage, but a benevolent realm: cloud gatherers, sacred keepers of water. In winter, deer and elk moved down to offer themselves to the communal hunt. In summer, rain—called by ceremonies of poems and prayer—walked from the summits to feed the crops.

The eastern slopes of the Sangre de Cristos descended to meet the high plains. Wet and green, the Mora Valley had the look of early pioneering. Smoke trailed from L-shaped adobes with high-pitched roofs. Narrow strips of land had been divided creek bottom to mountaintop through the generations. As families grew, each descendant received a slice of flat land for house and crops, a spring for water, a meadow for pasture, a wooded slope for timber. A farmer tilled with horse and plow. The sun blinked from a beaver pond. A log truck idled, loaded with freshly harvested fir. A group of kids peeked through a corral, mesmerized by the antics of a baby lamb. From the dusty window of the Hermanos Sanchez Mercantile, a paper Santa Claus waved. I opened my journal to write a few notes. It was April first.

Springs were plentiful, berries profuse, woodpiles high. Also piled high were the run-down automobiles, abandoned or undergoing restoration for so long that even their new parts had begun to rust. Slow gravel roads crossed plank bridges over creeks feeding stone gristmills, one of them operating. Satellite dishes and cell-phone towers were nonexistent. Trailer houses were just beginning to replace adobe homes. Land deeds were sketchy, plots were mostly horse-traded. Hayfields and work tasks were shared. When hand-dug canals were ready to deliver the spring melt-off, their wooden gates were opened and a priest blessed the *acequia madre,* the mother ditch. Each village had a Catholic church with a folk altar backed by painted wood panels and set with carved and lacquered *bultos* of the holy people: El Santo Niño, Saint Isidor the Plowman, La Señora de Guadalupe. Some churches were time-honored healing places. The Santuario de Chimayó held a basin of curative soil sought by pilgrims. Its uneven adobe walls displayed crutches, canes, teddy bears, rosaries, petitions from the sick, thank-you notes from the cured. Holy Week saw the church thronged with worshipers who walked miles shouldering kids, bearing crosses, praying the beads. This was the northern New Mexico I remember in 1971.

🦋

It was over the mountain from Chimayó that Gioia and I settled, precisely the area Steve Beckwitt described before we left California. We fashioned a shelter of plastic tarps, drew water from a spring, cooked over an open fire, built a makeshift sweat lodge, and eventually purchased forty acres of land at $50 an acre from a local farmer, Antonio Espinoza, who didn't quite have a deed, but that's how things were passed down. Paperless. By summer's end, on the brink of the first snowfall—September third— we had completed a one-room, pole-frame cabin—right out of my childhood drawings: no straight lines, a face-like array of windows, tin chimney, small sleeping loft, a fold-down spruce-plank kitchen table. With little know-how, it came to life: poles felled from the woods, timbers dragged by horse, stone hauled from a creek, clay from an arroyo, slabs from a local sawmill. Our home was positioned to receive the first sunbeams flaring over a sheer mesa above a meadow perfumed with a low, sweet-smelling sage. I often thought of the cabin as an ark flying a pirate flag against capitalist ideals. We were living off the grid, had kept things small, had gone against America's big-bucks economic system which fostered perpetual growth.

Our children, Giovanna and her beloved brother Joaquin, who was delivered by a local midwife, eagerly investigated their surrounds, learned the directional features, knew the seasons by the changing position of the sun. They were allowed to roam, no way-finding technology interfering with their ability to orient themselves according to landmarks, which they began to name: Split Rock, Toaster Rock, Copper Mine, The Valley. Gradually, they mapped the whole territory, learning the purple aster, girasol, penstemon, encino, piñon, alamo, and sumac— which they called the "vitamin-C bush" because of its sour berries.

They nibbled the watercress that wreathed our water source; gathered *hierba buena;* picked curly dock, wild onion, asparagus, *quelites,* and *verdulagas.* They recognized the planets by their size and color, named the constellations according to the designs they saw. They knew the coyote's cry, accepted the bear at the creek, the bobcat at the door, a skunk in the kitchen drawn by a warm apple pie. The Universe began from within. Home was every direction they looked from where they woke. They were not simply in touch with nature, they were held by it. They saw the fragility of it all, realized themselves as necessary participants. Their early experience was paramount to the rest of their lives. Their childhood geography, deeply internalized, is carried within them today, an oral map they pass onto their own children.

The cabin's "blueprint" harkened back to the hermit's abode my father hiked me to as a boy in Sequoia National Park. That den, the idea of solitude, would lodge in my psyche to be rekindled in college when Eric Barker arrived from the Big Sur to read his poems and describe his

Bohemian life in a cabin perched above the sea. A third awakening came in Ecuador when I met American expat Johnny Lovewisdom at his Vilcabamba hermitage, printing newsletters on a rustic mimeograph.

Five years after that encounter, I was deep in the mountains of New Mexico, printing on my own mimeo. The press I founded was called Tooth of Time Books, named after an igneous outcrop east of our cabin. One of the early poets to visit was Arthur Sze. We hiked through scrub oak, climbed Ocate Mesa, and sat on a stone lip watching light shift on the farmsteads in the valley below. Arthur was one of the first poets I published under the Tooth of Time imprint, an event that began our lifelong friendship. As more and more authors heard about the press, queries flooded in, so I printed a postcard reply:

> *Tooth of Time Press is devoted to poetry, prose, and alchemistic probings concerned with exploration/meditation/narration related to wandering/settling over/in astral & geographical hemispheres. Manuscripts are usually solicited. Authors are required to show up. Book production relies on participation in the form of typing, preparing stencils, sharing paper costs. We do not operate a dude ranch, there is no electricity or plumbing. Water is drawn from a spring; a small garden feeds us. As Jaime de Angulo would say: 'If you are looking for comfort, don't come here! You will have to sleep in a tent or under the stars. This place is far from civilization.'*

Authors whose work was accepted arrived one at a time, pitched camp in the meadow, editing their final drafts in pure mountain air at 7,500 feet. The routine included a mix of work and play: cookouts, readings of Shakespeare's plays, a dip in the creek, a print party, a collating and binding event, a poetry reading at a Taos bar, a book launch in Santa Fe—advertised by word of mouth and hand-printed flyers tacked to phone poles. One day ethnobotanist Richard Felger arrived with a gift of potted peyote; its offspring blooms in my studio today. His poetry book, *Dark Horses and Little Turtles* led to National Endowment for the Arts grants, which allowed me to publish trade-edition books beginning with Nanao Sakaki, Luci Tapahonso, Nathaniel Tarn, Harold Littlebird, and Rosemary Catacalos.

Our homesteading was largely independent of the New Mexico communes that flourished in the late Sixties. We enjoyed a fruitful bond with our Spanish-speaking neighbors, especially with seniors whose self-reliance had carried them through the Great Depression, World War II, lean years of drought, and bone-biting winters. With settlers like ourselves, we shared romance and butted heads over the pros and cons of off-the-grid living. A few stayed, many moved on, some are no longer alive. Years later, a fellow homesteader remarked, "It seemed so huge at the time. The whole experiment was—poof—just ten minutes."

Northern New Mexico winters were hard. So were the radicals who believed they were part of a unified revolution, only to discover not all revolutionaries shared the same values. You had peaceniks, militants, pragmatists, idealists, deer slayers, vegetarians, spiritual seekers, atheists, ex-cons, college highbrows, new-age yoginis, and dope-smoking dreamers seeking the pure life, keen on their own needs, eager to change their names, and live like Ishi or Gandhi. In the mix were those who wished to strip away a spoon-fed former life and get down to work in their new environs. But to begin to belong to a place where one was culturally aloof, patience was needed. It was easy to clean a spring and run a line to the house; it didn't take but a few years to restore a fallow field to yield a productive crop. But to work out the inevitable misunderstandings between people of vastly different backgrounds and nurture a neighborly exchange? Or become part of the already established movements founded by the Indians, Chicanos, and Brown Berets? Each was focused on a specific political, social, and economic agenda whose complexities were ungraspable to a newcomer.

Why had we come? Was it a longing for paradise, a need to create a utopia apart from a world gone awry? Most of us were of urban middle-class backgrounds, wanting out of parental expectations, life pathways we had not chosen, degrees too often rewarded with no jobs. We had migrated by thumb, rainbow-colored buses, sagging American behemoths, and restored hearses painted with mushrooms to a high country where we sought refuge from industrial decay, media wars, sidewalk wars, family wars, money wars, world wars—perpetual madness. We had had enough of righteous elders slapping us with moral-conduct codes, or trouncing us with make-it-or-break-it mantras for successful careers. Life wasn't what we were led to believe—at home, in the classroom, from the pulpit, and definitely not from the oval office. Nixon was a sham. His bombs and lies would soon turn on him.

The back-to-the-land movement wasn't new. It happened during the Great Depression when people fled hard economic times. It happened when farmers left the Dustbowl for California. The Sixties were different. We were fleeing hard political times, not hard economic times. And, we were turning our backs on prosperity—too much of it. Our movement wasn't driven by older mill workers or farmers who had lost their crops, but by under-thirty environmental and counterculture groups fed up with McCarthyism, racial inequality, proliferating consumerism, and a growing divide between rich and poor. But what did we know once we got to where we were going? Did anyone have a plan?

Few of us were familiar with farming, yet hard labor was a rule of thumb. "Do your own thing" took priority over working for a boss, which, as it turned out, many couldn't live without. For some a guru would do, a master to clock one in for morning meditation, and out after the evening lecture. For others a necessity arose to single themselves out as leaders, laying down stiff rules for the rest of us. My optimism was always balanced with a cautionary dose of distrust. I didn't take well to those who strong-armed the idea that to make things work one must stay home, tend the farm at all costs. Or that art must serve the community. Crafting a milking stool was favorable; framing a painting for a gallery was not. One was praised for schooling the kids at home, but scorned for leaving home to teach as a poet-in-the-schools. For me, home wasn't just a narrow canyon in the outback of Mora County. Home was the World, one big, multi-headed Imaginary Force. Paradise had its flaws, and few of us owned anything larger than a broken mirror to see the cause of these flaws. "We change our skies, not our souls," Horace warned.

In the Sixties and Seventies era of homesteading you didn't go to the Internet; it was all in your head. You spent little, you earned what you needed through honest labor: tree planting, waitressing, construction, nurse practitioner, carpentry, fence mending, teaching. You survived the ridicule of locals who thought it weird that you wanted in, while they wanted out: Denver, Albuquerque, Phoenix—a steady job, things to do, places to shop, a broader social life. Who could blame them? "Why do you hippies want to live in a culture that isn't yours, shoveling rocks, bathing in tin tubs, watching bugs eat your corn, freezing your ass in straw-bale huts in below-zero winters?"

Our neighbor Antonio never posed such questions.

As an elder attached to the land, he was eager to share his understanding of place: what crops did well, where and when to plant them, what animals could be raised, what protocols would allow entry into the social weave, who to meet, who to avoid. By his unassuming presence, he offered an example of how to give up urgency and go slow. Linger, listen. Enjoy knowledge that could only be gained by staying put.

Antonio and his wife Annie lived just over a wooded slope from our cabin. They were in their sixties, robust and of good cheer. They raised sheep, had a milk cow, a pig, a field of corn, fava beans, and alfalfa. They baled hay, dried apples, made jam from the plums. Without fail they rose at dawn to kindle the stove with slivers of resinous pine. After milking the goats, Annie made breakfast; Antonio planned his day over beans, potatoes, and eggs rolled into a tortilla. Work might include anything from repairing his tractor to hay bailing to rounding up a stray animal.

Annie made posole from hominy and pork; salsa from home-grown peppers. She roasted corn in her horno, an outdoor igloo-shaped earthen oven. She knew the native cures for *fiebre* and *mal de estómago,* and swore that water drawn from the earth was "better than city water infected with chemicals." Helping bucket water from her well, I asked why she didn't have it piped to the kitchen. "Sí, Antonio wanted to do that, but I refused. *Los tubos hacen mal el agua.*" The pipes make the water bad.

One day Antonio rode up on horseback, rope and a chainsaw strapped to his saddle. Pointing to a high rocky spur, he said: "See that dead tree up there? That's going to be our afternoon." The tree was a lightning-struck pine he aimed to fell, drag home, and saw up for firewood. His implication was not so much that I would be of help to him, but that I'd learn something by just being along. I was eager to go. Why refuse a chance to get out from under revising yet another draft of the latest poem?

The afternoon turned out to be a simple, well-paced work task shared by two men of very dissimilar upbringings—a college kid raised in suburbia; a Hispanic man raised in rural New Mexico with limited schooling. Working together, I learned about Antonio's upbringing, and his railroad jobs, woodcutting, and sheep-herding to ease the financial woes of the farm. And he learned a bit of where I was from, why I was here. The talk was slanted in his favor, of course, his wealth of tales: the locust plague, the blizzard of '56, the Rainsville cattle rustlers, the year the locals ran tax-assessors out of the valley. I think he was bemused to find himself telling stories, realizing that whatever he had to say would be so different from anything I grew up with.

Antonio and Annie were living proof that the arrogant catchphrase of the 1960s, "don't trust anyone over thirty," was off-kilter. How could I turn my back on my good neighbors, members of a previous generation who offered wisdom and benevolence? In a short span of time our own generation would be the older generation—over-thirty homesteaders ready to pass on a bit of time-tested insight.

Another neighbor, Mrs. Luisa Torres, born in 1903, lived with her husband on open land with low, spreading oaks and a few lofty pines. A forthright woman, she laughed easily and didn't hesitate to share her rural wisdom. She understood solitude, needed it, yet never shunned a chance for human exchange. We hardly passed a week without a visit, always greeted with a snack of whatever was on the stove: steamed *calabacitas*, corn tortillas, frijoles. During hunting season, Luisa invited us for fresh venison stew slow-cooked with roasted chiles, garlic, onions, and tomatillos. The *cocina*, just under seven feet, held a wood-fired cookstove. On each visit I would chop a few rounds of pine and refill her wood bin with kindling.

Luisa's face bore a perpetual smile. I sometimes saw her as a mischievous girl. Lines of sunny radiance spoked from the corners of her eyes. Hoeing the fields, she kept her hair in place with plastic nets saved from potatoes and oranges bought in bulk. Her hands, expressive works of art, gestured perpetually, hugging pumpkins, goats, family, friends, strangers, and the vanilla-scented ponderosas behind her home. Her linoleum floors she mopped with vinegar and hot water, the windowpanes were cleaned with ammonia, the furniture waxed to a gloss. Her miniature dinner bells—two hundred of them, each decorated with a city or country she had never visited—were always sparkling. The ancestors in their frames were dusted and straightened daily, as were the President Kennedy and Last Supper paintings on black velvet.

If the weather was cold, Luisa wore a vest over her blouse and a wool skirt over a cotton skirt, tied with an apron. She once giggled: "You could call me a hippie, I guess, because I never wear a bra." She wore tennis shoes at home, Sears work boots for the fields. On many days it was a pair of overalls over a plaid flannel shirt with a plug of osha in the top pocket: "Good for my sniffles, and it keeps the snakes away." When day was done, Luisa favored a short night of sleep. "Six hours, enough. Too many dreams make me heavy. I rise early, pray the rosary, make coffee. My husband gets up later. He drinks his coffee, and jokes, 'Yours tastes better because you've said your Hail Marys.'"

Luisa's motto: "I only tire when I *don't* work. If you come from a generation like mine, you don't sit around. Our whole family lived and worked together. What your commune people are trying out is what my generation did naturally: join hands, share the labor. In March everybody helped clean the *acequias*. Between work we enjoyed a birthday, a fiesta, or a *Quinceañera* to celebrate a girl's coming of age. We worked hard, so we laughed hard. And we danced hard too. On San Isidro Day we honored the patron saint with a procession in the fields. Families used the day to gather herbs and remedial plants. We had our own *curanderas,* so nobody had to go far for a doctor. A midwife gave basil tea to a woman in labor for her first pains, followed by vapors of spearmint tea. After the birth the mother drank blue-corn *atole.* She had special care for ten days. *Gracias a Dios,* we had no problems with births in our village. In a small place, where people help each other, you don't need much money. You can enjoy a humble life and be happy. If you stay put and live simply, you learn how to give and how to receive."

❦

After Gioia and I ended our marriage in 1979, I traveled to India for a period of self-reflection. I wanted a total break from the familiar, a culture completely foreign, no familiar footholds. I also wanted to follow my father's footsteps to the places he visited during his army furloughs: the holy rivers, Hindu temples, the Taj Mahal; the historic places where Buddha was born, gained enlightenment, began his teaching; and the places where Buddhism lived on. Ladakh was one of them, situated in the rain shadow between two Himalayan ranges in India's far northwest. Once part of Tibet, it had been annexed by India and was recently opened to foreigners. Almost directly on the other side of the world from New Mexico, it shared many similarities. A treeless plateau drained by a single river, it was home to a devout population who marked the seasons with music, song, and dance. Recent visitors to Ladakh described it as a country of its own; the roads few, the trails many; the people industrious, candid, and quick with laughter.

Leh, the capital at 11,500 feet, hugs a rocky cliff. A cubist collage of earth-brown dwellings crawling up a steep rise to the Potola-like palace, half melted by centuries of sun and rain. Leh had been recommended as a base, but it was the outliers that pulled me. On my first morning, I grabbed a bus out of town to Thiksey, a 500-year-old monastery southeast of town. It wasn't far, but the bus was a patched-together contraption, the going slow—a bumpy crawl, picking up and dropping off locals smelling of hearth smoke, dressed in woolen robes, thick sweaters, baggy trousers, work boots, and handmade wool shoes with leather soles. The little bus soon had me squeezed between a whole community, everybody in good cheer, chattering under stovepipe hats with upturned corners, their amulets tinkling, stones of turquoise, coral, and amber catching the morning sun.

At one point the bus detoured slightly. The driver was doing what one does on foot, a Buddhist tradition of respect when approaching a stupa: walking around it in a clockwise direction. In this case the bus had approached a mani wall, a flat-topped berm plastered, and covered with river stones carved with *Om Mani Padme Hum*. As we slowly jerked and bounced clockwise around the wall, a few passengers twirled their prayer wheels. Ah, I realized: to turn in accordance with the earth's turning, and with its circumambulation of the sun.

Within an hour Thiksey appeared on a steep knoll, a snow-white monastic assemblage of crumbling *chortens*, a nunnery, a jumble of monks' quarters stepping up into azure clarity, narrowing at the gompa proper, its red and yellow prayer hall capped with gold finials. WAY UP read a hand-painted sign. I climbed to the roof and inhaled the view. Burnished sand every direction, an occasional pencil-mark of dervish wind, ghost peaks glinting distantly, a hundred kilometers a stone's throw. Everything flame vivid. In the silence, only the sound of light. Everything suspended.

Downstairs, to the side of the prayer hall, a lone monk sat in the lotus pose shaking a tiny hand drum in a murky chamber, chanting before an array of statues. The room felt millennia old. The deities were veiled, too fierce for the human psyche. One peeked from its shawl, open-jawed, eyes rolling upward, a black cane painted with skulls in one hand. Other icons—half-wrapped, puffed cheeks, ogling eyes—disappeared into a ghoulish darkness of frayed drapery. Very much a dream world. The adjoining chapel was a contrast. It housed a brightly colored statue of Maitreya, the Future Buddha (*maitri*, Sanskrit: friendly; *metta*, Pali: loving kindness). As if waiting for his time to come, he gazed serenely outward under a crown of painted deities. "Wisdom Buddhas," explained the attendant monk. "Each has a special power to help the meditator change negative energy into positive. Hate, pride, lust to love, understanding, trust."

I returned to Leh on a footpath skirting the fields along the Indus, a peaceful hike—plenty of birdlife in the berry bushes hugging the irrigation ditches: warblers, wag-tails, bluethroats, and mountain chiffchaffs. On a grassy bank a group of ladies enjoyed a picnic, laughing and ca-joling over dumplings, fruit, and thermoses of tea. Farther on, at a diversion of water reserved for washing, a woman slapped her laundry with a paddle and hung it on low shrubs to dry.

In Leh I lunched on noodle soup, picked up my backpack, and ambled north, following canals fed by springs in mountain cleaves marked with shrines. An hour's walk brought me to a hamlet where a potato harvest was in progress. A man called out *Julay!* and led me through his apple trees to a well kept two-story adobe.

These were the days when Ladakhis were beginning to open their doors to travelers. His family consisted of his wife, elder son, and two daughters—both studying in Buddhist nunneries. One of them, Dawa, was home to help with the harvest.

She showed me to an upstairs room. "Just you see." It was freshly swept with juniper boughs and filled with light. A futon was made up with pillows and a Tibetan spread. Next to it a wooden bench held a kerosene lamp. Overhead, the ceiling was that of a traditional New Mexican home: peeled log beams and a weave of poplar limbs. Stepping onto the sun-warmed balcony, I faced the 20,000-foot Zanskar range gleaming above the plain. In the foreground, cobbled alleys wound through a maze of picture-puzzle rooftops, each with a golden square of drying grain. A whitewashed stupa stood at the center of the maze. Strings of colored prayer flags radiated from its dome, giving it a playful look. "Not new," Dawa said. "Many hundred year old."

I took the room without hesitation. Dawa brought *solja*, a salty pink butter tea, and two flatbreads. She wore a maroon robe and Chinese tennis shoes. Her hands were rough, her cheeks sunburnt, her face lit with a smile—exactly how I had imagined Luisa Torres as a youth: pretty in a hardy way, dutiful by nature, at one with her surrounds. Over the next few days, I watched Dawa move effortlessly about the house, maximizing every action with grace, humming mantras as she worked; Buddha in mind, I imagined, as she kindled the stove, trimmed the lamp wicks, climbed the roof ladder with bundles of fodder to add to those drying on the parapets.

One evening—kitchen chores finished, plates, cups, and pans stacked—I sat with Dawa while she rolled lampblack over a woodblock carved with a spirit horse and a Tibetan prayer. Transferring the image to colored squares of cloth, she set them aside to dry, then sewed the prayer flags to a cotton cord: yellow, green, red, white, blue. Earth, water, fire, cloud, sky. Next day we strung the banners over the upstairs balcony. They pattered gayly in the breeze, spreading good wishes into the universe. I tried explaining how the pattering of the banners was like the sound we made as kids to imitate a horse's gallop. Dawa giggled—I will never forget that giggle—as I pointed to the spirit horse on the flags, cupped my hands, slapped them against my legs, and skipped around the orchard trying to pantomime a gallop. That time, those days!

A few weeks later I was homebound, the plane lowering toward Albuquerque's Sunport, rocking in the usual high-desert turbulence. After twenty-five hours of flying— Ladakh to Delhi and over the Arctic to Chicago—I peered from the plane's window in the half-stupor of travel, only to wonder if I had left Asia at all. The smooth plateau below had the same treeless mineral sheen as Ladakh; the Sangre de Cristos we had just flown over, coated with the season's first snow, could have been the Himalaya. To the west, rising alone, was Tsoodzil, Turquoise Mountain, sacred to the Diné. With a stretch of imagination, I saw it as Nanga Parbat as viewed from the flight out of Leh—a 26,000-foot sapphire massif set like a jewel on the plateau between the Karakoram and the Himalaya.

I spent a few nights in Santa Fe relaxing and visiting friends, then drove north to settle back into my old homestead in Mora County, and pay a visit to Luisa Torres. New Mexico's autumn sky was that of Ladakh's spotless cobalt. The land lay quiet, timeless as always, adobe homes dotting the forests and fields like miniature clay sculptures, wood bucked and piled high, sandhill cranes circling above, headed south to Bosque del Apache Wildlife Refuge on the Middle Río Grande. Despite a nip in the air, morning glories blossomed on trellises, sunflowers bobbed on thick stems busy with ants, and pink dianthus brightened planters made from recycled automobile tires laid flat, painted pink, and filled with soil. Even the abandoned shell of a pickup, rusted to a golden sheen, looked good among the purple thistles.

Very few people had phones in those days. (Even in the early 1980's I had yet to achieve such prosperity.) This may be why rural New Mexicans adhered to the stalwart custom I embraced as I approached Luisa's house: pull up, park, leave the motor running, give a honk, wait until the door opens. That's country politeness. You don't want to catch anybody in their knickers. I sat for a couple minutes, then noticed Luisa waving from the rear of her house where she seemed to be sanding a large chest. Her orchard, like those I had just left in Ladakh, had turned yellow, the apples ripening, almost ready to pick. When I went up to greet her, I was taken aback. It wasn't a chest she was sanding, it was a casket—her casket!

"No te preocupes" she exclaimed, "Don't worry. I am of good health. I still feed the chickens and goats and care for my herb garden. *Todo va bien, hijito.* But I am getting older, and I need to take responsibility for my own death, just as my ancestors did." She explained that with a little help from her family, a pine was felled behind her house and cut into boards at her son's mill "to make this lovely box for me." She was obviously having fun with this project; one most people would rather have the funeral home do. "How useless it is to bury a body in a costly casket, something that happens in these modern times," she chortled.

The casket smelled sweetly of pitch and sanding. On the hill behind Luisa's house stood the copse of pines from where the boards were cut. A pair of crows wheeled past the sun as Luisa took a seat. "In the old times it was very easy to live in this beautiful place. And easy for a family

317

to lose a loved one. But the relatives of the deceased had continual company to assist. Neighbors helped make a coffin. The village cemetery was well kept, the church always open, the padre always here to perform the rites. The family was not left with debts as happens now."

As I was saying the last of a half-dozen goodbyes to Luisa Torres, she returned my extended adios with a curious beam and a tug at my sleeve. "Wait, I want you to see something." I followed her, surprised as she walked toward the coffin and climbed into it. There she lay, miming herself in a departed state—resting peacefully, eyes closed, hands crossed on her lap. Unable to hold a serious pose, a smile grew from the corners of her mouth. She looked up at me, bright eyed, with an impish laugh. "Don't worry, not yet!" she laughed. "This box is going to be perfect for storing apples until I'm ready to go. It's going to be a good refrigerator. It'll soak up their flavor, and when I'm ready for it—this wood is going to be sweet, a very sweet resting place for me."

CHAPTER NOTES

YOUNG BLOOD: A PREAMBLE

Sections of this chapter appeared in *Reflections in the Lizard's Eye* (Western Edge Press, 2000) and in *A Wild Delight* (The Bancroft Library Press, University of California, 2019). Michael McClure quotes are from *Scratching the Beat Surface* (North Point Press, 1982). Bob Dylan's "Masters of War" appears on *The Freewheelin' Bob Dylan*. Lew Welch quote is from *Ring of Bone: Collected Poems* (City Lights Books, 2012). Jack Kerouac's words are from *The Jack Kerouac Collection* (Rhino Word Beat records, 1990); John Muir's words from *The Mountains of California* (The Century Company, 1917). Among my childhood books: *A Child's Garden of Verses,* illustrated by Myrtle Sheldon (M.A. Donohue & Co., 1939); *Treasure Island,* illustrated by N.C. Wyeth (Charles Scribner's Sons, 1911); *Famous Paintings: An Introduction to Art for Young People,* Alice Elizabeth Chase (Platt and Munk, 1951); *Homes and Habits of Wild Animals,* Karl Patterson Schmidt, illustrated by Walter Alois Weber (M.A. Donohue & Co., 1934); *The Golden Geography: A Child's Introduction to the World,* Elsa Jane Werner (Simon and Schuster, 1952). For an engaging account of early rock and roll, see Greil Marcus' *The History of Rock 'n' Roll in Ten Songs* (Yale University Press, 2014).

THE TAJ MAHAL: ENIGMA & REALITY

An early version appeared in *A Question of Journey* (Light and Dust Books, 1995); it was reprinted in *A Question of Journey: Travel Episodes, India, Nepal, Thailand & Bali* (Book Faith India, 1999).

MULTITUDE & SOLITUDE

Previously unpublished. Baudelaire quotes are from his *Intimate Journals,* translated by Christopher Isherwood (City Lights Books, 1983); Jack Kerouac from *Pomes All Sizes* (City Lights Books, 1992); Jayanta Mahapatra from *Jayanta Mahapatra Selected Poems* (Oxford University Press, 1987).

ABODE OF THE PERFECT SUBLIME LOTUS

Early versions appeared in *The India Journals: West Bengal, Orissa, Sikkim* (Tooth of Time Books, 2007, limited to twenty-two copies) and in *The Way to Thorong La* (Empty Bowl Press, 2020). Nicholas Roerich quote is from *Himalayas: Abode of Light* (Nicholas Roerich Museum, 2017).

HIMALAYAN SKETCHES

Some of the *haibun* were issued as broadsides by Tangram Press and by The Press at the Palace of the Governors. Others appeared in *The World, the World* (White Pine Press, 2013), *The Great Unrest* (White Pine Press, 2019), and *The Way to Thorong La* (Empty Bowl Press, 2020).

THE SHATABDI EXPRESS: RUMINATIONS

An early version appeared in *Kyoto Journal No. 99: Travel, Revisited*, Dec 2020; and in *The Indian Journals III* (Tooth of Time Books, 2010, limited to twenty-two copies). Versions of Bashō's haiku are my own. Santōka's haiku are from *Mountain Tasting*, translated by John Stevens (White Pine Press, 2009). Ho Yuan Huong poem is from *Spring Essence*, translated by John Balaban (Copper Canyon Press, 2000). Xuangzang was a renowned 7th-century Chinese Buddhist monk, scholar, traveler, and translator. Joseph Campbell quote is from *Baksheesh & Brahman: Asian Journals – India* (New World Library, 2002). Goethe quotes are from *Italian Journey*, translated by W.H. Auden and Elizabeth Mayer (North Point Press, 1982). Nanao Sakaki poem appears in *Break the Mirror* (North Point Press, 1987). Non-italicized haiku in this chapter and throughout the book are my own.

KERALA'S THEATER OF THE DOUBLE

An early version appeared in *Kyoto Journal*, No. 76, 2012. Buson haiku is my version, based on R.H. Blyth's translation, *Haiku, Vol. II* (Hokuseidō Press, 1950). Antonin Artaud quote is from *The Theater and Its Double*, translated by Mary Caroline Richards (Grove Press, 1958).

RHYTHM IN STONE

Previously unpublished. My versions of Santōka's poems are based on those in *Mountain Tasting: Haiku and Journals of Santōka Taneda*, translated by John Stevens (White Pine Press, 2009). Gary Snyder's comments are from *Passage Through India* (Gray Fox Press, 1972). As I was about to leave for India in 1979, I wrote Gary asking for advice. "Be prepared for great travail," was his reply, which I misread as "Be prepared for great travel." Both turned out to be true. The Upanishads quote is from *Tantra Asana*, Ajit Mookerjee (Basilius Presse, 1971). "There is no word in Sanskrit for obscene," is a quote from Joseph Campbell, p. 214, *Baksheesh & Brahman: Asian Journals – India* (New World Library, 2002). Many Sanskrit scholars offer a contrary opinion. The Indian love poem is a composite based on excerpts from *Sanskrit Poetry from Vidyakara's Treasury*, translated by Daniel H.H. Ingalls (Harvard University Press, 1968) and *Grow Long, Blessed Night*, translated by Martha Ann Selby (Oxford University Press, 2000). I highly recommend Andrew Schelling's compelling translations of Indian love poetry. *The Cane Groves of Narmada River* is a standout, offering a superb selection of poems, insightful notes, extensive bibliography (City Lights Books, 1998).

TIME, TRANCE, AND DANCE IN BALI

An earlier version appeared in *Kyoto Journal*, No. 42, 1999. Quotations are from: *The Masks of God: Oriental Mythology*, Joseph Campbell (Viking Press, 1962); *Balinese Music*, Michael Tenzer (Periplus Editions, 1992); *The Sacred and the Profane*, Mircea Eliade (Harper & Row, 1961); *The Theater and its Double*, Antonin Artaud (Grove Press, 1958). Renée Gregorio and I were married in Munduk, Bali, 1996, in an abbreviated traditional ceremony at Tana Barak waterfall; details appear in our chapbook *Unmasking the Fire* (Yoo-Hoo Press, 2000).

SEARCHING FOR GHALIB'S HOUSE

Previously unpublished. Original draft appears in *The Indian Journals III* (Tooth of Time Books, 2010, limited to twenty-two copies). Bashō versions are my own, with thanks to: *Bashō and His Interpreters: Selected Hokku with Commentary* (Stanford University Press, 1992) and *Bashō's Haiku: Selected Poems of Matsuo Bashō*, translated by David Landis Barnhill (SUNY Press, 2004). Kabir excerpts are from *The Kabir Book*, versions by Robert Bly (Beacon Press, 1977). Ghalib excerpts from: *The Lightning Should Have Fallen on Ghalib: Selected Poems of Ghalib,* translated from the Urdu by Robert Bly and Sunil Dutta (The Ecco Press, 1999) and *Ghazals of Ghalib, Versions from the Urdu* edited by Aijaz Ahmad (Columbia University Press, 1971). Twelve years after my visit to Ghalib's house, a new book on Ghalib appeared: *Faces Hidden in the Dust, the Selected Ghazals of Ghalib,* translated by Tony Barnstone and Bilal Shaw (White Pine, 2021). A refreshingly crisp, high-spirited, engaging read.

BEAUTY ASKEW: THE HAIKU EYE

Portions of this essay appeared in *The Unswept Path: Contemporary American Haiku* (White Pine Press, 2005); *El Palacio* magazine, Vol. 113, No. 4, winter 2008; *Blue Sky Ringing* (Punjabi Haiku Forum, 2010); and *Seeding the Cosmos: New & Selected Haiku* (La Alameda Press, 2010). All non-italicized haiku in this essay are my own. The Sappho fragment is my version; see *Sweetbitter Love: Poems of Sappho,* translations by Willis Barnstone (Shambala, 2006). Bashō's haiku are found in his *Kashima Journal* and in R.H. Blyth's four-volume *Haiku* (Hokuseido Press, 1950). Elizabeth Searle Lamb's poem is from *Across the Windharp* (La Alameda Press, 1999); Renée Gregorio's, from *The Storm That Tames Us* (La Alameda Press, 1999); Nanao Sakaki's, from *Real Play* (Tooth of Time Books, 1981); Steve Sanfield's, from *Postage Due: the continuing poetic correspondence of John Brandi & Steve Sanfield, 2007-2011* (Backlog/Tooth of Time Books, 2011); Bashō's words are rephrased from Nobuyuki Yuasa's *The Year of My Life: A Translation of Issa's Oraga Haru* (University of California Press, 1972); Gary Snyder's Han Shan translation is from *Riprap, & Cold Mountain Poems* (Four Seasons Foundation, 1969); Jack Kerouac, from "Belief & Technique for Modern Prose" (*Evergreen Review,* Vol. 2, No. 8, 1959); David Meltzer, from our personal correspondence; Margaret Randall from *Lost and Found,* Series 2, No. 1, 2010; Issa, from *Inch by Inch: 45 Haiku by Issa* translated by Nanao Sakaki (La Alameda Press, 1999); Santōka (my versions), from *Mountain Tasting: Haiku and Journals of Santōka Taneda,* translated by John Stevens (White Pine Press, 2009); Chiyo-ni (my version), based on Patricia Donegan's translation with Yoshie Ishibashi in *Chiyo-ni: Woman Haiku Master* (Tuttle Publishing, 1998); the Aztec poem is from *Flower & Song: Aztec Poems,* translated by Edward Kissam and Michael

Schmidt (Anvil Press Poetry, 1977); Steve Sanfield, from *A New Way* (Tooth of Time Books, 1983); Penny Harter, from *The Unswept Path* (White Pine Press, 2005); Moritake, from *The Unswept Path* (White Pine Press, 2005).

A LUMINOUS UPLIFT

Early versions appeared in: *Shaman's Drum* magazine, No. 28, 1992, *In the Desert We Do Not Count the Days* (Holy Cow! Press, 1991) and in *Reflections in the Lizard's Eye: Notes from the High Desert* (Western Edge Press, 2000). D.H. Lawrence quote is from *D.H. Lawrence in Taos*, Joseph Foster (University of New Mexico Press, 1972); Ed Abbey from *Desert Solitaire* (McGraw-Hill, 1968); Wordsworth from *Selected Poetry of William Wordsworth* (Modern Library, 2021); Vincent Scully from *Pueblo/Mountain, Village, Dance* (University of Chicago Press, 1989). Lorca from *Federico García Lorca Collected Poems*, p. xii, edited by Christopher Mauer (Farrar, Straus and Giroux, 2002). *Kachina* is also spelled *Katsina* or *Katcina*, according to the Hopi pronunciation.

SOUTHWEST SKETCHES

My *haibun* are excerpted from *Into the Dream Maze,* designed and printed by Tom Leech (The Press at the Palace of the Governors, 2015) in an edition of thirty-five copies hand-bound by Rosalia Galassi and presented in a clamshell box covered with Japanese Asahi silk. John Nichols wrote the preface. Madeline Durham created the paste-paper book covers and box liners, using colors to match New Mexico's sandstone cliffs. James Bourland made the plates of my fifteen pen-and-ink drawings that were printed opposite the haibun. To finalize the production, I spent a month-long daily routine hand coloring each drawing in all thirty-five copies.

MORITZ THOMSEN, LIVING POOR

Previously unpublished. The original draft, written in Corrales, NM, 1986, was to be included in a tribute to Moritz Thomsen, an anthology proposed by author Tom Miller. The project was abandoned after publishers turned it down. Moritz's review of *Desde Alla* appeared in *The San Francisco Chronicle,* Sunday, April 30, 1972. The letter I quoted with details of Moritz's "tower house" is from Jeffrey Ashe.

PLANET PILGRIM, NANAO SAKAKI

This remembrance appears exactly as published in *Planet Pilgrim, Nanao Sakaki*, a chapbook designed, printed, and bound by Tom Leech (The Press at the Palace of the Governors, 2017) using handmade papers from the Tibetan Handicraft Industry, Kathmandu. Gary Snyder's quote is from his introduction to *Real Play* (Tooth of Time Books, 1981), revised and expanded for *Break the Mirror: Poems of Nanao Sakaki* (North Point Press, 1987). Nanao's poems are from *Real Play: Poetry & Drama by Nanao Sakaki* (Tooth of Time Books, 1981). Direct quotes from Nanao were excerpted from my journals and from an interview with Nanao conducted by J.B. Bryan and myself, published in *Inch by Inch, 45 Haiku by Issa* (La Alameda Press, 1999). Issa's comment about "Saigyō's shadow" appears in *Oraga Haru, the Year of My Life* (University of California Press, 1972), as does Bashō's dictum "Keep the mind high."

THE COMING OF THE DEER

Appeared in *The Madrona Project* magazine: *Human Communities in Wild Places*, Vol. II, No. 2 (Empty Bowl, January, 2022).

FINDING NEW MEXICO, 1971

Previously unpublished. For Shelley's preface to "Alastor" see Bloom and Trilling's *Romantic Poetry and Prose*, pp. 401, 402 (Oxford University Press, 1973). Leonard Bird, a dear friend, was one of many U.S. military veterans who died of cancer resulting from the Nevada nuclear tests. He authored *Folding Paper Cranes: An Atomic Memoir* (University of Utah Press, 2005), an essential read. Pablo Neruda excerpts are from *Alturas de Macchu Picchu*, translated by Nathaniel Tarn (Farrar Straus & Giroux, 1968; see p. 43). *Banisteriopsis caapi* is described in my "Ayahuasca Reverie" (*Shaman's Drum* magazine, No. 59, 2001). For Thomas Merton's journal entries, see *Woods, Shore, Desert: A Notebook, May 1968* (Museum of New Mexico Press, 1982) and Tony O'Brien's *Light in the Desert* (Museum of New Mexico Press, 2011). Lorca's stanza is from "Canción de Jinete," *Selected Poems of Federico García*

Lorca (New Directions, 1961). Machado quote is from *Times Alone: Selected Poems of Antonio Machado,* translated by Robert Bly (Wesleyan University Press, 1983). D.H. Lawrence quote is from "The Princess" (page 507), Vol. II, *The Complete Short Stories* (Penguin Books, 1977). For recommended reading on the Counterculture in New Mexico, see: *Utopian Vistas: the Mabel Dodge Luhan House & the American Counterculture,* Lois Palken Rudnick (University of New Mexico Press, 1996); *Scrapbook of a Taos Hippie,* Iris Keltz (Cinco Puntos Press, 2000); *Voices of Counterculture in the Southwest,* edited by Jack Loeffler and Meredith Davidson (Museum of New Mexico Press, 2017); *Planet Pilgrim, Nanao Sakaki,* John Brandi (Press at the Palace of the Governors, 2017); *The Milagro Beanfield War,* John Nichols (Henry Holt, 1994); *That Back Road In,* John Brandi (Wingbow Press, 1985); *Mostly Mules,* Tom Ireland (Lama Foundation, 1974), a spunky tale by a fellow homesteader whose take on Colorado still rings true: "In Colorado the fence posts are straighter, the grass greener, the mountains are more mountainous, the cows fatter. Everything in its place. That's why I like New Mexico." See also his *Birds of Sorrow: Notes from a River Junction in Northern New Mexico* (Zephyr Press, 1991). For the history of the back-to-the-land movement, see *Back to the Land: The Enduring Dream of Self-Sufficiency in Modern America,* Dona Brown (University of Wisconsin Press, 2011). For Thomas Merton's trip to Asia after he left the Monastery of Christ, see *The Asian Journal of Thomas Merton* (New Directions, 1973). Luisa Torres quotes are from my journals and from "The Words of an Old One," *El Palacio* magazine (Museum of New Mexico, Fall 1978).

A NOTE OF APPRECIATION

I'd like to acknowledge the following persons who helped bring this book to fruition: to Renée Gregorio, my wife, confidant, traveling companion and homemaker extraordinaire for your patience, reassurance, innumerable readings, and careful critiques of this book in its various stages; and to Arthur Sze, Anne Valley Fox and Marilyn Stablein for your close evaluation of the manuscript and suggestions toward final editing. Thanks to my brother Jim for reviewing my Hopi notes and "The Coming of the Deer," and for family photos and genealogy discussions; to my sister Maria for her gifts of vintage books of Western Americana; to my daughter Giovanna for her suggestions on "Finding New Mexico"; to my son Joaquin for a flight over the Taos Gorge; to Bob Shurtleff for additional family history; to John Nichols for *Sibley's Guide to Birds* and our many afternoons of comradely brouhaha; to Jeff Ashe for comments on Moritz Thomsen and the Ecuadorian agrarian reform; to Don Briddell for leading me to Johnny Lovewisdom; to Kay Muldoon-Ibrahim for her photos of Chile, 1960s; to Michael Scott for his photos of New Mexico, 1970s; to Peter Garland for provocative missives, edge-walking travelogue and his beautiful String Quartets; to Bill Porter for pointing me to ancient Chinese road scholars; to Jacquie Bellon for her eagle-eye view of the Sixties and the joys of our moveable feast; to Carol Moldaw for Jane Belo's *Traditional Balinese Culture*; to Nancy Noyes for casita #6; to Janet Gregorio and June Zaccone for generosity, encouragement and advice; to Ed Kissam and Jo Ann Intili for far-reaching travels and continued support of my artistic endeavors; to Jerry Reddan, Tangram Press, and Tom Leech, Press at the Palace of the Governors, for exquisite printings of my poems and prose; to Ken Rodgers for the care with which he published my writing in the *Kyoto Journal*; to Michael Daley, Finn Wilcox, John Pierce and Holly Hughes at Empty Bowl; to Miriam, Joan and Renée at Tres Chicas; to Jeff and Cirrelda at La Alameda: long live the independent press! Finally, my thanks to Dennis Maloney and Elaine LaMattina at White Pine Press for your friendship and steady commitment to the publishing of my work—a gift and a treasure.

John Brandi was born in Los Angeles, 1943. He received a B.A. from Cal State Northridge, 1965, and joined the Peace Corps. First poems published while living in the Andes. Settled in New Mexico, 1971. Worked as a poet in rural schools, prisons, urban colleges, Alaska outback, Navajo Nation schools: 1973-2020. National Endowment Fellowship for Poetry, 1979. Poetry readings in U.S., Paris, Guadalajara. Visual art exhibited at the Moody Gallery, University of New Mexico, San Francisco Public Library, Roswell Museum, Claudia Chapline Gallery, NM History Museum. Lecturer for US students studying in Indonesia and Mexico. Keynote speaker for haiku symposiums in Canada and India. Touchstone Distinguished Books Award for *A House By Itself, Selected Haiku of Masaoka Shiki*. His many books include: *That Back Road In*; *Reflections in the Lizard's Eye*; *Seeding the Cosmos*; *Water Shining Beyond the Fields*; *The World, the World*; *The Great Unrest*; *The Way to Thorong La*; and I*nto the Dream Maze*, a collectors' edition of his handcolored haibun.

Photograph: Lawrence & Regine Brandi, Los Angeles, 1935.